FORTY FATHERS

FORTY FATHERS

Men Talk about Parenting

FATHERS

As told to **Tessa Lloyd**, with a foreword by Peter Mansbridge

Douglas & McIntyre

Douglas and McIntyre (2013) Ltd.
P.O. Box 219, Madeira Park, BC, VON 2H0
www.douglas-mcintyre.com

Edited by Silas White
Cover design by Anna Comfort O'Keeffe
Text design by Brianna Cerkiewicz
Printed and bound in Canada

Douglas and McIntyre (2013) Ltd. acknowledges the support of the Canada Council
for the Arts, which last year invested $153 million to bring the arts to Canadians
throughout the country.

*Nous remercions le Conseil des arts du Canada de son soutien. L'an dernier, le Conseil
a investi 153 millions de dollars pour mettre de l'art dans la vie des Canadiennes et
des Canadiens de tout le pays.*

We also gratefully acknowledge financial support from the Government of Canada
and from the Province of British Columbia through the BC Arts Council and the
Book Publishing Tax Credit.

Library and Archives Canada Cataloguing in Publication

Title: Forty fathers : men talk about parenting / edited by Tessa Lloyd ; foreword
    by Peter Mansbridge.
Names: Lloyd, Tessa, editor.
Identifiers: Canadiana (print) 20190159774 | Canadiana (ebook) 20190159812 | ISBN
    9781771622431 (hardcover) | ISBN 9781771622448 (HTML)
Subjects: LCSH: Fathers—Canada—Interviews. | LCSH: Men—Canada—Interviews.
    | LCSH: Parents—Canada—Interviews. | LCSH: Parenting—Canada—Anecdotes.
Classification: LCC HQ756 .F67 2019 | DDC 306.874/2—dc23

This book is dedicated to

Fathers & Children

who I hope will experience the true abundance
their relationship has to offer

and to Peter,
who would have made
the finest of fathers.

Contents

Foreword by
Peter Mansbridge

One weekend when I was about ten years old, I remember being in our basement watching my father at his workbench. He was trying to deal with a piece of woodwork and was very focused on his goal. But I noticed something that had me worried: I was sure I saw his hand shaking, which I'd never seen before. *Only old men shake*, I thought.

Like many other kids my age, I saw my dad as my hero and was crushed by the thought that he was aging. When I went upstairs, my mother could tell right away that I was upset. I told her what I'd seen. She smiled and said I shouldn't worry, he was fine, just a bit tired from a hard week at work. And she was right. Stanley Mansbridge lived a long and very productive life for almost another half-century.

He was a good father and a good husband; he loved his family and loved his job. There's no doubt that the centrepiece of his life had been the experience that had framed him, but at the same time one he rarely discussed. He'd been a member of a bomber crew for the Royal Air Force in the Second World War. He'd seen horror and he'd created horror. He'd made friends and he'd lost friends to the point where he stopped making friends altogether; it was just too hard losing them.

Sometimes I'd sneak into his room and look for where he kept his medals. I'd take them out of the little cardboard box that had come through the mail at the end of the war, take them out of their individual wrappings and just hold them in my hand. I'd think of how I wanted so much to make him as proud of me as I was of him.

Sixty years later, I've got three children of my own and three grandchildren. I've been far from the perfect father, and I will always regret that. For starters, I should have spent far more time at home doing the things fathers are supposed to do. But what are those things? Well, there is no computer printout that pops out a list detailing correct fatherly behaviour. Why? Because nothing is really "correct," it's personal. Different fathers do different things. So much depends on their own circumstances, their own experiences and yes, how they were shaped by their own fathers.

Expressing that was the goal when Tessa Lloyd canvassed forty Canadian men for their personal narratives about achieving fatherhood. They are a very diverse group of men with different thoughts about how we prepare for and execute our roles. Drawing upon their own experiences, they give us some advice on what we might do differently.

When *my* son was ten years old, our family was on a holiday in France. We'd been shopping and were crossing, jaywalking really, a main street. Suddenly I tripped and fell flat on my face. With oncoming traffic getting uncomfortably close, my son stood between me and the traffic with his hand up in the stop position. As it turned out, all was fine. I got up and we were on the sidewalk long before the traffic reached us. But in that moment I saw a familiar look on his face—it was that same worried look I'd had in the basement with my father.

Oh, and one last thing. My dad's medals. I'm their custodian now, and every few months I go through the same routine I used to as a child. I open that little box and hold the medals in my hand, connecting, in a way, with fatherhood.

Introduction

Parenting is the hardest job I've ever done, as well as the most rewarding. From the modelling provided by my own mother and the nurturing skills that were encouraged when I was a child, to the plethora of resources about parenting that I happily absorbed, I felt confident and supported as a mum.

Caring for children is generally depicted as a given for mothers but as a *choice* for fathers. Boys have different childhood experiences than girls that influence how and what they learn about being a parent. Once they are adults, institutional, familial, social and economic factors make it harder for men to be nurturers. Community and health programs focus on the needs of mothers, and fathers are not given as much support to be positively and effectively involved.

I decided to write this book because I believe that it is especially valuable for men to fulfill their unique potential as fathers. As a counsellor, I work extensively with fathers, and my impression is that many of them have nowhere to lean. When my own sons-in-law became fathers, I thought about what might support and inspire them in this transition. Like the fathers I work with, I didn't picture them seeking advice from other men, and expected they would shy away from books on parenting. One thing I thought might inspire them—and others—was reading about the experiences of fathers, men they knew and respected. When I looked for it, no such book containing a collection of intimate stories from Canadian fathers was to be found. The more I thought about the idea of creating such a resource, the more it resonated for me and propelled me forward. I wanted my book to be a departure from any prescriptive how-to manual about parenting. My idea was to help shine light on the transmission of beliefs, values, attitudes and patterns of behaviour between generations of men. I set out to interview forty fathers about their relationship with their children and with their dads. Many people asked me the question, "How can you, as a woman, come up with a book about a male experience?" The answer is that I can't, but viewing the experience of fatherhood from the outside, I could ask men candid, well-crafted questions about their distinct and deeply personal experiences, so that they could tell it like it is, from the heart—in their own words. The result is *Forty Fathers*, a chorus of diverse voices of Canadian men, ages twenty-nine to eighty-nine, who describe how they are figuring out their relationships with their fathers, and with their children.

I have experienced first-hand some failures of fatherhood. In 1926 when my own father was six years old, he was witness to his mother being knocked to the ground and losing teeth from a blow by his father. She left, with three small children in tow—and they never saw their father again. The emotional scars of having witnessed family violence and the sorrow of growing up without a father left a long shadow over my dad. He was angry, detached from, yet defensive about his emotions. As a child, he got into fights and was expelled from school. He was confrontational and combative with me, my three siblings and my mum. The fury he exuded made family life incredibly tense, and my relationship with him was forever a challenge.

I left home at age eighteen and immigrated to Canada at age twenty-one with my new husband, Stephen. We had four gorgeous daughters between 1977 and 1983, but Stephen was a reluctant dad; he didn't devote energy, time and attention to parenting. His relationships with the children suffered, and this did not improve when we split up in 1994. In 2003 Stephen became ill with a brain tumour, and he died two years later. In those last years of his life Stephen reached out to our daughters in ways he had not done before, and they achieved much happier and more positive relationships. It was hard not to lament the years when Stephen was detached from our children, when they had so much room in their hearts for their dad.

I'd be the first to agree that it's a confusing time to be male. As a counsellor working with boys and young men, I have been repeatedly reminded of the identity issues they face as they attempt to

Interview with Robert Bateman

absorb a socially constructed model of masculinity. Boys get very mixed messages about *who* to be and *how* to be. Mainstream media continues to provide us with images that emphasize male dominance, power, competition, strength and hypermasculinity. These influences limit male potential, and carry significant costs to males and the health and wellness of society at large. Males take more risks and injure themselves. They experience more disease, have a shorter life expectancy than women, and take their own lives at four times the rate of women.

In my thirty-year career with children and families, issues about parenting have been central to my work. While I have had the pleasure of experiencing many family situations that are blessed with whole and happy father-child relationships, I have also been witness to persistent themes of detachment, alienation and dissatisfaction between fathers and their children. While working with a father, it's not uncommon to discover that he has a poor relationship with his own father. Comments surface like "I could tell he was uncomfortable with me," "He left all the parenting to my mum," and "I just learned how to avoid him."

If separation and divorce come into the picture, fathers who have been strongly attached to their children can struggle to maintain that relationship. One divorced man told me, "During the most troubled times I was going to write a book about fatherhood myself and call it *Vitamin F*. At the time, it felt like the whole world didn't seem to understand. Fathers can get shut out and our contribution is not always valued."

A weak father-child connection can be a significant negative influence throughout life. Children raised in father-absent homes are more likely to have behavioural problems and suffer abuse and neglect and they are at greater risk of experiencing poverty and twice as likely to drop out of high school. Conversely, children with involved fathers get better grades in school, relate more empathically to others and have higher self-esteem than children whose fathers are not involved.

For the 8.6 million fathers in Canada, significant shifts have occurred in the last fifty years. Statistics Canada reports that more fathers are taking time off work to care for their newborn children, the number of stay-at-home fathers is on the rise, and a growing number of children say they find it easier to talk to Dad.

I know that it felt good for the fathers who share their experiences in this book to talk about this vital part of their lives. It's not for everyone to reveal their thoughts and feelings on this topic, so I celebrate the fathers who have allowed their story to act as a beacon for other men. These conversations (almost all done in person) were intense, dynamic and often cathartic. They weren't always easy. Regrets, doubts, longings, hopes and promises were expressed. There was laughter, contemplation and tears. These exchanges also elicited insight and clarity, where satisfaction, joy and fulfillment were recognized and celebrated. In short, they were beautiful and life-affirming. I am honoured to have shared these moments.

Fatherhood is central to the human experience, and while each man's story is different, the themes that emerge are universal. I hope that any father picking up this book will find himself reflected somewhere in its pages, and that this will lead him to find his own way to greater joy, purpose and satisfaction for him and his children.

This book has been pieced together around the arrival of grandchildren, several family weddings (including my own), as well as my work as a counsellor in a primary school and in private practice. Phew! An unexpected outcome has been achieved, as I recognize the interviewing and writing process has been therapeutic for me. I have arrived in a place of peace, acceptance and forgiveness for the errors and omissions of my own father and for the father of my children. The happy postscript is that I have married an amazing man who has fully embraced every aspect of being a *grandfather* to our six grandchildren—and who in return is adored.

Alan Doyle

St. John's, Newfoundland

Musician, 50

||||||||||||||||||||||||||||||||||||||||||||||||||||||||||||||||||||||||||||||||||||||

Alan Doyle was born on May 17, 1969 in Petty Harbour,
Newfoundland. In 1993 he and his friends Séan
McCann, Bob Hallett and Darrell Power formed the
band Great Big Sea. Alan has also released several solo
albums, and has been involved in a variety of stage,
television and film productions. Alan is the author of
Where I Belong and *A Newfoundlander in Canada: Always
Going Somewhere, Always Coming Home*. In 2016 he
was named a member of the Order of Canada for his
contributions to his province's musical traditions and
for his commitment to many local charitable initiatives.
Alan is married to Joanne and they have a son named
Henry, born in 2006. Alan calls him "The Prince."

||||||||||||||||||||||||||||||||||||||||||||||||||||||||||||||||||||||||||||||

My childhood was very typical for kids growing up in Petty Harbour
in the sixties. It was considered a safe community and we were
allowed to roam. Mums and dads practised "benign neglect." It
wasn't that they weren't interested, and we certainly were and are
close, but we just got on with our separate lives. Where we came
together was through music; my parents were both musicians. No
one had much money. When I had the opportunity to replace my
father in the band he played in with my uncles, I was flying. I was
fourteen, and playing in clubs.

I was from a small town, but by the time I got into high school I realized us Petty Harbour kids were light years ahead of the others who'd grown up in the city. In grade ten, the other kids were sneaking off to get a case of beer. I'd already quit rum twice by then, so was like, "What are you doing that for?"

The fathering paradigm was so completely different for my father than it is for me. I dropped in on my father a few years ago with my son. At one point I was in another room and he called out to me, "Alan, what the heck are you doing?"

I replied, "I'm doing something you have never had to do your whole life, Dad."

"What's that?" he said.

"I'm trying to occupy my son," I replied, "finding him something to do."

"You're right, son," my father said. "I never had to do that one time in my whole life. I never had to find anything for you to do."

My dad worked twelve-hour shifts. I got practical help from him, but we didn't talk much. We didn't have much to talk about. I didn't have heart-to-hearts with my father; that didn't happen with anyone I knew. There was nothing to fix—I was just a happy kid. Any personal stuff you had, you'd work out with your siblings.

In 2006 I was ready to be a dad, I had a career, a wonderful wife, a house and I was ready to get on with it. There's a radical difference between my life as a parent and my father's life as a parent. One may as well be from Mars and the other from Jupiter. I think that this is a big change in one generation. I don't believe my father would say there was much difference in the way he was expected to act and what was expected of my grandfather—or his before him.

As I compare myself at the age of ten and how my son is at this age, there's a huge shift in how our lives flow. One big difference is because where I grew up was very rural and my son is being raised in the city, St. John's. But these days, you're expected to program every minute of your kid's life. We get a bit of a break because we live on a quiet street, so usually once a week for a few hours we can just chuck him out on the road. Someone will be out there for him to play with. All the rest of it is school and activities.

Alan Doyle, 2018

Kids are so used to having a schedule imposed upon them. It's worrying. Their instinct is to wake up every morning, look at someone and get that person to tell them what they're supposed to do. I never had that until I was twenty! All the direction I had was "Just go do something." It's up to you what you are doing. The only rule in our house was "The only thing you can't do is *nothing*." That's it.

These days, kids are so conditioned to someone doing the programming for them and to praising their every move. It terrifies me to think what all this scheduling is doing to my son. Shouldn't we be worried about the fact that they don't have any free time? I try to create it for my son, but I think I fail miserably.

It's considered irresponsible to let kids out of your sight. You've got to know where they are at all times. There's no "collective will" to make it happen, so if I sent Henry out at any old time of day, he'd be on his own. His peers are all doing some organized activity. I know it's trite to say, but *when I was a kid* my parents knew where I was: I was in Petty Harbour, somewhere. It all worked well. I made choices, learned to handle risks. We were totally set up for it.

Henry and I, our childhood realities are so far apart. My family was relatively poor, living in a small house in a rural town, my parents scraping by to make ends meet or to afford one instrument—or guitar lessons for me. Almost forty years later when my son arrives, his father is a rich rock star who has a big, fancy house, paintings on the wall and a recording studio in the basement.

I had lots of people, including my mum, telling me how my life was going to change when this child arrived. "Yes," my brother Bernie added, "let's hope it doesn't upset his delicate routine. He hasn't had two days the same since 1989."

Then I get an infant. And I'm like "What do you mean, it's different?" Nah, not really. I'm in a band for Christ's sake. There's always someone out there in the middle of the night crying about something, someone else pissing themselves, someone can't talk, someone else is falling down. I've got to take someone's pants off and put a new pair on them or something like that. I just get on with it.

It's kind of true, if you're in a band you really don't know what's going down. It's like some days you have to be up at four a.m., you've got to leave or be on TV, the next day you can sleep for seventeen hours and the day after, there's no sleep at all. It's not like being a touring musician is supposed to be prep for parenting, but that's what it did for me. I learned to sleep when it was available to me, and to get up for a border crossing or to get off a flight. Discomfort, sleep deprivation? It was happening to me anyway.

When Henry was born, I loved my new role, but I didn't love my job any less. Was I supposed to? Because I didn't. He's awesome. So's my band. Henry came into my life when it was booming, and my personal career outside the band was taking off. He was two when I got my first acting job.

I live and die by the calendar and the clock. I know where I'll be at 8:10 p.m. next March 16. I am super-programmed. Being a young adult trying to make a living in the arts, I was conditioned to be so hungry for it—any opportunity, a gig of any kind—so when they come, you have no muscle to say "No."

One of my biggest challenges as a father has been learning to say no to awesome stuff that I've wanted to do since I was ten years old. Once I missed out on a tour with Sting. If you'd have told fifteen-year-old me that, I'd have shot myself.

As a father I get another version of awesome stuff. I learned to put family time on my calendar. It'll have days blocked off with *Dad*. I have to do it, or it won't happen. If you are not careful, you can miss it all.

All my parents ever wanted was for me to be happy. I thought this was something that parents just said but for them it's not: it's the truth. When I was sixteen, if I'd said I wanted to be a drywaller, and then I'd shown up at Sunday dinners happy and content, talking about the cool drywalling gig I was doing, they'd be totally happy.

Now it's my turn to be the parent. I get such a kick out of watching Henry. He's in the odd music thing, choir thing, and I can see how good it makes him feel. It's always thrilling for me, undeniably. He keeps saying he doesn't want to be in a band, but maybe the emcee. That's cool, whatever. I'm going to keep my ego out of the way.

W. Brett Wilson

Calgary, Alberta

Philanthropist, *Dragons' Den* emeritus, 62

||||||||||||||||||||||||||||||||||||||||||||||||||||||||||||||||||||||||||||||||||||||||||||||||||||||||

W. Brett Wilson was born in 1957 in North Battleford,
Saskatchewan. He earned a degree in civil engineering at
the University of Saskatchewan, then worked for Imperial
Oil before completing his MBA in entrepreneurship at
the University of Calgary. Brett married his engineering
classmate Pam in 1981. They had three children together
before they divorced in 2001. Brett co-founded the
investment banking advisory firm Wilson Mackie & Co.
and FirstEnergy Capital Corp. For three seasons he was
a panellist for CBC's television program *Dragons' Den*.

||||||||||||||||||||||||||||||||||||||||||||||||||||||||||||||||||||||||||||||||||||||||||||||||||||||||

My children were eight, eleven and thirteen when my marriage
ended. A failed and failing marriage had allowed me to lose myself
in my work with no remorse. It's a horrible excuse, but it was easier to be at the office, come home late and leave early. Work was
extraordinarily rewarding, a big boost to my ego and my wallet.
The rewards were so tangible, a few more hours, another deal...
The children, my ex-wife, me—we were all losers. I could go entire
weeks living in the same house but not see my family. We didn't
do things together, and if I did end up being left with my children
I was resentful.

A pivotal moment for me came one day when I was actually at
home, or as I referred to it, I was stuck at home "babysitting" my

own children. My daughter answered the phone and told someone I needed to speak to that I wasn't there. I lost a piece of art I was trying to acquire because of her, and when I found out what she had done, I blew. "What the hell are you doing, telling someone that I'm not home?" And she said, "Well, you never are." I raged at her to the point of scaring and scarring her before I realized she was right.

I hit the wall that day and acknowledged that my life was a train wreck. Thankfully, I had the sense to get myself into a treatment program. I spent eight days working through the Hoffman Process. I got help with defining my priorities, dealing with patterns in relationships, confronting negative themes from my childhood and gaining skills to deal with my emotions. I did a whole lot of work on myself— particularly around who I was as a father and what it meant to be a good father.

One of the activities we were asked to do involved writing our own obituaries. Most people, including me, shed tears working on this, and when we came back to the group we were asked to read them aloud. There were highly charged moments for everyone in the room as we grappled with the idea of our own mortalities. Then came one of the most emotional experiences I have had, as our group leader tore all these obituaries in half and sent us back to write a second one. This one would be the obituary our children would write for us.

Whoa. It was a brand-new exercise that forced me to think about how my children felt and where they were coming from. It was so simple yet so powerful. The gap between these two obituaries, that's where my work lay. I had to look closely at the way I had approached the role of fatherhood, dissecting my attitude and looking at my values, beliefs and behaviour.

I had to elevate parenting in my own mind, because until this time it had barely even been on my list of priorities. This was when I was able to bring conscious choice into my life, come to terms with who I wanted to be, and appreciate that the most important part of my life was my children. I was rethinking my identity. The word that defined me at my essence was not *engineer*, *banker* or *businessman*. It was *father*.

When I left the program, what happened to me next was another game changer: I was diagnosed with cancer. One thing this diagnosis did was help give me permission to say no. I had to focus on my physical, emotional and spiritual health for the first time in my life. It was too late to save my marriage, but at least I got a good divorce. Then I started to get my children back, and work on my relationship with my dad.

I began to appreciate what an amazing father he was. My father was away working in the oil patch for the first four months of my life. Apparently when he came home, I put up a big fuss and wouldn't let him touch me. That day, he quit his job and moved back to North Battleford. He got a job working as a salesman for a car dealership.

We lived in low-income housing at the time, but after a few years my dad bought a small, older house for 12,400 dollars. A new subdivision got built close by with houses twice the size of ours. Because of the way the catchment boundary got drawn, I ended up going to school with all the rich kids from this new subdivision. Children of doctors and lawyers. They all had allowances, fancy clothes, travel, adventure, those sorts of things.

I was so hard on my dad: *How come we don't have...?* I judged him harshly for not making the big bucks. I was so focused on what we didn't have, I didn't appreciate what I did have: a father who was always there. He coached, he helped us with our homework, he went door to door fundraising for our sports, he was always *present*. It didn't really occur to me at the time, but the other kids—their parents were hardly ever around.

No one ever said, "You're lucky to have a father like that." There was no metric for understanding, measuring that. I was going through my own stuff, being bullied, feeling inadequate. I was small for my age, and I couldn't wait to get away. You know, that's the Joni Mitchell song: "You don't know what you've got till it's gone."

My parents had a really strong marriage. They were such good friends to each other and knew how to have fun. The only time my parents argued was about money. Eventually, my dad became a sales manager at the car dealership. My mum went back to work as a social worker, we got a cabin, a second car and a colour TV. But I wasn't celebrating, I was still judging my father harshly.

He quit work the day my mum died at the age of fifty-six. I was thirty then and I had lost all the relationships in my life. People would call; I'd always be at the office. I'd get home at ten and never return the calls. It wasn't animosity, it was complete indifference. As a father, all that mattered to me was being a good provider. I was doing it for them. Why else would I work so hard? Because I loved them. Why didn't they understand I was doing it for their benefit?

I was asked to coach my elder daughter's slo-pitch team. I missed three out of four games, I was late, had an event, was always getting someone else to substitute. I just didn't make it a priority and my daughter saw that. It would have been better if I could have just said, "I'll come and watch when I can." I wanted the glory but didn't have the guts.

Meanwhile, I never gave my father credit or valued what he did, but I've done that now—and in front of big groups of people. I have been able to tell him how proud I am of him and how ashamed I am of my former self. I have to reckon with the fact that I am the one who caused us to lose fifteen years of our relationship. I don't live with shame and regret anymore, thanks to the work I did in the Hoffman Process. I am in a place of acceptance.

You know that idea about kids needing *quality* time? That's just an idea invented by businessmen to excuse their absence. Kids need quality *and* quantity! They also need their parents to focus on them when they are together. This means no screens. I know so many men whose lives are supposedly on track. They have the toys, the lifestyle. The number one challenge they have? Parenting. Lots of them just can't figure it out.

I have been completely committed to being healthy, and to building strong relationships with my children. If I have the chance to do something with my kids, I cancel everything! We have travelled the world together. I have stared cancer down and got to a healthy place, spiritually and emotionally; if I have to go tomorrow, I'm okay. I have had the chance to do it well, and there's nothing more important to me than being a father!

Greg Wells

Toronto, Ontario

Exercise physiologist, kinesiologist, 48

‖‖

Dr. Greg Wells is an assistant professor at the University of Toronto, where he studies elite sport performance. He also serves as an associate scientist at the Hospital for Sick Children, where he and his team explore how to use exercise to diagnose, prevent and treat chronic illnesses in children. Greg is the author of *Superbodies: Peak Performance Secrets from the World's Best Athletes* and *The Ripple Effect: Sleep Better, Eat Better, Move Better, Think Better*. He lives with his wife, Judith, and children, Ingrid and Adam, in Toronto.

‖‖

I had a charmed childhood. We were a close family, doing lots of travelling together and enjoying long camping trips every summer. I've had a great relationship with my dad; he's always been a very involved parent, there for me every step of the way. Playing catch stands out as a way we connected—I have vivid memories of him and me playing catch from the time I was really little.

When I got into swimming, he took me to all my practices, four days a week leaving at five a.m. We didn't say a lot. There's not much to say at five a.m., but he never complained about it or said no. I'd wake him at 4:50 a.m. and after the practice he'd come home, shower and go to work where he was a senior bank executive.

I trained so hard when I was a teenager, I was never home. Then I left for the University in Calgary when I was seventeen. I remember that year I turned seventeen, my grandmother—my dad's mum whom I was super close to—was dying of a brain tumour. It was a hard time for our whole family. My dad and I had some tough times, but after I got to Calgary we got past our discomfort and back into our groove.

When my dad got upset you knew it was *big*, that you had screwed up. He made it obvious that whatever it was that I'd done wasn't acceptable, and I was highly motivated to get my act together.

Dad was very driven during his career. He's a pretty emotionally stable, highly principled guy who's provided me with a very strong moral compass. I watched how he handled things at work and respected that a great deal. He taught me there's a way to handle things that's right, ethically and morally—even if that might compromise your progress. It's true that people can cheat and get ahead—there was none of that in my world. I think about my career and how I have applied all that he taught me. There were definitely some points where I could have got ahead faster, at someone else's expense—but that was not for me.

Dad's in his mid-seventies now and has an unbelievable bond with my kids. It's so cool to see him engaged, playing, hands-on—there's no plugging them in front of screens.

One of the most powerful human needs is the need to be listened to. This is something my father was good at, and I have worked hard to develop myself. Throughout my career as a coach, scientist at the hospital and especially with my own children, I have learned to just listen. Now my daughter, Ingrid, calls me on it if ever I speak over her—it's good, it keeps me honest—and it means that once she has been heard, she is ready to listen.

My wife and I had a very tough time getting and staying pregnant. Our first baby died shortly after birth. It was crippling, and we felt very alone. It's a weird thing in our society; this is a more common experience than you would ever think, but no one talks about this happening to them. One of my ways to handle this loss has been to throw it out there when speaking in public, and to talk about it.

Eighteen months later we were expecting a baby again. It was an insane year. I was working like a maniac, renovating our house, creating a series for CTV called *Superbodies*, and then when Judith was seven months into this high-risk pregnancy, I left to commentate the 2010 Olympic Games as a sports-science analyst—with a pager.

I'd had no interest in being a dad when I was in my early or even mid-thirties. I was just not ready. If I thought about becoming a dad I was like, *NO*. It was a visceral reaction. But I was thirty-nine by the time Ingrid arrived. My career was stable and I was ready to rock at being a father. "Bring it on, I'm all in" was how I felt, in a way that I could never have imagined ten or even five years earlier.

I had zero preparation for parenting. We were too frantic, and there was so much emphasis on getting through the pregnancy, ensuring it was healthy for mum and baby. You don't have a clue about what's coming. Becoming a dad, it was a massive shift. It was the hardest thing I have ever done in my life, and I've done crazy, hard stuff like riding my bike through the Sahara Desert.

In the early years, parenting was pure survival. You're exhausted; you don't sleep. There's life *before* you have children and then there's life *after*. There's no connection between the two. I think about who I was before kids and I can't understand how I ever had a hard time functioning!

I had no idea what fatigue was back then. I'd *say* I was tired, but I had no idea. I was dancing to my own drum, doing 100 per cent of what Greg wanted. Now that there's Greg with kids, it's all about them, every decision I make, every penny I earn and every action I take. In that instant I caught Ingrid as she popped out into the world, I was a different man.

There were times in the first few years when I had to dig deep to survive. Picture this: tiny baby, early hours of the morning, about three a.m. Ingrid is screaming, I'm holding her down on the change table, there's urine and feces flying around, but it's not the baby or me that I am worrying about. Judith is standing at the door of the room and I can see she is cracking. In that moment, I am calmer than she is, and I say "Judith, you can leave now." I gave her permission to exit the scene. I literally kicked her out of the room, and we were all fine.

Since then the switch has been flipped on many occasions, and she's kicked me out instead when I have been in the deepest of frustration and fatigue. We have learned to give each other that space to de-stress and regroup. You have to take yourself out of the scenario, look at it from six feet above your head. Something has to pop the pressure.

Everything goes better when I exercise, so on occasion Judith has the wisdom to say to me, "Take your bike, Greg, and get out."

Here's another scene: Ingrid's about two, I'm putting her in the car, I'm late for work, and she's screaming. I'm sweating buckets as I've got Ingrid literally pinned because she's arching her back and squirming so much as I'm bolting her into the car seat. Judith is at the door watching and our next-door neighbour who's a clinical psychologist comes out of her house just as I yell, "Fuck, Ingrid!" They both look at me. I'm like, *Oh my God, I have permanently damaged my child.*

Sometimes you beat yourself up because you did something that wasn't perfect. You know it was wrong, but you have to just let it go. Does every dad have those moments? I think so. You're never going to be perfect. You do the best you can in any single day, you don't judge yourself, you're exhausted. You try and keep your head above water.

Being *present*—it's very much a buzzword these days. I run between two labs, I'm flying all over the world, I'm speaking to large groups, I'm writing books—I'm trying to help a billion people! I have learned that when I'm with my children, it's critically important that I am actually *with* them, not just physically but completely. Yes, the phone needs to go away; Ingrid busted me on that once when we were at the park. She was really into *Shrek* at the time, so much so that she had memorized some of the lines, like when the princess tells Shrek, "Your job is not my problem." Ugh, I pulled the knife out of my heart and ever since then, any time we are together, the phone is not around.

I am very deliberate about getting the children outside, but most especially introducing them to adrenalin-based sports like mountain biking, surfing, skateboarding, skiing and climbing. I

Ingrid, Greg and Adam, 2017

started teaching Ingrid to paddleboard when she was two and by the time she was four, she had the confidence to jump off the board in the middle of the lake and swim away from me thinking she could make it to shore, about fifteen-hundred metres away. She's surfed in Nicaragua, and at the bike park she tries to keep up with the teenage boys.

I made a decision about wanting to get them happy, excited and engaged in outdoor activities, and we make it a priority to spend money on good sports equipment. They've got unbelievable winter gear because in the winter we play outside for hours. We don't spend our money on theatres, sports games, none of that spectator stuff. I've no clue what will happen later on, but I think this will mean they'll be better able to take care of themselves emotionally. Instead of sinking into a deep dark depression and disappearing into their rooms, I hope they'll be more likely to grab a paddleboard or a bike and head out.

I can see it paying off already. A couple of times Ingrid has come home in a foul mood, and I get her on her bike, and the bad mood evaporates. It's amazing. In the house it would be so much harder to manage—"Stop doing that," "Put down the remote," "No, you can't have screen time"—but we get outside and the energy shifts to a positive place right away. It is infinitely easier to be a good parent outdoors! My kids have very little screen time, but if we are taking a flight, all bets are off—they can have the iPad as much as they want.

My son, Adam, he's calm, gentle, and much more go-with-the-flow, while my daughter, Ingrid, wants to dominate and take over everything—she's viciously competitive. I'm trying to teach them that it's okay to push yourself and try really hard—but that failure is awesome. It's so easy to be terrified of kids failing; we think that if they go down they'll stay down. I remind myself that the people I am fortunate enough to know who have been wildly successful are people who have failed the most, spectacularly. I want my kids to be 100 per cent okay with that, regardless of how they approach life.

I see such a pattern of people putting others down in order to feel good about themselves. I can't stand that—for me, competition is about testing yourself against people who are better than you. Philip McKernan is a filmmaker and speaker who made an impression on me by talking about our need for external validation. As an academic I am constantly having my research reviewed by my peers. When I was cycling across Africa I was trying to get into *The Guinness Book of World Records* (which eight members of our expedition did), and then my first book had to be a bestseller (which it was).

While listening to Phillip I realized that I had always looked for a lot of external validation. I dropped my pen; I started thinking, *Oh my God. This is why I am constantly trying to achieve more and more...* Don't get me wrong: I love everything I do. I wouldn't change anything in my past, but it made me realize how I have been driven by external validation and that what I do has to be only about what gives me joy, satisfaction and fulfillment, not all about what anyone else thinks. I overcame this need in five minutes when the light went on for me.

Now I am able to bring this consciousness to being a father. I want to make sure that my kids are free from the need for external validation in their lives. The intrinsic stuff is way more powerful. I am well aware of what can happen for girls, especially the beating they can take in their teens, so I am helping my daughter to tune in to what she wants, feels and thinks, so that she looks within and is never dependent or striving for that high from "someplace else."

On one of the nights that shit was happening at my house, I took Ingrid out in the stroller. It's three in the morning and I'm walking through the neighbourhood where we used to live. I'm feeling alone and pretty sorry for myself. I have to work the next day. There's no sign of life block after block and then somewhere in the distance I see someone walking toward me. As we get closer I see that it's a male figure. It's a dad, he's holding a baby, and he's out walking as well.

We get close and then, as we pass each other, we exchange a nod. In that moment it's like we share a deep, deep, deep understanding. It's a split-second glance, but we exchange empathy for each other's exhaustion and experience. I'll never forget that moment; it helped me to realize it's all so worthwhile.

Men—most of the time our conversations are about sport, business, our careers. The men I know want to be good dads but we don't easily talk about it or support each other, me included. We ask questions about each other's kids when we get together: *"How is he doing in sports?" "How's she doing in school?" "Does he have a girlfriend?"* But it's hyper-superficial—there's no discussion whatsoever about any of the challenges we are facing in our parenting.

I have struggled at times. Sport psychology has helped a lot but the complete game changer for me has been meditation. I started a daily practice eight months ago. That's what's giving me the few seconds I need between a trigger and my reaction. The thing that really bothered me from my childhood about my dad is that those times when he really lost it—we don't get to repair, there is always a scar left behind. As much as I can, I want to stay calm in that crisis moment, to not lose it, to be able to make conscious choices about what I do.

There is magic in all moments, we just need the perspective to realize it. If we can access it when we are with our children and share the magic with them—even if it's just a tiny bit of it—then I think we can live differently and be way better dads.

Art Napoleon
Victoria, British Columbia
Cultural educator, co-host of *Moosemeat & Marmalade*, 58

||||||||||||||||||||||||||||||||||||||||||||||||||||||||||||||||||||||||||||||||||||||||

Art Napoleon is a TV producer, songwriter, adventurer, wild-game foodie and "extreme berry picker." He was formerly a chief of the Saulteau First Nation in northeastern BC. Art is as comfortable on a big-city stage or boardroom as he is skinning a moose in a hailstorm— with a pocket knife. He has a growing résumé in the film industry and has most recently been a co-host and producer for the Aboriginal Peoples Television Network show *Moosemeat & Marmalade*. Art is father to six children: Julian, born in 1984, Niska in 1986, Quanah in 1988, Dakota in 1994, Nipiya in 2006 and Sipin in 2007.

||||||||||||||||||||||||||||||||||||||||||||||||||||||||||||||||||||||||||||||||||||||||

I grew up on the East Moberly Lake Reserve in the foothills of the Rockies of British Columbia—very isolated, no running water, no electricity and no paved roads. It's fifteen minutes from the little town of Chetwynd, where there's only about five thousand people.

My dad was a distant figure in my life, fading in and out but casting a long shadow. When I was eight months old, my mum died. Her death was unexpected and apparently it left my dad in really bad shape. He took off, not even going to her funeral. From what I know now, my guess is that he was running away—from himself.

My grandparents took on the role of being my parents. Their background was Cree and Dane-zaa, and Cree was the language they spoke in the home. Grandpa had a wealth of traditional knowledge and a certain way of holding himself that I revered. I sort of felt intimidated when I was around him, and my voice got so soft I could barely be heard. He had a strong impact on me. He was a gifted story-teller and drummer—one of the things we did together was make a drum. My grandfather was an alcoholic, however, and things were rocky between him and my grandma. He would disappear for days on end, selling things to buy booze.

When I was eight years old, my grandparents split up. I still saw my grandpa but his drinking was getting a whole lot worse and often he'd be in rough shape. Once when I was in high school I saw Grandpa staggering along downtown, and I took the long way around. I would have been so ashamed to let my friends know, *Hey that drunk guy over there, he's my grandpa*. He drank himself to death, eventually. I was in college at the time, and I got a call from the RCMP telling me he'd been hit by a bus—drunk, wandering on the highway.

I thought my grandparents were my parents. My grandparents didn't really explain things. "Real" to a child is who tucks you in at night, who reads you stories. It was a bus driver who broke it to me that my real mum was dead. My father reappeared for the first time when I was about four years old. I didn't know who he was. I thought my grandpa was my dad. I was surprised that this man could be my father, a white guy I'd never seen before!

My grandmother was amazing. She was the matriarch and every-thing centred around her way of doing things. As for males in my life, good guys that I could look up to, they were thin on the ground. At the time I didn't know what I was missing, but in retrospect I can see that sure had a marked impact on me. My uncles—they were hunt-ers, trappers, hard workers. They gave me a strong work ethic and self-sufficiency. But none of them have been able to live in a family and raise children, not one.

I was a quiet, shy, sullen and withdrawn little boy. I had no confidence at all. What happened in my childhood shrank my spirit, bringing despair and suicidal thoughts. The influence of coloniza-tion, the church, being oppressed, harassed—they all factored into my childhood. I had a grade five teacher who strapped me, singled me out to receive his racist comments and used any opportunity to let me know, *You don't count.*

My dad continued to appear about once a year. In my later teens I spent more time with him, and when I reached adulthood we actually bonded a fair bit. He didn't maintain ties with his own family; apparently his Irish parents didn't want anything to do with me or my mum. Where on earth could I find a good example of a healthy man? Certainly not from my dad or from my grandpa. At the age of seventeen I knew that wasn't how I was going to be as a man.

I had a burning curiosity about the world. I needed to explore and fantasized about escaping. I had some persuasive powers and managed to get myself a sponsor so I could move to Victoria and finish high school at Vic High. It's a miracle that a spiritual and philosophical mentor named Calvin came into my life, a teacher and basketball coach whom I admired and who believed in me. He introduced me to Buddhism and Taoism. He fostered my cultural pride. He encouraged me to think in new ways, taught me self-renewal and how to change my script.

My confidence soared. I began taking better care of myself—and life improved. I found a place where I fit. Also, I had one magic moment to return to. When my grandpa was close to the end of his life, and sober, he said to me, "You know you're always reading and going to school—you're going to be someone someday." He said it in a way that wasn't just his opinion; he said it like he really knew it. Thank God for that moment. The hope that his comment gave me continued to bear fruit years later.

Each holiday I'd be back up north, drawn by my connection with my grandma and my longings to be in nature. I still valued the culture I'd grown up in, and I knew I had more to learn. Whenever we were in the woods we were in our element, and we really bonded. When we returned to our traditional practices, berry picking, moose camp, that's when the beauty of life emerged.

My father drank hard all his life and hung out with countless heavy-drinking women, all short-lived relationships. He'd been stabbed, probably shot at, lived in a rickety old motorhome. He was a self-destructive, wild white redneck who never learned how to be a very good dad. He had a heap of offspring—I don't think even he knew how many. It's not a pretty story. I don't think he really knew how to show empathy. Most of his kids have had really rough lives—some were raised in foster homes, some had addiction issues, one died of exposure on the streets in Vancouver. But some of them are doing quite well, have careers and are enjoying life.

When Dad died in 2015 all of my half-siblings were at his funeral. Some of them I had never met my whole life. He sure was well loved by his clan. Although my dad didn't give me much that I'd want to bring to my parenting, there are things I respect about him. He was quite a character and had a very sensitive, highly intelligent side to him. He loved learning and history, and he was very well read. He was a skilled carpenter. He hung out with Natives all his life and was a good trapper. I value that. Over the years I have learned to focus more on what he did give me rather than on his deficits.

Then there's me as a father. It's been chaotic—children of all ages, unwed couplings, broken relationships, a convoluted series of blended families—this is my life. I didn't know I'd become a parent in 1984 until my son Julian was about six months old. I'd had a brief fling with his mum and she'd decided not to let me know I was the father of her baby. The door wasn't open for me to play an active part of Julian's life. I had become a raging alcoholic, but after I started to put a cap on it in 1989, I was able to build a stronger connection with my son, despite the difficulties and distance between us. He'd come up north for spring break and the summer holidays, and we had great times together, a lot of it about being together in nature: hunting, fishing and camping.

From 1984 to 1989 I was with another woman, Roxanne, and together we had a daughter, Niska, in 1986, and a son, Quanah, in 1988. Although I felt like a dad for the first time, their early years were really rocky because of my drinking and the tumultuous relationship I had with their mum. I worry about them a lot, because they experienced me at my worst.

In my mind, a real dad is someone who teaches and protects, who is available, who pays attention, nurtures and supports. Those years when I was with Roxanne, I wasn't doing those things—and

FROM LEFT: Quanah, Niska, Sipin, Nipiya and Art, 2019

I didn't even recognize it. When sobriety came, that was hard too: lots of emotions to handle that I'd learned to mask, and memories that I'd buried.

I disappointed myself as a parent. Still to this day I feel remorse and guilt, but beating up on myself doesn't do my kids any good, does it? I'm trying again, even though I screwed up. I'm taking another shot at redemption. They see that. It's possible because of how they see me parenting their younger siblings. I am the most stable I've ever been. Now I am able to be a better father.

I am sure Julian feels I should have been more available. I feel good that I have given him his Native roots, and even though we gravitated to cities, Niska and Quanah got their moosemeat culture too. I know how to pick myself up when I fall, and I have learned to be both mother and father to my children.

To this day, we still have issues to work on but we are able to express love for each other. Both Niska and Quanah have budding entertainment careers of their own. Julian is enjoying his career working on the land, in fields related to environment and conservation, and he's hitting the speaking circuit. My other son, Dakota, is still looking for his niche, but he is intelligent and has a kind heart so I have faith he will find his way. No parent ever wants to see their kids struggling because of what we put them through. It gives me great joy to see them succeed at careers that give meaning to their lives.

Because of my abusive and neglectful behaviour especially in Quanah and Niska's youth, they had every right to be hateful and resentful toward me. Quanah rightfully kept her distance from me. Quanah and I made a breakthrough in the latter part of her teens during a time when *he* became *she*. That's one of the steepest learning curves you can get as a parent. My dream is that one day we will be able to communicate more effectively, be free to talk about the past in a way that continues to bring healing and to have a more full relationship, adult to adult.

Nowadays, I like myself much better as a dad. I have somewhere along the line absorbed enough good stuff from other dads around me: men who were so close to their children and who knew how to be gentle and show affection. Grandpa helped give me patience, playfulness and songs. When my children were small I used to get down on the floor and play lots of different characters that I could turn into, like the "river giant" or "Mungo."

I am able to connect deeply with Nipiya and Sipin through good conversation. They have been able to hold their own with adults in conversation since they were very young. The girls are extremely talented with music, dance and acting. High achievers. We have great fun.

I don't want to micromanage my children. My job is to teach them their connection to culture and the skills they'll need to face life. I try and give them just enough latitude to roam, and the opportunity to make good choices and to know that the world does not revolve around them.

I still have to deal with the after-effects of a painful childhood and generational alcoholism. I had a lot of demons that overpowered my good intentions. I believe a lot of men have them; I am not afraid to acknowledge their existence. I manage them better now, and I know how to take care of myself.

Art Napoleon

As a society we have somehow minimized the importance of fathers. Many of them show up in comedy as clueless buffoons. There are a bunch of mothers raising kids with no men in sight. Men must be aware and not fall for the unhealthy things that are often glorified about masculinity, that don't fit with being a good father and a healthy person. Men are shown that vulnerability is a weakness, but I believe it's a strength. Men should step up to the plate and embrace every aspect of being a father.

Justin Trudeau

Ottawa, Ontario

Politician, teacher, 47

||||||||||||||||||||||||||||||||||||||||||||||||||||||||||||||||||||||||||||||||||||||||||||||||||||||||||||||

Justin Trudeau was born on December 25, 1971, the eldest
of three boys. He grew up at 24 Sussex Drive while his
father, Pierre Elliott Trudeau, was prime minister. His
parents split up in 1977. Justin has degrees from McGill
University and the University of British Columbia. He
worked as a teacher before entering politics in 2007. He
has been prime minister of Canada since October 2015. He
lives in Ottawa with his wife, Sophie Grégoire Trudeau,
and their three children, Xavier, Ella-Grace and Hadrien.

||||||||||||||||||||||||||||||||||||||||||||||||||||||||||||||||||||||||||||||||||||||||||||||||||||||||||||||

What my brothers and I got from my father was the purest intent
and complete and absolute love. I'm of two minds about whether
that means "unconditional": I knew that there was nothing I could
do that would make him love me less, but at the same time I felt the
pressure to do the things that I thought would make my father happier, more proud, so that he would love me more.

When my parents' marriage was breaking up, I remember the
fighting. The differences between my parents were obvious to me: I
could see when my mum was in pain, but my father didn't show it,
even to us. He was an extremely sensitive, emotional man, but he
was trying to be so together and so reasonable. He kept it all inside.

Like any young kid impacted by divorce, I felt helpless. While
Sacha lashed out, and Miche became more independent, I tried to
hold myself to the highest standard, to varying degrees of success. I

faltered more often than not; I was angry and hurt. Once when I was about five years old, I smacked my father in the face. He reminded me about it years later, and told me he knew I was trying to communicate something I couldn't get across any other way.

Save for the occasional outburst, that high standard followed me into my teen years. But living up to it became harder as I got older. When it came time to choose a career, my father passed on wisdom he had received from his own father, saying that a law degree could "get me anywhere." Maybe he was right, maybe he wasn't. As directionless as I may have been, all I knew for sure was that law school just didn't feel right *to* me or *for* me. For a few years I struggled to find my own path, torn—I was determined to become my own man, yet still chased the approval of my dad.

Eventually, at the top of a mountain while I was backpacking overseas, I made an important decision that would change my life: I decided that I would become a teacher. In that moment, it all seemed to click. Becoming a teacher made sense to me—it reflected who I was as a person, and what I believed in. I was aligning myself not with my father but with my maternal grandfather and a long line of teachers before him. Thankfully, my father was supportive of my choice. I wanted his approval, but at the same time I needed to carve out my own identity in the shadow of his larger-than-life personality.

Teaching was not only the way I chose to contribute to society— it would also serve as a pillar on which my own, unique identity would be built. I remember once my father visited me while I was teaching in Vancouver, and I had an opportunity to be seen for who I was while in his company. A student caught up to us on the school grounds, calling "Mr. Trudeau..." We both turned around thinking that she wanted to get my father's autograph, or shake his hand, but it was *me* she was addressing. I was *Mr. Trudeau.* The slight smile my father gave me spoke volumes. I had finally found my place in the world, and I had done it on my own terms.

Fatherhood was next for me. And luckily, I had not one, but two examples to follow. My father's staunch Catholic upbringing had left him clearly conflicted about sexuality and relationships. It was a hard topic for him to get into. In conversations, I often found

Justin with wife Sophie, daughter Ella-Grace and sons Hadrien (CENTRE) and Xavier, 2018

myself protecting him from his own discomfort. When my mum remarried, my stepfather became a father figure to me. Happily, his way of being and relating to us boys complemented and stood in contrast to my father's approach. With him, conversations about sex and girls were much more easily accomplished.

When it came to fatherhood, I remember the evolution of my thinking as a young man. It used to be that the most important thing for me was *having kids* rather than *being a father.* But in my late twenties and early thirties, it evolved into being the right person to *become* a father; it wasn't just about being a dad, it became about being a *good* dad. To me, being a good dad means shaping the world around my kids in whatever way I can. I owe it to them to try to make this place that they inhabit better, safer and more just. This core belief, I know for sure, I inherited from my parents.

These days, when I come home from work, my kids, Xavier, Ella-Grace and Hadrien, always have new tricks to show me—things they've learned at school or with their friends. I miss out on things, no doubt about it. I'm not there with them all the time, but I'm constantly asking myself, *Are the things that I'm doing at work making a real, meaningful difference?* I want to work hard every day to create a better country, and a better world.

And as I navigate the complex world of leadership and governing, I look to my dad as a good example of parenting in political life. After my parents split up and my mum moved out, every single weekday evening my father would come home to 24 Sussex at 6:30 p.m. We would swim, read and do homework together. On these weekday nights, "the prime minister of Canada was not available." Now that I'm prime minister, I understand fully the hoops that he—and others—had to jump through to make this happen. But it was essential to us then, so I try to be as disciplined in my schedule with my own kids now—in that, Sophie is an essential partner.

That's not to say there's no overlap between work and family. I remember my dad bringing my brothers and me on work trips, not only across Canada, but to countries around the world. He was determined to make time for us and give us a peek into his job. We were incredibly fortunate to have lived that experience, and it's something I'm trying to replicate now with my own kids. Sometimes the whole family will come on one of my work trips, and they get to learn about other cultures while I'm busy in meetings. But oftentimes I bring just one of my kids along. It's important for them to have one-on-one time with their dad, and for us to share experiences that are ours and ours alone.

In this job, being fully present for my children is paramount. It's a work in progress, but I'm mindful of it every single day. When my dad was with us, he gave us 100 per cent of his attention. It was a beautiful gift. Now I'm trying to develop that same capacity, though I admit that sometimes my work phone is too close by. I often find myself looking to my dad as an example of how to find balance and remain an effective leader. I want to hold on to all the things my father did right. He was an incredible role model for me and my brothers. My dad was calm, wise and rational—some would say to a fault. He tried to make things equal with his pure intent.

But I'm also deviating somewhat from his mould as I raise my own kids. My father once took me on a rafting trip on the

Tatshenshini River when I was still a teenager. None of my brothers, just me and my father and a range of fascinating people—scientists, environmentalists, academics and of course river guides. Sometime later, he told my mother how impressed he had been to see me connecting and holding my own with such a range of interesting people. It's that kind of comment I wish I could have heard directly from him—and that I am going to make sure my children hear from me.

I try to be more emotionally engaged than my father was. More relaxed and spontaneous, too. I want my children to see me in a happy, successful relationship with their mum—that's very important to me. Sophie is my love, my equal and my life partner. When I met her, I knew pretty quickly I had found the right woman to be the mother of my children. She's been by my side throughout this incredible journey, and there's no doubt in my mind that I couldn't have done it without her patience, her guidance and her grace.

When my father was dying, I was at his side. He was eighty, I was twenty-eight. It was a beautiful time. I tried in those moments to return the love he'd given us, and to reassure him that we'd be okay. I miss him like you wouldn't believe, but I am also very much at peace. Parents are the centre of our solar system, even when we're adults. Being a father—nothing else matters as much. I get that now, and looking back, I see that same belief in the actions of my father. If I can follow his lead and strive every day to be a good husband, friend and father, I will proudly consider this a life well lived.

Bret Hart

Calgary, Alberta

Wrestler, actor, author, 62

||||||||||||||||||||||||||||||||||||||||||||||||||||||||||||||||||||||||||||||||||||||||||||||||

Bret Hart was born in 1957. He is a retired professional
and amateur wrestler, well known as Bret "The Hitman"
Hart. He is widely regarded as one of the greatest pro
wrestlers of all time, having cultivated a legacy over a
twenty-three-year career. Bret married Julie in 1982.
They had four children: Jade, born in 1983, Dallas in
1984, Alexandra ("Beans") in 1988 and Blade in 1990.
He and Julie split up in 1998. In 2010 Bret married
Stephanie Washington. Through his daughters, Bret is
now a grandparent to Kyra, Grayson, Bo and Vylet.

||||||||||||||||||||||||||||||||||||||||||||||||||||||||||||||||||||||||||||||||||||||||||||||||

What a childhood I had. I was number eight of twelve children. Our
house was wild. I didn't appreciate how hard it was for my parents until I got older. Maybe I don't truly even now. My mom never
learned to drive. My dad worked and did all the driving and all the
cooking. It was so busy. Sometimes dinner didn't get onto the table
until 9:30 or 10:00 at night. I was often short on sleep, and my teachers never understood what my life was like.

My dad was my superhero. You didn't cross him—totally the
wrong guy to dig a bigger hole with, and if he told you to jump you
said, "How high?" He was firm in a good way: how else do you handle twelve kids? The most important thing for Dad was to be with us.
The wrestling was just a job, everything was about being a father,
but running the wrestling business took him away far too often. I

saw the effect that this had on our family and vowed I'd never do the same.

Sunday evenings were a favourite of mine. First we wrestled and then we'd play a hot game of dodgeball using a medicine ball. After that, Dad scrubbed us down in the shower. Later, our treat was watching *Bonanza* and *The Untouchables*. It was a big challenge keeping us all fed, and sometimes things got tough. There were some really lean times. Dad picked up big boxes of distressed fruit from Safeway. We didn't care.

I have some great memories. It was freezing cold one winter. There were a number of cars on our property in various stages of disrepair and Dad couldn't start any one of them. Our neighbour loaned him a vw Beetle and my Dad managed to get ten Hart children packed in. It was so tight that when a door was opened we slithered out, all of us laughing helplessly.

I had lots of respect for him but I was also a bit intimidated, scared to mess up and fail. He was so disciplined and had such a strong work ethic. My dad was so proud when I won the city championships. That's when we truly bonded. He became my biggest supporter. I became a great wrestler because of him. He had a knack for steering us in the right direction, though I didn't always appreciate it at the time. I learned the hard way by ignoring his advice. He was so opposed to me getting married at twenty-five, I eloped. He knew I was making a mistake. But he didn't rub my nose in it. He showed respect by never bringing it up with me again. That's the kind of man he was.

He was the calm in a storm and there were many occasions when he not only stopped someone from doing something stupid, but managed to have things end on a positive note. An example of this is when we woke one winter's night around two a.m. to the sound of spinning tires. My father thought it was one of my brothers stuck in a snowdrift, but when he went out to help he found a kid trying to steal his car. My father hauled this kid back to the house, but instead of calling the police like most people would, my dad used his own form of discipline and "stretched" him. After that, he called the kid's parents to come and pick him up. Later on, he gave this kid a job as an usher at the matches.

FROM LEFT: Alexandra ("Beans"), Grayson, Jade, Steve, Bo (on Jade's lap), Bret and wife Stephanie, Blade, Lindsay, Vylet (on Lindsay's lap), Dallas and Kyra

Wrestling wasn't classy in the late seventies: rough people doing it, rough people watching. I wanted to help my dad by working hard for him. My whole ambition was to be a stay-at-home dad, I wasn't going to miss out on my kids growing up like my dad did. My career with WWF took off in 1992 and there was a lot of travel involved. I decided I would only do it for four or five years. But then I started making decent money. I bought way too big a house and I became a slave to it. I had no choice but to do the work and travel, but here I was, missing out on my kids growing up. All those special occasions like birthdays and Halloween—they passed me by. After all the times I had told myself that it would never happen... I had the same problem as my dad.

After my dad sold Stampede Wrestling, he lived vicariously through my wrestling career. Whenever I returned from a trip, I headed over to the Hart house to regale him and my mom with my stories. My first marriage didn't last and the breakup got pretty nasty.

FROM LEFT: Blade, Alexandra, Bret, Jade and Dallas

My kids went through a lot. Of course I have many regrets about what I did and didn't do. But the biggest regret I have is not my failed marriage, it is missing so much of my kids growing up.

That gave me a big burden of guilt that I have worked hard to dig myself out from underneath. Despite my absences, I have always been very close with all my kids. The meaning of "home," Dad created it, and I think I'm doing the same for my children. When I was away I would get so homesick: that long and winding road that led to the Hart house—it carved out a big space in my heart. I'm lucky that my kids all live in town. Now they come here! It's my privilege to make big Sunday dinners for my family just as my mom and dad did for us.

Marc Kielburger

Toronto, Ontario

Humanitarian, activist, 42

||||||||||||||||||||||||||||||||||||||||||||||||||||||||||||||||||||||||||||||||||||||||||||||||||||||||

Marc Kielburger grew up in Toronto, graduated from
Harvard University with a degree in international relations
and won a Rhodes Scholarship to complete his law
degree at Oxford University. He and his brother, Craig,
co-founded WE Charity, which is helping to lift more
than a million people out of poverty in Africa, Asia and
Latin America. In Canada, the US and the UK, WE Schools
and WE Day provide service learning programs to fifteen
thousand schools, engaging four million children in
becoming makers of change. Marc is married to Roxanne
Joyal, whom he met when they were teenagers working as
parliamentary pages in Ottawa. They have two daughters:
Lily-Rose, born in 2012, and Violette, born in 2015.

||||||||||||||||||||||||||||||||||||||||||||||||||||||||||||||||||||||||||||||||||||||||||||

My dad is a teacher: a loving, gentle, inordinately kind man. From
the time I was a little boy I have always viewed him as a terrific role
model. Whether we were at the grocery store, exploring a foreign
city or in the local park, he would be reaching out, engaging others
in conversation and helping wherever he could. He has a strong
sense of social justice: not out there protesting, but effecting change
in a very quiet, understated way, and certainly asking the right questions of my brother and me.

He's the son of an immigrant. His father worked very hard
and my dad inherited the strong work ethic and amazing sense of

purpose. I am not sure he set out to make activists of us, but what he did from an early age was involve us in discussions about what was going on in the world. He'd spread the daily newspaper out on the kitchen table and as he read it, he'd involve us in discussion. What was happening in the world was deeply personal to him. Once a week, he stepped it up by asking us to pick an issue we had discussed and say what we would do to change the problem.

He has provided his positive energy over the years, supporting us getting involved in pretty radical travels for young boys—Craig taking on the issue of child labour in India, and me, at age thirteen, travelling to a leper colony in Jamaica. He didn't shelter us, but instead was incredibly brave letting us grow up as "children of the world."

We had few rules and no curfew. There was no sense of "You have to do your homework." Anytime there was an issue, we'd talk. He had high expectations for us, but he communicated them well and if I did step out of line, he'd come alongside me saying "Let's solve this together," or "Maybe I wasn't clear enough. How can I support you better?" It was collaborative, and it's instilled good habits in both my brother and me, and paved the way for self-actualization. It was a white-picket-fence, *Leave It to Beaver* kind of childhood. No dysfunction, drama or big fights.

There were some things Dad didn't do. I was the only boy my age in our neighbourhood whose father didn't take him to play baseball. He's not a jock. I had to teach him how to play baseball, then basketball. I was very sporty and competitive, and he stepped willingly into my world.

Nowadays, he's worried about the state of the world, especially what's happening in North America. That's what we talk about, Canadian politics and the decline in moral authority. He still clips articles from the papers and every time I see him, he's got a stack for me. "Here's the seventeen articles you need to read," he'll say.

I have oodles of respect for him, especially since becoming a dad myself. I know there were times when I was a pain in the neck, for example when he took us to France for six weeks when I was sixteen.

Marc with Lily-Rose (BELOW) and Violette, 2018

The museum and galleries were not my idea of fun, and I was not the most gracious. By way of apology, this past summer I took my dad back to those same museums. I truly appreciate now what he was trying to show us.

I'm terrified, being a dad right now. My daughter, she's got my dad's outgoing personality and my sense of conviction, and she'll talk to anybody. The whole business of social media and bullying, I'm really scared she'll walk right into it. Even though it was simpler when I grew up, I think my dad's advice makes sense, and it's what he did with me: keep the communication open and comfortable.

I was very ready to be a dad. I'll never win the prize for the quantity of time I spend with my children, but I sure hope to win in terms of the quality of time when I'm with them. They adore me, and I make sure I am truly present when we are with each other. I know I take equal place as the strongest role model in their lives, and how I interact with my wife provides an example to my daughters of the people they'll one day marry.

In my work I have recognized that the most powerful people in the world are not politicians or CEOs, they're *parents*. The world needs your child and your child needs you! My brother and I wrote a book on this topic. We interviewed two hundred people on how to best promote prosocial behaviour, confidence, self-efficacy and sound decision-making. There's no magic formula, but having awareness, teaching compassion, understanding the language of feelings, and being able to effectively manage and express emotion— those ought to be on every dad's list.

Out there in the world, I see fathers who don't value their children, who abuse them, who sell their kids. My dark moments are when I observe this gross abdication of parental responsibility, of humanity—and of course it even happens in Canada. In North America, child-rearing is very personal and often private. Beyond immediate family, no one really gets involved or offers an opinion. But in Kenya, a baby belongs to the community. It's practically a civic duty to lend a hand, and advice. Despite our North American sensibilities and precautions, we learned to relax with our first baby on a visit to Kenya a number of years ago when she disappeared into a crowd after we handed her over to a friend.

Fathers have a challenge—they are not doing well in terms of developing empathy, particularly with young boys. My advice to new fathers is to be involved; your actions speak volumes. Nurture empathy; get your child thinking about others. Let your child take care of a pet, volunteer with your family, get them involved in their community, and set them up when they are little as useful and capable members of the family who have responsibilities. I

Marc Kielburger with brother Craig (LEFT) and father Fred

like the idea of creating and setting in motion rites of passage like Indigenous populations do across the world so that your child can graduate to different activities as they come of age. My hope is to see fathers open their hearts more, shed the tough-guy persona, and embrace the love and warmth available to them—investing in it deeply and wholeheartedly.

Susur Lee

Toronto, Ontario

Chef, restaurateur, 60

‖‖

Susur Lee was born in Hong Kong in 1958. He began
cooking in hotels at the age of fourteen and apprenticed
in prestigious luxury hotels before coming to Canada in
1978. Here, he worked his way up to the role of executive
chef at a number of restaurants before opening his own
establishment. He now runs several Toronto restaurants
(one with two of his sons) and his signature style of fusion
cuisine is very popular. Susur has competed on cooking
shows such as *Iron Chef Canada* and also acted as a judge
(*MasterChef Asia*). He is married to Brenda Bent and
they have three sons in their twenties: Levi, Kai and Jet.

‖‖

My boys, they put me to the test—quite often; they know my weak
spots and use gentle humour to nudge me along. We are in a very
good space. I certainly feel accepted by them. It's hard to believe
my babies are grown men, all of them now much bigger and taller
than me.

I grew up the youngest of six children in a very industrialized
part of Hong Kong, a lower-class area. Hong Kong, it's a city that's
"on" twenty-four hours a day, so vibrant. Everyone is industrious and
entrepreneurial—and in our family we were all expected to produce.
My parents would bring home boxes of plastic flowers and we'd put
them into bouquets and take them back to the factory where they'd
pay us ten dollars a dozen.

I have lots of special memories of my dad, a very lovely man, but in my book, too nice. Looking back I can see it was because he was just not that engaged. My mother, she was the powerful one in the family. I didn't feel that he was doing his part. As a male, I knew he was expected to stand up for what he believed in. He couldn't make decisions and I resented that. He was really nice to me, but very quiet, and he failed to inspire me. A little playful from time to time, and he loved to dance. That was one joy we shared: my greatest memories of him are when he would put on a record and we would dance.

By the time I was fourteen, all my siblings were working and I was the only child left at home. Capitalism was everywhere, and there wasn't much of a focus on education; it was all about making a living. I was rebellious and independent, and ready to spread my wings, so I left school and moved in with some friends. When that didn't work out, my brother took me in and said, "You've got to be a rat and work in this restaurant." That's how I got started. I never decided I was going to be a chef, it just happened.

My father never challenged me or reached out to me. He was just detached. My impression is that he kept everything inside. I don't think he had a clue how to handle his feelings. It was hard to read him, but I have a sense that he was consumed with guilt because there was trouble between him and my mum, and he had taken a mistress. I knew about this. It didn't sit well with me, under-standably. I imagine if his conscience had been clear, he'd have been a way livelier and happier person. He passed away when I was about fifty.

My mum, she's still going strong. I go to see her twice a year in Hong Kong. She's still the powerhouse; she never fails to amaze me. In some ways I look to her for my strength—what we culturally imagine comes from a father, in my family comes from her. She's very natural and aware of people emotionally. She's been much hap-pier since my father died. She's so witty and smart, but she missed out on her education. She doesn't even know how to write her name, and she uses her fingerprint when she goes to the bank to get cash.

FROM LEFT: Kai, Susur and Jet, 2017

My father came to Canada only once. I'm so glad he got to see me being a dad, completely invested in my children. He could see I was doing a great job. Although he didn't say much, I could tell that he was proud of me. No hugs, no compliments, the Chinese don't do that. But I got squeezes on my shoulder or a pat on my back as he passed by—and those meant a lot to me.

I had some challenging feelings when I was about to become a father for the first time. I was young, and my love was my kitchen. How would I cope? How would I handle being tied down? I wanted freedom. I felt daunted at the idea of responsibility. In 1990, right after Levi was born, I went out and bought the biggest motorcycle. My wife was so mad: "What the fuck are you doing? Are you crazy?" We were already in the game, Levi had arrived—what was I trying to prove and to whom?

My work was very important to me. It was flourishing in that period. I had so much creativity, so many things I wanted to do, but my wife is tough, she's very tough. She had a career, too, as a well-known designer in Toronto and she was not giving up her career, so we were both in it, we parented together.

We shared everything, all the duties; anything she could do I did, too. We had no family to lean on around us, we relied on babysitters or we took Levi with us; Brenda took him to the studio or I took him to the restaurant. She'd do the night duty because I needed to be at the market at six a.m. We were going *flat out*. But then magic happened. I remember it clearly with Levi. As soon as he got past the boring baby stage and he was interacting with me, I started to feel the love from this little boy. He gave me so much it filled my heart. I was in love.

I only rode the motorcycle a few times. It was a BMW off-road travelling bike; I had liked the idea of being an explorer. Each time I rode it I kept thinking, *This is ridiculous*. Then I put it in storage, and there it stayed for twenty-seven years. I sold it only six months ago! Looking back, I can see that this was a symbol of—and a statement I was making about—my freedom. Ultimately, I used my freedom to be with my boys. I wanted to have a strong connection and be a great example to my children. This was the most important job of my life.

I just love it when the boys reminisce about the fun we had when they were little and our lives were a whirlwind. They didn't miss anything. "Dad, remember when we did the game on the bed and I jumped around you and you rolled everywhere?" This from Jet, who is now six foot five and too big to jump on any bed. Their playfulness touches my heart. I was way more physical with my children than my own dad ever was.

People have asked me about raising children with my demanding career. Sure, I was short on time to spend with them, but I made certain when I was with them that I was 100 per cent present, even if I was tired. Of course I learned some tricks: I'd get myself a little nap by playing a game with them. I'd be lying on the couch: "Daddy's dead for fifteen minutes," then they would be hysterical if I started snoring.

I would watch other families and sometimes I would get nervous. *How do I get my kids to read a book? Play nice? Make friends?* I worried that I didn't know how to parent like other dads. It was most important to me that they have a good education, which they got,

FROM LEFT: Jet, Susur and Kai, 2017

but what I am most proud of is they have the life skills and character to live life to its fullest, in the style of their own generation. They've got the people skills, the business sense; they are good at making decisions. Some things they do I don't totally agree with, but I am able to let it go. We talk often and I am proud to say they reach out when they need help or advice. Since I never had that with my dad, it makes me feel I have succeeded with them.

When I was a child and did stupid things, there was no discipline from my father. He didn't react, nor did he help me fix my problems. I am making a point of following through with my boys. I teach them how to problem-solve; I teach them how to fix things.

We have a close emotional bond and we are very close physically. There's a level of intimacy we have achieved by using nicknames for each other. It's like we have a private family language that brings us closer together. All three boys have them. When someone is really mad, when you use their special name, it's like a reset button, it brings harmony. It works and it comes very naturally. They do it to me, too! It helps a lot; it breaks a boundary. "Yes, Chef," they'll say. It's tender, intimate, very close.

My values are from Asia. A really solid work ethic, dedication, not giving up, but I also try not to be so *Chinese* with my children. I have been here longer than I ever lived there. They sometimes wonder how their mum and I can be together. Me from Hong Kong, their mum from Winnipeg with a redneck background. We couldn't be more different! In many of the ways I think and behave, I am still very Chinese. In the way I do business, my Chinese-ness comes through. The boys have learned from me that there is always a bargain to be had. I'm still so strongly connected to Asia—that's where all the things I love to eat are from!

My biggest worry about my boys growing up took care of itself. My kids are not big drinkers. At home, we provide sound role models. I didn't dictate to them about drug use, but we did discuss how people feel about "using" in this industry. No one trusts a druggie. I've been able to plant my values. I encourage them to travel, to experience life to its fullest. I never interfere in their love lives. I can talk about sexuality with them indirectly using my playfulness and sense of humour. Mostly, I've wanted to normalize healthy sexual relationships.

They've grown up in restaurants with lots of people and chances to learn from many others besides their parents, just like I was influenced by the older men and women who mentored me when I lived and cooked in Hong Kong. In the kitchen you feel the full consequences of your actions very quickly. Those are the really important life lessons you don't get in school.

It was years ago, when Levi was very young, that I was cooking abroad. I was lined up to do a cooking event with a highly accomplished chef and it was arranged for us to have dinner together the night before. On occasions such as this we eat well, and the mood is usually light and fun. When we sat down together that evening, this man's mood was dark, kind of heavy, very serious. As we shared our food, he opened up to me. I remember that conversation so vividly. He began to talk about his life, how frantic it was, how little free time he had and how he hadn't paid much attention to his daughter, thinking everything was fine. Now, she was suffering. He told me, "She's not happy with her life or living in this world."

His pain and sorrow were so huge and apparent. I realized very quickly that it didn't matter that he was a great chef; none of that was important. Our stress level at home had been really high, but here was a lesson I could apply right away to my own family life. Food is love. It's how I show love, cooking for my family. I do it a lot, they can rely on me, but what I love most of all is that they can rely on themselves. I chuckled when my youngest son asked recently, "Is there anything wrong with living with your parents forever?"

Trevor Linden

Vancouver, British Columbia

Former Vancouver Canuck, 49

||||||||||||||||||||||||||||||||||||||||||||||||||||||||||||||||||||||||||||||||

Trevor Linden was born in Medicine Hat, Alberta in
1970. He played twenty seasons in the NHL from 1988
to 2008, sixteen of those with the Vancouver Canucks,
earning him the nickname "Captain Canuck." Trevor was
president of hockey operations for the Canucks from
2014 to 2018. He also has business ventures in Vancouver:
Club16 Trevor Linden Fitness and Orangetheory Fitness.
Trevor has been married to Cristina for twenty-three
years and they have a son, Roman, born on July 12, 2017.

||||||||||||||||||||||||||||||||||||||||||||||||||||||||||||||||||||||||||||||||

Fatherhood has changed since I was born in the 1970s. People look
at it way differently now than they did back then, at least I think
most do. Fathers didn't put so much into fatherhood, and they didn't
get so much out. My dad and my grandpa were in a business venture
together that didn't go well. Dad set out on his own in the oil and gas
industry. He was very honest, hard-working—grinding every day just
to keep a roof over our heads and food on the table. We lived very
modestly; it was tough at times. I was the second of three boys. Dad
was always supportive and interested. Mom was the one who did
the hands-on parenting, acted as the disciplinarian, and she was
the glue in the family. She was athletic, really sports-minded. She
was also the bookkeeper for the business.

I had a great childhood growing up in Medicine Hat. My parents
gave us every opportunity we wanted, a lot of it to do with sport. My

father tells the story of me at about age four insisting on going out on the ice at the outdoor rink. It was thirty degrees below zero, but I was one determined little boy, so my father took me down to the rink and put me on the ice while he jumped back in the truck to watch me while staying warm.

Life was simple compared to what it is now, and people didn't expect so much. I never felt hard done by, not at all, but there wasn't as much time made for "fun." In fact when I think about it, fun was considered a luxury. I never went on a plane until I was twelve years old. For us, holidays were going out to our land or my uncle's farm—he had a big spread and we'd participate in the branding, fix fences, pick rocks...

One of the highlights of my childhood was going out to the shop with my dad. On one occasion my mom said, "You can't go, he's going to be leaving at five a.m." That didn't matter to me. I was so keen to go anyway, out to the gravel pit where he kept all the equipment. He taught me how to run a front-end loader, and once he got a motorbike out there and taught us how to ride that. I loved being around the equipment. My brothers and I were so glad to be a part of a lot of things in Dad's world. I admired his business sense and as I got older he explained things to me, like bidding on a job or buying a new piece of equipment from an auction house.

Dad supported us 100 per cent, but he wasn't an athletic guy, not a sports fan, not into hockey. Sport didn't come naturally to him. The nice thing about that was because he didn't know a lot about hockey, he didn't push me one way or the other. He didn't tell me what to do or how to do it, there was no pressure from him whatsoever. That contrasts sharply with some of the over-the-top hockey parenting of today. What Dad did or didn't do has served me well. I was a self-starter; I pushed myself to achieve. It was all about me, not him!

I don't think I learned much about handling conflict from my dad. He deferred to my mom, and she took a "tough love" approach. She is an amazing parent. She grew up with six siblings on a farm in southern Alberta—the family lived in a granary after their house burned down. She's very practical and down-to-earth. I hope I can have some of those same qualities as a father.

Love wasn't something you talked about when I was growing up, and there wasn't room for public displays of affection. We weren't a touchy-feely kind of family. Occasionally I'd get a rub on the back of my neck from my dad, which I just loved. Typically, in the seventies in southern Alberta people showed their love through what they did for others. In our family there was a tremendous amount of love, support and caring. Dad worked his ass off to provide for us; Mom worked extremely hard, put food on the table, packed great lunches every day: that was the language of love in our family.

Feelings weren't something that anyone made much room for—nobody really thought too much about them. If we were sick we just got on with it—we still had to do our chores and go to school. Dad and I, we talked about business, equipment, trucks and cars. Cars were a big thing in our family. I had a job by the time I was ten at the golf course, picking up range balls. I became a club cleaner at age twelve, all so I could save enough money to buy a car when I was sixteen. Dad drove me to Calgary in March 1986, just before my sixteenth birthday. We found a car, and I took all of the money out of my bank account (three thousand dollars) to pay for it!

I was a good kid, I was so into sport; I wasn't out partying, drinking or smoking pot. I pushed myself hard to be as good as I could at whatever I was doing. I made it easy for them—we all did. I know Dad was exasperated with me at times, but he never lost his cool in a scary way. I find the relationship I have with my dad challenging; it's been a bit of a struggle. I know I've been a bit impatient with him at times, which doesn't help.

We are all broken people because of the places we come from. Our imperfections create the environment for our own children. If you don't address those imperfections, you take them into your own parenting. I see my dad's challenges and I see where they come from. I understand more now about why they are there. Both his parents came from families where there were issues of alcohol addiction and violence. It's affected him; it manifests in very different ways, but I understand that now. I love him.

Discussing his feelings is not something my dad has ever been comfortable with. I can talk openly with him about reaching out for help, about the benefits of counselling, about what's worked for me. I go to a therapist once a week; I've done so for a long time, and it's been invaluable for me. What's not to love about being able to talk about where I am at, why something is going on for me and where my feelings are coming from? It's helped me to be able to understand myself a whole lot better. I think what holds my dad back is the old stigma about mental health issues, about asking for help and about admitting vulnerability. It's changing—the old myths are breaking down—but for men of his generation those barriers have been pretty significant.

I think about how it's so important to continue to grow, learn, change and evolve throughout life. I'd like to see my dad be able to explore who he is. The wonderful thing is, it's not over. My relationship with my dad, his well-being, it's all a work in progress. I fully expect things will improve. My dad, brothers and I, we all keep working at our father-son connection. Believe it or not, Dad took up cycling about five years ago, already in his seventies. In the summer of 2019 my brothers, my dad and I are taking a trip together. We are heading off to France to cycle a Wounded Warriors journey from Dieppe to Juno Beach. How many families do that kind of thing together?

Cristina and I had been married for twenty-two years. We wanted a baby but we started late. The chances of it happening were getting slimmer, and we were "running out of runway." Cristina wasn't able to carry a baby so we went the surrogate route to become parents to our son Roman, who arrived in July 2017. I was so scared about having a baby and disrupting what seemed to be a perfect life. It was a scary transition. I had heard some stories about dads who couldn't cope with babies, and I was afraid I'd be one of them.

I had no clue about babies. I liked children, but babies? I've always been scared to death... I never wanted to hold one in case I did the wrong thing; they are so fragile! I froze when someone put a baby in my arms. *Holy shit*, I was thinking. *What have I got myself into?* To make matters worse, we'd have people actually say things to us like, "Forget about having fun," and "Your life is over!"

Trevor and Roman, 2018

When Roman was born in July 2017 I was off work and able to be there twenty-four seven and because we were bottle-feeding, I had the great joy of being the one to get up with him every single night for the first few months. I can't believe how much I loved that phase. It was just like magic from the day he was born, how comfortable I was with him. I guess I was a natural at forty-seven years of age! I love the time I get with just Roman and me. If Cristina is away, Roman and I are fine.

Of course our lives are different than before he arrived, but it's all for the better. We support each other in parenting, and we support each other in having our alone time. This little guy, he's a dream. For the last ten months, he's slept from seven p.m. to seven a.m. He loves to eat, he loves his car seat, he's happy being out in the stroller, he really is an amazing kid and he's brought so much joy to our families. I never thought my brothers would be that keen, but they adore him. My older brother even makes special visits once a week to spend time with him. For Cristina's parents, he's their only precious grandchild.

I am proud of making it work. I am not holding back on life at all. We take Roman everywhere. Cristina and I both love hiking, biking, skiing, camping. We are already introducing Roman to the outdoors and getting him out into the mountains. I did a lot of worrying about being an older dad, but I'm fit and active and I expect to be so for a long time. When Roman's twenty, I'll be sixty-seven. I do the math all the time. I hope he'll still want to do things with me.

I want to create a different experience for him; not the screen time or the fancy holidays. Four Seasons Hotel in Hawaii? If you go there, you could be anywhere in the world and not really know the difference. I have no interest in Roman playing hockey at all. I'd prefer him not to, but I'll support him in doing what he wants to do. I'd love for him to play baseball, as I want to be one of those dads out there at the baseball diamond! Most importantly, I want to have a relationship with my son where he can talk to me about anything. I want to build trust and foster closeness. That's a hard thing to do, and I know I can come across as a bit intimidating at times.

Quite honestly, I have been so driven, so goal focused my whole life that I need to learn how to have more fun. From the time I was ten years old, I was super responsible, hard-working, wanted to please people, do the right thing. Roman is bringing out the kid in me and I want him to view me as a fun dad. With Roman, my life is in a different groove altogether. I never imagined I could be sitting on the floor singing songs in a music class with my child, five moms and their babies. Never thought I'd be that guy. I feel incredibly lucky and happy to have this time in my life, to be a dad.

Charlie Demers with his daughter, Joséphine

Charlie Demers

Vancouver, British Columbia

Writer, comedian, activist, 39

|||||||||||||||||||||||||||||||||||||||||||||||||||||||||||||||||||||||||||||||||||||||||

Charlie Demers is a writer, comedian and political
activist born and raised in Vancouver. He frequently
performs stand-up comedy in live venues across Canada
and appears on CBC Radio's comedy show *The Debaters*.
He is the author of *Vancouver Special* (2009), *The
Prescription Errors* (2009), *The Horrors: An A to Z of Funny
Thoughts on Awful Things* (2015), *The Dad Dialogues: A
Correspondence on Fatherhood (and the Universe)* (2016;
co-written with George Bowering) and *Property Values*
(2018). He lives in Vancouver with his wife, Cara,
and daughter, Joséphine, who was born in 2014.

|||||||||||||||||||||||||||||||||||||||||||||||||||||||||||||||||||||||||||||||||||||

When I became a father, I began looking at life through a whole
new lens. Before becoming a parent, I thought of life in a linear way.
Since Joséphine was born, I've seen life as more of a spiral, like
the back of a seashell. I see myself coming back to the experiences of my childhood as she experiences her "firsts." In September,
school will start, but this time it's our daughter who attends, and
I see myself returning to the same experiences I had as a child,
one layer removed. I am hoping it'll spiral around again for me as
a grandparent.

I have hypochondria, I catastrophize. We had a very difficult
birth and the whole while, as it was happening, I was telling myself
there was no way she'd live. Joséphine was about as late as they'll

allow a baby to be. She was due December 22 and didn't arrive until January 3. By that time, we had heard every platitude imaginable. Everyone told us that "babies come when they are ready"... *unless you need synthesized oxytocin*, I told myself. Yeah, they come when they are ready, *unless you need a balloon behind the cervix*, or they come when they are ready, *unless you need an obstetrician roused from their bed at four in the morning.* While I was imagining the worst, there she was on January 3, none the worse for wear.

In the first years of her life, Joséphine had a number of health scares, which made it easy for me to project a lot of my health panic onto her. We reached the high-water mark of infant medical terror one day when she was eighteen months old and had a strong allergic reaction to eating walnuts, and she had to spend the night in a hospital in Berlin, where we were staying. Thank God, Joséphine has been very healthy ever since.

Of course, when you are expecting a baby, you receive so much advice about what's going to happen to you, some of it useful but 90 per cent of it just common sense. One important piece of knowledge shared with me by my friend Seán Cullen was, "You are now the second most important person in two people's lives." It felt very true for the first couple of years. It was nice at around the age of three, when there was no longer the same kind of biological determinism and I became as needed by Joséphine as my partner was. Now, when I am being beckoned out of bed or whatever it is, it's a special thing to be needed in that way. It's what I always wanted but it's a lot of work!

When Joséphine was little, I was struck by how much of herself she really was. I had kind of thought you moulded the baby you had into the person you wanted them to be. One of the things I realized almost right away was that they come with personality. She came out as Joséphine. I am more following than leading. I had to let go of the idea that this child was some kind of blank slate, and she's stuck with her path. I have stopped expecting there might be a 180 or a U-turn. We are a feminist household. We think about the kind of messages we are sending her explicitly and tacitly about gender. We lay the various options out, but she hasn't given us much of a chance to be as "hip" as we thought we'd be. She is so clear about being a girl and wanting the girls' toys, it's been kind of like raising a gay son—she's so hyperfeminine, it's almost like she's doing drag. But I really believe now that they come as who they are and it's up to us to create the conditions for those characteristics she came with to express themselves.

Joséphine is the opposite of a shrinking violet! She has a distinct insistence on her own sovereignty and ownership of her body. If you are trying to get her into a shirt she doesn't want to wear, or to get her to take a bath when she's not in the mood, she'll let you know. These characteristics may make her a challenge to raise, but isn't it especially true for fathers of daughters that those characteristics are the very same ones we want our daughters to take out into the world? I can't help but think, *man, I hope she holds on to this.*

I have been very lucky with male role models in my life, beginning with my dad. If there was any concern I could identify with me taking on my father's example it would be that he was a superhero who did it all. When my mom was sick, he was working full-time, going to school, looking after a wife in hospital and raising two boys. I took his example of grace under fire in an emergency situation and tried to make it my game plan. Instead of reading it as, "you *could* do something like this if you had to," I took it to mean, "you *should* do something like this."

When Joséphine was born, I had this almost avaricious approach to making money in my professional life. "Get out there and earn," I said to myself. This was the biggest mistake that I made. Because I was a freelancer, I'd say "yes" to absolutely everything, and as a comedian, if I am earning it means I'm away from home—either I'm on the road or I'm performing late nights. I did my first comedy festival when Joséphine was five weeks old. Those career commitments I made, I couldn't disentangle until she was about two years old, and I won't ever get that time back. It was brutal and really tough on our marriage. I would get home and think, *finally, I can sit down and relax*, and Cara was like, *finally, here's someone to hold this baby and give me a break*. Cara and I were like two people drowning three feet apart from each other.

I am grateful for the sage advice that came from a friend who told me how to keep my relationship with my wife from being entirely subsumed by a new relationship with her as a co-parent. The advice I'd give to my thirty-three-year-old self is that feathering the nest is less important than being in the nest. In those first few years, you need time more than you need money. If only there had been an unbroken span of time to have been able to care for Joséphine on an hour-by-hour, minute-by-minute basis.

I have OCD so I am a naturally talented worrier. When we were expecting Joséphine I worried about a lot of things, like health, money and survival. A big fear I had is that things wouldn't last—that like me, and like my mom, Joséphine would lose a parent early. I wish someone had pulled me aside and said "relax, slow down."

It's a very interesting time for fathers. We are being fed a few different lines. One is that we have to be our best selves as earners, and another is that we need to shake that caveman idea of a father's distant, perfunctory role in the raising of children. The truth is, we are being sold a version of fatherhood that is really only accessible to those who already have money. Those are the fathers who can afford to invest that time in "being present."

Some guys who are becoming fathers are saying to themselves, *what can I do to be nothing like my dad?*, whereas my dad was 95 per cent the kind of dad I wanted to be. The question became more about how could I be more like him. With his being a closeted gay man in the eighties and nineties, for me it was like he was the text-book Goldilocks of masculinity and femininity. I just felt that he was the perfect blend. I never thought of him as being any less strong or tough or manly, but he was so sensitive and so attuned to the beautiful things in life, so attuned to people's feelings. That gave me a huge start in life. I didn't have the same complexes about asking for help, expressing my feelings or whatever. It was very balanced.

My dad's particular manifestation of manliness—for want of a better word—is always something I aspire to. Never a meathead, but he wasn't a weenie, either. Even before he came out, when he displayed characteristics that could be considered more along the feminine gradient, it was always with such confidence and style, it

Charlie Demers

never seemed to be a sacrifice of what made him a man. To me, he always seemed to be a great example of what a man should be. He knew nothing about cars or sports, but that didn't make him nervous at all.

He was loved and respected by my friends. A kid I was at school with called my dad one night when he was drunk at a party to get my dad to pick him up and take him home. This was long after we had stopped being friends, but my dad had made it clear that he could and would do that. He didn't do it in a way that sacrificed distance between us. He didn't try to be one of the kids, he was just someone who understood the humanity of young people.

I feel very lucky to have him. I am very aware what a privilege it is.

All the stuff that guys complain about their dads not doing, I could never relate to them. I have always felt I could talk to Dad about anything and everything, never feel judged by him, I never felt his love for me could be lost, it was totally unconditional. He was cool when other people's dads weren't. He had style, charisma, never the kind of dad who'd embarrass you. He took us to concerts, to the symphony, film festivals, the library. We weren't a rich family, but we sure had access to this rich cultural world that he saw as important.

My dad and I came to an early understanding that I would never lie to him and that he would always trust me. That created such a mutually beneficial bond early on that it never occurred to me to put that at risk, it was so good for us both. When Mom died, I was ten and my brother was seven. Overnight it was like I was eighteen and my brother was four—we broke in different directions. Dad basically, tacitly said, "I'm going to need you to do some more grown-up stuff, and in exchange I am going to treat you as more of a grown-up." A year later, he started working on his master's degree and I would have to make dinner for my brother and myself. When I look at my friends' kids who are eleven years old, I think, *Jesus Christ, I can't imagine them being anywhere close to doing that kind of thing*. At the time it was all very natural. I would get the job done, Dad would be at school. Of course, it changed the dynamic between us, it had to.

I'd describe Dad's parenting style as being at the far end of the libertarian continuum. Once I was in my teens, there was very little he'd say no to, or that I needed direction with. I had a long leash, but I never had the sense that he was absent. When I was going to a concert in grade ten, he said, "You know, there's a very big difference between smoking grass, which is a natural substance, and doing chemical drugs." His honesty in that moment made so much intuitive sense, I never tried anything harder than marijuana. Very indicative of his style is that when I didn't go straight to university from high school, he charged me rent to live at home. When I decided to start my degree, he gave me back all the rent I had paid for my tuition.

We could talk about anything, but if you look back at our house, technically we were all keeping some very big secrets from each other. My brother was gay, my dad was gay and I had ocd. I was hiding it from everyone in the world. Dad came out in 2000, when I was twenty, my brother just about six months before him. Maybe

Dad would have disclosed it sooner, but he was a teacher, and in the nineties there was still this idea that gay men could not be trusted around children. Anyway, we were all dealing with the trauma of my mom's death.

The only real negative side effect for me of Dad being in the closet was that it would have been good for me to know that the relationships he was having after Mom died were not just close male friendships—to have known they were romantic would have helped. I am afraid I thought of him as being kind of a Sicilian widow who after losing the love of his life had sworn off romance and had never moved on. That gave me a warped sense of how to continue to show your love for someone you have lost.

Dad's happily married now to a great guy, my stepdad. He lives in Nova Scotia and we have a few visits with them each year, and in between, lots of FaceTime with Joséphine.

Turning thirty-nine this year felt significant for me because that was how old my mom was when she died. I think back to my dad and how he coped. I am amazed at the job he did.

Robert Bateman

Salt Spring Island, British Columbia

Artist, 89

||||||||||||||||||||||||||||||||||||||||||||||||||||||||||||||||||||||||||||||||||||

Robert Bateman is an artist and naturalist living on Salt Spring Island. He was born in Toronto, Ontario in 1930. His first marriage was to Suzanne Bowerman, with whom he had three children: Alan, Sarah and John. In 1975 he and Birgit Freybe were married. They had two children together: Christopher and Rob.

||||||||||||||||||||||||||||||||||||||||||||||||||||||||||||||||||||||||||||||||

My father was a taciturn engineer, not noted for introspection. My mother did most of the hands-on child-rearing with positive energy and caring. Dad and I had a good relationship, but he didn't say much. We didn't argue, nor did we go deep. And we weren't physical. His family were farming stock from the north of Ireland. I think of them as salt of the earth.

Family was all-important to my dad. My parents had a good marriage and worked well as a team. Unlike many men of his generation, he did not balk at domestic tasks. I have vivid memories of him at the kitchen sink, happily engaged in his task of washing dishes after Mum had cooked a delicious meal. He had a gentle presence and a strong sense of social justice that I appreciated. He wasn't a loquacious man. Like I said, there weren't any arguments, but neither were there any philosophical discussions, which I would have loved. There were lots of topics that you just couldn't talk to him about.

He was moderate in absolutely everything, including moderation: two glasses of sherry a year, one beer, two cigarettes. He was very even, no big show of emotion, and avoided arguments if at all possible. My dad was a putterer, always accomplishing something. We were always expected to be busy, accomplishing something—with that old Protestant work ethic. I remember him telling us to "get your hands out of your pockets" and "take a 'holt.'" There was no blasphemy allowed and certainly no swearing.

My most endearing memories of childhood are of being in the outdoors, of being at our summer cottage, where we began going for holidays in 1938. That's where my deep and abiding connection with nature began. I don't have one ounce of jock in me. I was never comfortable on the playing field or in the locker room. I was a boy birdwatcher.

The pursuit of the traditional definition of masculinity is socially destructive. It might have been fine for cave dwellers, but in this day and age it gets men into a lot of trouble. We don't need to be out there being brutal buccaneers, but somehow we seem unable to reinvent a popular alternative. It's even *dangerous* to be male! I saw a cartoon not that long ago: two young boys playing, one says to the other, "What are you going to be *if* you grow up?" It's a bad idea that most countries in the world are run by men who are *still* boys with toys—like in the Pentagon. Too much testosterone for their own good, and our own good.

It's so counterproductive for nations. The Taliban have no trouble getting recruits from young men who think it's fun to be violent. We can follow it back to Genghis Khan and the Vikings—plenty of young men who somehow found it rewarding to hurt and kill. It's past time to stop fostering aggressive behaviour in boys. I wince when I hear about some of the things boys are routinely exposed to. Turn off the TV and get rid of these violent video games! Pay attention to the kinds of toys you put in the hands of your children and think about the messages those things communicate. Get your kids outdoors! Nature is pure magic.

Even with only one child I already thought of myself as the patriarch, perhaps aided by the fact that I was the eldest of three boys. I love the role, and although I believe in zero population growth, I've produced five children (with two different wives). My children, all

Robert, wife Birgit and children, 1975

adults now of course, were "free-range" kids long before the idea became popularized. Like me, they were out at all hours and in all weathers.

I'm a chronic scheduler and my kids would probably say that I should have been more spontaneous. When they were young, I needed to see them being busy and engaged. I couldn't tolerate "lazy bones" or the remote appearance of them. Sometimes I was busy imposing the Protestant work ethic that my father had put in place without really thinking about whether that worked and if that were really how I wanted to raise my children. Giving orders only backfired. Instead, I would give my children choices, but I chose what was on the menu. That way the kids felt they had some control, but I set the standards.

My dad died when I was forty-five. One thing I am so glad to have done with Dad in the last bit of his life was to go down memory lane with him. I took a tape recorder and went around all his boyhood haunts near Tweed outside Belleville. I heard all the stories, saw the barns he played in, his house growing up, the river and lakes he fished in. I wish I'd known more about what he thought and what he believed in. He rarely gave advice and actually I wish he had given me more. My kids would probably say I have done the opposite, dispensed too much. I usually work hard to consciously resist the instinct to interfere, but not always with success.

Over the years, my kids and I...we've worked things out. When there's a problem we talk, we don't let things linger or go underground, we deal with things. I make suggestions and I receive theirs. I don't harbour resentment and I never, ever use putdowns. We have open, deep and trusting relationships. My son Christopher, almost from the time that he could walk and talk, I thought of him as a sort of superior being, kind of an old soul: I remember going to him for advice when he was about six years old!

I think approaching parenthood free from gender stereotypes is the healthiest way to go, both parents pulling their weight, because mostly both parents are working, so it's pointless to divide labour along old, worn-out gender lines. Fathers should be engaged, get off their phones, take an interest, be great listeners (men often aren't), communicate and share, share, share. Be yourself, communicate your own hopes and dreams. Don't tolerate mediocrity!

It's been important to me to be involved in the lives of my children, to give them advice even if they don't ask for it or take it. My sons are great dads and I like to think I have set a good example for them. You never set out with this in mind, but really when I think about it, that has to be the bottom line, the joy and satisfaction of seeing your children becoming good parents. Each will leave the world a better place, I am convinced.

The best advice I can give to new fathers is what I heard many years ago from June Callwood at a Christmas party, and I read this repeated in *Chatelaine* after she died. It's ridiculously simple: "Be kind." If only we could all do it, it would change the world.

In the last stages of his life, I didn't want to say, "Hey Dad, I've always wanted to say how much you have meant to me." He wasn't the type and with him, I wasn't that type either. I remember my last time of what felt like an intimate encounter with him. He was dying of cancer in Princess Margaret Hospital in Toronto. I grabbed him by

Bateman children, 1977

the big toe and shook it. "So long, Dad," I said. "I'll see you tomorrow." Nothing really left unsaid.

Koji Masuda

Vancouver, British Columbia

Real estate developer, 49

||||||||||||||||||||||||||||||||||||||||||||||||||||||||||||||||||||||||||||||||||||||||||||||

Koji Masuda was born in Yokohama, Japan in 1969, and is the elder of two boys. He is a real estate developer who divides his time between Vancouver, Victoria and Japan. His paternal grandfather was a great entrepreneur who lost everything to the US government at the end of the Second World War, and made his fortune over again. His father took over the business when his grandfather died; at the time it was worth four hundred million dollars. Koji is the father of two children, Leanne (born in 2000), who lives in Okinawa, Japan, and Maho (born in 2010), who lives in Victoria, BC.

||||||||||||||||||||||||||||||||||||||||||||||||||||||||||||||||||||||||||||||||||||||||||||||

Before we get to my father, a little background about my grandfathers. My maternal grandfather was an entrepreneur—amassing his wealth in advertising—and an elite Second World War veteran. He was a very private person who was hard to get close to, a man who held his feelings inside and I think suffered from post-traumatic stress disorder—PTSD. He would never complain about anything. Even on the hottest day in Japan he would never say, "I'm hot." Some of this had to do with his martial-art discipline but I think also because of what he experienced during the Second World War when he became the sole survivor of his battalions.

I never met my grandfather on my father's side. My grandmother refused to have anything to do with him because of his extramarital affairs. My grandmother kicked my grandfather out, and he died when I was twelve years old in the care of his mistress. My father was the dutiful son, even after he died, looking after my grandfather's interests and taking care of his mistress. Was it the honourable thing? I don't know. Even now I am conflicted and confused by the ideas of duty and honour, Japanese values and Canadian beliefs. But I think it was the right thing to do, as she had cared for him.

When I heard that this grandfather of mine had died, I was furious. I was so sad not to have met him. I confronted my father, and there was a big scene at home. My father raged at me but then he raged at my mother because she was the one who had told me the family truths.

My grandfather amassed a great fortune. He had many employees and they called my father the "little prince." As a boy my father didn't even have to dress himself. He never had to think of anyone else but himself. Anything he wanted, he could do. It's left him to this day with a "take it or leave it" mentality: I'm right and you're wrong. He has made lots of enemies. Even though he spends time in North America, he has never been able to embrace Western ways. He can be a kind, gentle and sincere man. He's family-minded, no question, but you cannot query what he says or oppose him. He believes that children should be deferential and obedient. He needed to control me, my brother, his employees. He has expected complete loyalty and submission, and managed to burn through a whole lot of staff, especially secretaries.

My upbringing was very tough and militaristic. My father was barely ever around. When he did come home, everyone was supposed to be at his beck and call. Women were subservient and considered inferior to men. My father didn't know how to show empathy, accommodate others, or be flexible.

It was obvious to me that my parents' marriage was in trouble. They broke up in 1983 when I was thirteen. My father told my mum, "Up until now you have raised the boys. Now I'm going to do it." Then he sent us to boarding school in Canada and moved in with his mistress in Tokyo. He'd been having affairs for years. This, for him, was an acceptable means of handling stress.

Koji and Leanne, 2009

Dad had tried to paint a rosy picture of Canada, but when I arrived it was a brutal transition. I'd been happy at my school in Japan and learning English proved a huge challenge. At my school I had to work hard to find my place, to make friends, to fit in. I had to fight for my rights more than once. Although I spent my teenage years here in Canada, I brought my Japanese culture with me. One of my teachers remembers me always stopping when I saw her ahead, stepping aside and bowing. I hung on to many traditional values and practices, without examining what they were and if they worked for me. Over the years I have learned to discard the ones that don't fit.

My father could not handle it when I showed that I was different from him. He expected me to embrace the same values and methods as him, whether I believed in them or not. I have the same goals as my dad, but different ways of achieving them. Like him, I want to preserve the family business, look after the employees, make their families happy. Raise a happy family.

I was supposed to consult with him about my choice of partner, but I got engaged to Yoko when I was twenty-seven without even telling my parents. I was working for my father at the time, as an executive in Seattle, and as soon as my father found out, he sent me back to Japan on a one-year assignment for "more training" on one-tenth of my previous salary. The job was not what I'd been promised. I left after three months to forge my own path. Free will was so important to me I was willing to let everything else go.

Yoko and I got married, and we had a baby, Leanne. The early days were wonderful, and I was very happy to be a hands-on father, doing everything for my baby and reaping the benefits. However, Yoko experienced anxiety and postpartum depression. We didn't handle it well. When things became really tough for us, I was not there to resolve any issues and I let Yoko down. Like my father and grandfather had done, I looked elsewhere for intimacy, which of course drove a huge wedge between us. We separated, a bitter divorce followed and I was shut out of Leanne's life.

Since coming back to Canada, I have made regular trips to Japan in the hope of seeing Leanne. I support her and have continued to write to her every month. I am determined not to disappear. Even if we have little chance to see each other, brief exchanges can sustain me. Our emotional connection is deep, and the love I have for my daughter burns brightly and will not fade!

I married again in 2009 here in Canada and our daughter Maho was born a year later. Sadly, that marriage also went sideways. It was a devastating experience to put Maho through our divorce; however, this one was more of a "good" divorce. Her mum and I share custody and Maho spends many of her days with me.

My father and I remain estranged from each other. It really does hurt me. I wish that he could get rid of his ego and pride, and just be a father. When I was small I wanted so badly for him to notice me, to want to spend time with me. I would like him to recognize that being a father is bigger than who you are or what you are. Being a father, bringing life into the world gives you a responsibility to disregard your own needs, to go beyond your ego.

Children teach you a great deal—as much as you try to raise them well, there are no guarantees. Parenting is an art, not a science. You must be willing and committed to staying the course. I believe in

Maho and Koji, 2017

my children so that they can challenge themselves and live to their potential. I am their believer, their coach and their cheerleader. I love the pleasure of providing a positive and encouraging environment for their growth and development, knowing that I have a place in the future through my children—that through these beautiful little people, I have made a contribution to life itself.

Larry Goldenberg

Vancouver, British Columbia

Urologist, founder of Canadian Men's Health Foundation, 65

‖‖‖

Dr. Larry Goldenberg grew up in Toronto and is the
child of Holocaust survivors. He is an award-winning
researcher in the field of medicine and prostate research
and a member of the Order of Canada. He is professor
and past head of the Department of Urologic Sciences
at the University of British Columbia. In 2014 he
established the Canadian Men's Health Foundation to
build awareness and help change attitudes and behaviour
to improve the overall health of Canadian men. Larry
lives in Vancouver with his wife Paula. They have two
sons: Adam, born in 1987, and Mitchell, born in 1989.

‖‖‖

I like what you are doing with this book. You know, I have been
working on issues related to men's health and well-being—it's my
passion—and I've discovered that in order to reach men, you have to
line up your message at least six different ways to be sure they receive
it. Men are morphologically different, psycho-morphologically different. We've done some research related to this. It's similar to the
retail sector: no matter what the issue, you must find a variety of
ways to get the message across.

I've always wanted to be like my father. I've never met anyone who disliked him or didn't respect him. This basic need to be
respected, to be liked, is what's driven me to succeed in medicine
and care for my patients. I am the son of Holocaust survivors. My

dad survived in hiding in Europe. He came to Canada after the war, twenty-one years old with no money, no English; all he had was creative energy and street smarts. The only word he had in English was *Coca-Cola*. He started as a painter, learned to build houses and soon had his own company, self-taught all the way.

He had many skills that worked for him in his work, especially his enormous energy. I always thought he was trying to work enough for two people, himself and his brother who died in the war. And he had diplomacy. Although he was the one making successful business decisions, he had a knack for letting his partners feel like they were the ones in charge. He is a quiet, gentle man. Decent. Ethical. Not incredibly scholastic. But he made sure his children would get the education that he was denied by Hitler.

He's a family man first and foremost. He taught me to respect my elders through the way he took care of his father and his father-in-law. He's a very humble man who instilled in me the main attributes of Judaism: respect for education, understanding our history and traditions, being charitable to all. He showed great appreciation for his community—a community that had helped him to overcome the horrors of his early life. He got involved in charity work, built a synagogue and participated in the Jewish National Fund. He has blown the ram's horn in synagogue for fifty years. He's so well loved in his community.

He taught me that humanism is not a separate ideology but part of being a good Jew, citizen and leader. He's the kindest person I know. The love in our home was palpable. He and my mom were married when the vows *until death do us part* really meant something. He always put my mom on a pedestal and after forty-two years in my own marriage, I know how important that is.

At home, Dad was strict. He never hit us but he'd take his belt off and snap it. He had our attention and respect, and we'd be running. He was frugal, never wasteful and generous with his help. He demonstrated a great sense of duty and taught me "no pain, no gain"—take chances, make decisions, stick with it. He was determined to get back what he had lost. He's got a great sense of humour. I just love his laugh and his smile.

Until a few years ago he never spoke about the war years unless we asked him. He just wanted to get on with life; it didn't work to dwell on what had happened. Recently, he's been telling me more. He's thinking about his whole life as he comes closer to the end of it.

His mother had died before the war. Then after war broke out, his brother was taken away by the Russian army. He was in hiding with his father and sister. They changed his birth certificate to make him younger so they wouldn't take him as well. They ended up in Austria in 1950 in a displaced persons camp, and family members who were already here helped them come to Canada. They came through Pier 21 in Halifax, and his welcome to Canada was an order to "Open your pants," whereupon a bunch of DDT was dumped in to kill the lice he was suspected of carrying.

The challenges he faced make me appreciate what I have and the differences between his early years and mine. That drive to make up for what had been lost was so strong for him—it can fade in a generation. As a result, he almost made life too comfy for his kids.

We didn't do a lot of those typical father-son things because he was always working hard. He never taught me how to fix things, hunt or camp—we were not that kind of family, but every winter we'd drive down to Florida and have great family holidays. As far as fishing goes, neither one of us would ever touch a worm, so our attempts at fishing on Lake Simcoe involved using salami as bait. Then we'd eat the rest and be out of bait, so the whole expedition wouldn't last long. He'd watch the news and talk to my grandfather. I loved listening to them and watching the two of them roll quarters from the laundry machine in the apartment building they had built together.

We don't have a lot in common. He's in construction, I'm in medicine. We'd often walk together without much to say, but there was so much love between us. No hugs, but recently that has started to change. A few months ago when I was in Toronto we went to the synagogue together, and Dad took my hand and held it. It was a small gesture, but so special for me.

Being a father is the most amazing thing that's happened to me. Adam is thirty-one and Mitchell is twenty-nine. Love has been a central pillar in our family and one of my biggest pleasures is seeing the love between my boys, the strength of their relationship with each other. They've always got each other's back. Both of them are musical and were involved in theatre: Adam the intellectual, a lawyer and debating champion, is into social issues and politics; Mitchell, quiet and smart as a whip, an athlete, full of surprises, is following in my footsteps to become a urologist.

Any man can be a father, but it takes a special and very conscious effort to be a dad. We are an incredibly close family and the communication between us is easy and comfortable. Nothing matters to me more than knowing my boys love me for who I am and cherish being part of our family.

They respect the traditions of Judaism, but I recognize that it looks different to them than it did to my generation. My Jewish education went right through to grade thirteen in Ontario, and I had no friends outside our religion. I speak Hebrew fluently. I started the boys at the Hebrew school here in Vancouver, but after a bullying issue we moved both boys to St. George's and they never looked back.

One of the main loves in life that we shared, and still share, is hockey. Mitchell played hockey and we all watched *Hockey Night in Canada* while the three of us sorted hockey cards. Mitchell learned to read with them. I don't drink, I don't take drugs, but I'm addicted to hockey cards. I'm a collector; it gives me peace.

Both boys have had chronic pain issues to deal with—back problems for Mitchell and neck issues for Adam. Mitchell was complaining about pain after a hockey injury, and in typical medical father style, I said, "Come on, suck it up. You need to work harder!" I didn't stop there. Next I told him he should be doing more abdominal exercise and that he was getting fat.

Soon after, while playing hockey, Mitchell fell to the ice, crawled to the boards and couldn't move. At the hospital they discovered he had a congenital back condition that had caused malformed vertebrae that were millimetres away from damaging his spinal cord. So at sixteen, he had major surgery to repair the problem.

Even though he's never blamed me for not taking him seriously, it was a dark time for me coming to terms with how I had treated

Larry (LEFT) and father Mark, 2008

him—my assumptions and my willingness to draw erroneous conclusions. I felt like a bit of a fool, and of course felt I had let him down. The shoemaker's children go barefoot, indeed.

Another challenge I have faced as a father was when Adam came out to us as gay at the age of fourteen. I can't say I'd had any idea; he didn't fit the admittedly cartoonish stereotype I carried in my head of how a gay man looked, sounded or behaved. He's very much a "man's man" in his approach and appearance. He had known for a while and had been closeted in fearful silence. We had just arrived for a holiday in Palm Desert. "I've got something to tell you," he said. "I'm gay." Paula and I were in shock. His brother's response? "What's for dinner?"

He is who he is, and I wasn't going to love him any less. But this was hard. There are many layers to it. Feelings of disappointment surfaced when I realized that his genes may not pass on to the next generation, and as I considered how this news would be received in the Jewish community. To my parents, homosexuality is not normal.

FROM LEFT: Larry, Mitch and Adam, 2019

They would refer to gay men in derogatory Yiddish terms, and others in my family were clearly homophobic. My brother's brother-in-law is gay, and when he was present for family dinners I could feel the tension in my parents.

We didn't tell anyone in the family. In my heart of hearts, I wished that my parents would live many years, but that they would pass away not knowing. As it does, time went on. I said to Adam, "You know what? It's up to you if you want to tell your grandparents, if you want them to know who you really are." And he did. He went to talk to them, and they accepted his truth immediately. There was no looking back. They talked a bit about what he had said, how he'd explained, "I was born this way, there's no one to blame, and I am not making a choice."

I was the one who didn't know how to bridge the gap from today's generation, that accepts homosexuality so readily, to my parents' generation. It was a big deal but it worked out beautifully. If anything, their bond is stronger. Adam's response to me was, "You underestimated your parents." And now that Adam is engaged to be married to Alex, we're thrilled to see him so happy and we look forward to welcoming our new son-in-law into the fold—and to the process of having a same-sex wedding in our family.

A different struggle between the old and the new is that Mitchell's wife is not Jewish. Interfaith marriages can be a challenge, and are considered by some to have a negative and erosive effect on the world's Jewish demographics. But we love Mitchell's wife Brittany. I cross my fingers that this special, beautiful young woman who has captured Mitchell's heart will convert, but even if she doesn't, they'll raise their children to appreciate and understand their Jewish heritage. It's a challenge, and it shows me how as a father you can't project your wishes, hopes, dreams onto your children. I am there for my boys, no matter what. I trust that they'll make all the right choices. I am very blessed.

Peter MacKay with son Kian and daughter Valentia

Peter MacKay

New Glasgow, Nova Scotia

Lawyer, former politician, 54

||||||||||||||||||||||||||||||||||||||||||||||||||||||||||||||||||||||||||||||||||||||||||

Peter MacKay is a lawyer and former politician living
in Toronto. His father, Elmer MacKay, was a member
of Parliament for the riding of Central Nova in Nova
Scotia for over twenty years, and a cabinet minister in the
Progressive Conservative government of Prime Minister
Brian Mulroney. From 1997 to 2015, Peter was the MP for
Central Nova and served as minister of foreign affairs,
minister of justice and attorney general, as well as minister
of national defence. He has been married to Nazanin
Afshin-Jam since 2012. In 2013 they became parents with
the arrival of a son, Kian, followed by a daughter, Valentia,
in 2015, and second son, Caledon Cyrus, in July 2018.

||||||||||||||||||||||||||||||||||||||||||||||||||||||||||||||||||||||||||||||||||||||||

My dad was a far-off heroic figure in my early childhood, always off
on an important mission somewhere. He was consumed by his work
in politics, law before that, and his life didn't appear well balanced.
He was kind of a mystical figure coming and going in the wings of
our lives. With his Protestant work ethic and gruff exterior, I realized
early in life that if I wanted attention or affirmation from him, the
way to get it was through hard work.

When he was home on the farm, we were always busy as he
assigned tasks and put my siblings and me to work outdoors: gar-
dening, watering, weeding, tree planting and fencing, bringing in
hay and taking care of cattle. It's not unusual of course, especially for

rural families, for everyone, even the little ones, to pitch in. Neither was giving boys different jobs to do than girls—which my sister, two years older, reacted to strongly. Anything I could do she could do better. Good lessons for me as a child, watching her do just that.

I was eight in 1972 when my parents split up. I blamed my mother because she was the one who took us away from what I felt was an idyllic life. The farm, my grandparents, friends, school, the forest, streams and fields, that was my playground. My mum made what was in retrospect the only decision she could. Her strength and silent dignity in what clearly shattered her inspire me to this day.

I don't remember anybody explaining why or what had happened at the time. I just remember the moving truck arriving, and everything being loaded in. In fairness to my mum, she needed to get away and return to her home in the Annapolis Valley, a three-hour drive away, where she had the support of her family and community. That's where she grew up, in Centreville on her parents' blueberry farm.

After the divorce, contact with my dad was sporadic, not regular or sustained. I always felt torn; a certain amount of stress came from never quite knowing where I should be or where I belonged, especially in the summer... Playing baseball with my new friends in Wolfville, or back on the farm with my grandparents, or maybe with my dad? I feel I grew up faster than I would have otherwise, and I assumed I was the man in the family at a very young age. Much of that assumed responsibility was in my mind: watching out for my younger siblings, being the responsible one and setting a good example.

There were tough times when things were chaotic, and it seemed like we were quite alone. My mum was very sad. I remember her crying sometimes at night, but for quite a while I blamed her for moving us away from the farm. Eventually when I understood what had happened, I felt guilty and realized how unfair I'd been. My mum was blameless.

My mum—she was the *one*: my omnipresent, compassionate, nurturing confidante. She was both parents to me, coming to sports matches and school functions, and encouraging me through all life's trials and tribulations. Later in life, I would celebrate my love and appreciation by sending her a card on Father's Day.

My father has been a very driven and disciplined man throughout his life. He has a strong sense of right and wrong and tried to instill that in all his children. He tried to teach us some of life's hard lessons and was always a realist and pragmatic in his view of the world. I believe the relentless, fast-paced and often unforgiving world of politics inevitably shaped him and hardened him. He respected toughness above most things—the ability to persevere in the face of obstacles and setbacks.

He certainly idolized both his parents and made extraordinary efforts both to please them and to spend time with them, particularly as they grew old. He had a very close and caring relationship with his mother, yet a much different, more formal one with his father. Gaining his father's respect and approval was a lifelong mission for him. In some ways, I unknowingly emulated that path in my life and relationship to my father as well.

I am not sure my father ever truly knew how proud his father, my grandfather, was of him. I don't know whether it was the aging process making him more reflective and pensive, or just his emotional makeup, but I saw such a difference in my grandfather near the end of his life. He was much more affectionate, open and free with his words. He would speak to me in ways I don't think he ever could with his son. He would tell me how proud he was of both of us and that it gave him great satisfaction to see us succeed. He was a giant in my world until his passing.

It doesn't matter whether you are four or forty, when it seems that your father is disappointed with you or when he is choosing someone else at the expense of his relationship with you, it's brutal. It is particularly hard at a young age when you are not armed with all the facts, or are simply immature with a self-absorbed desire for all your father's attention. One way my father and I did connect over the years was through our shared passion for sports—baseball in particular. Even into my thirties when we got together I'd bring my baseball glove and we'd throw a ball in his nine-by-nine backyard at the farm, and have a conversation at the same time. It was easy and light, with the rhythmic hit of the ball in the glove, and it was the time I was most comfortable with him.

I suppose, like many people, I have some regrets. That's a hard thing to reconcile later in life when it comes to family. It can be excruciating to say certain things to loved ones, but it's even worse to leave things unsaid. I have come to that realization late in my life, but it has certainly been a positive revelation when it comes to my relationship with my kids. Sometimes the hardest, most painful lessons in life come from your parents, as do the very best and long-lasting examples of how to live your life.

I am grateful for both. I believe strongly that your parents' influence never ends and is embedded deeply in your DNA, for better and sometimes for worse. You really have elements of both; you can cultivate and bring out the very best, strive to emulate and cultivate those positive qualities, but lurking in your subconscious and your soul, those darker traits remain.

I don't think it's ever too late to reconcile or forge a new type of relationship in a family dynamic. The alternatives are much worse. I feel blessed to have had strong role models, and very real—though sometimes raw—relationships with both parents. In the end you take all their lessons and examples with you on a separate journey with your own children and the relationships you build with them.

I have grainy but beautiful memories of my mum's dad who died when I was about five—of him being kind, close, very approachable and truly *present* with us on the blueberry farm. He would take us on his knee and bounce us and tell stories in a soft yet animated voice. He had such a kind face, and eyes that drew you in as he spoke. It was novel and extraordinary to me as a child that this grown man would get right down at eye level and play with us on the kitchen floor, spinning the lids of pans with a wooden spoon or juggling items as he danced. His movement and grace were like magic to us before the days of video games or action movies.

His playfulness shone through in his rich Irish brogue as he encouraged us to make a hole at the other end of an empty eggshell to allow the good fairies to fly out. He had such a hold on our attention and I can still hear the gales of laughter we produced whenever

Peter MacKay

we were with him. The only other man I remember being able to engage us in such a way was John Diefenbaker, whom I met when I was a little boy.

Meeting my wife, having children—nothing comes close in terms of happiness, fulfillment and joy. Nothing truly prepares you for being a father. The love I feel for my children is almost overwhelming: the sensation of leaving the hospital with that little bundle, my son, stepping outside into the world and thinking, *They're actually going to let me take this child home.* There was no one coming along with the instruction manual telling me, "Here's how you are going to do it!"

All the prenatal advice and coaching was about labour. Nothing to prepare me for the shift in identity or the real parenting skills necessary; it was all flying by the seat of my pants! Then the truth starts to take hold, who you are, with this separate and completely dependent little being now living under your roof. Amidst the sleep deprivation and fascination came the realization just how much of my life had changed—and that it was permanent.

It was a very special time. I was totally engaged. These were the last couple of years of my life in politics, living in a tiny one-bedroom apartment in Ottawa and shuttling back and forth between Ottawa and Nova Scotia. Kian travelled so much in that time he earned his own Air Miles card. I was already forty-eight years old when I became a dad, quite set in my ways, a total workaholic—and used to being able to do my own thing, like a lot of watching the news, hockey or baseball games. Giving that up doesn't seem like a sacrifice; it feels like becoming truly mature and complete as an adult.

In addition to relentless work commitments in my constituency and in the capital, I played sports much longer than I should have. I kept playing hockey and rugby well into my forties, and maybe that was to fill a bit of a void. I didn't have kids, I wasn't married... But maybe that's why I wasn't getting married? They were clearly the wrong priorities, but sports were my outlet—where my father would take an axe and go to the woods, I would get out to rugby practice, play hockey at night, or run—I ran a lot. Looking back, I can see that I was also burying myself. It was a selfish and emotionally unhealthy way to live. These days I get a workout playing with my children—and I am much more fulfilled.

My life is wired differently, but old habits die hard and I have to be very disciplined not to fall back into spreading myself too thin by saying yes to every ask. In the past it was all very routinized and formulaic. I can't believe I conducted my life that way for so long.

It's hard to imagine my life before the arrival of my kids. I just don't see being a minister and having children as compatible; something would have to give. Sadly, it's no surprise that the divorce rate is so high in politics, as it is in many high-pressure professions. I have become a much more emotional human being as a father. I notice things I never did before. I watch other parents with their children; I see the struggles of families in a different, more empathic light.

My younger brother, who is very deeply involved in the raising of his children, acts as my coach and mentor. He's been a great role model for me as a father. He is a disciplinarian but is also very supportive and caring. Children push you to the brink, and you have to keep a clear head so you know what to do when you get there. I have had to work on my patience. I slow myself down, tune in to them and go at their pace. You adjust to *them*, not the other way around.

Peter with Valentia (LEFT) and Kian

I hope that, as they grow, we form close trusting relationships where my kids can come to me, feel safe talking to me about anything, though I recognize I might not always be the ideal person. I want to make sure my kids are surrounded by people who love and can support them.

I don't want to be a helicopter parent, but I'm extremely worried about the online world and hypersexualization of children that is exploding around us. We are on sensory overload with the internet these days. I am amazed to see my little ones navigate online so adeptly. It's so tough to think about children's vulnerabilities and the access points for those who prey on them. I worry about my kids, but I worry about everyone else's kids as well. Their innocence and wide-eyed thirst for knowledge and interaction with the wider world thrills me, inspires me and also scares the hell out of me.

My kids have taught me so much about myself and provided me with a path to being a better and more productive human being. Children are truly life's greatest gift, and when one makes the effort and fosters healthy relationships with them, they never stop giving.

Jeffrey Molloy

Gabriola Island, British Columbia

Artist (deceased)

||||||||||||||||||||||||||||||||||||||||||||||||||||||||||||||||||||||||||||||||||||||

Jeff was born January 16, 1957 in Ontario and died
on August 3, 2016 at his home on Gabriola Island. He
worked as a pipefitter and later as a home energy
inspector before becoming a full-time artist. In his
artistic practice, Jeff developed a distinct aesthetic
that drew wide acclaim: using mixed media, painting
and assemblage, his work took a critical approach
in exploring social, cultural and political issues. Jeff
married Kathryn in 1980 and together they had three
children: Jules (1980), Kate (1982) and Gavin (1984).

||||||||||||||||||||||||||||||||||||||||||||||||||||||||||||||||||||||||||||||||||||||

I see no difference between the canvas and a blank day—you bring
yourself to both. And fatherhood is the place where all is revealed.
Recognizing what is actually important when you sit down and look
at your life: *Who am I? Is this what life is all about? When do I know
if I have "done it"?* On some levels I still don't think I have done it.
In terms of my art or my career, I can pin that down, but in terms
of my fatherhood? When did I realize my mistakes or things I had
done right? I am still in it, I am still making it up as I go along, now
nearing the end of my life.

Fatherhood—I was lucky to make it through, you know. Same
thing that comes up for a lot of guys: alcohol, drugs, they take you
away... Everything is a little more real for me right now than for most

people. I am not giving up, but I am not an idiot; I know I am not winning this. *[Jeff had been fighting cancer for several years.]*

I was adopted at six days old; I think my grandmother knew the family I was from. People went to church, they kept quiet about these kinds of things. My adoptive father, John Edward Molloy, was born in 1928 and died in 1993—he "died young" at sixty-three. My relationship with my dad—it was complicated. He was a wonderful guy in so many ways, but fuck he had some demons. He could be quite abusive. Came by it honestly: his father could be a bit of a prick too. I don't know much about my great-grandfather, but it seems that each generation was meaner than the one before.

I am happy to say that's not the case anymore. I have broken the pattern. Happily, my father was also incredibly loving. And if there was anyone I got my artistic background from it was him, oddly enough because he was a mechanic kind of guy, great with his hands. He also had a fabulous voice, opera kind of sound, big, powerful and beautiful. He was a happy guy a lot of the time, singing, putting on music, but he was Irish; there were big mood swings. If you got his temper up, he'd burn a hole through you. When he got that look in his eye, you thought, *Holy shit, I'm out of here.*

When the outbursts came, really they had nothing to do with us kids; it had to do with my parents' volatile relationship, the underlying fuel that we were in the middle of. I bore the brunt of it. I was a difficult kid, I pushed his buttons and he got me back. He was big and strong, and I wasn't. I'd be pinned and given a brush cut. You know the residential school thing, the piece I produced with the priest cutting the child's hair? It wasn't a priest who did it to me, it was my dad. I was the child being held, him cutting my hair and taking my power. To me it was subjugation. It seemed designed to make me inferior, wipe away the identity I was trying to claim for myself. Hair, my fucking hair, I have lost it all I don't know how many times, yes, and now it's grown back again.

One time as he was knocking me around when I was sixteen, I finally stood up to him and said, "Go ahead, hit me again, and then I'll knock the shit out of you." There was no way I could ever have done that, but after that, he stopped.

Jeff with grandson Luca, 2013

He could cry, he could laugh, he could do it all but he couldn't *tell* anyone how he felt. He knew he needed help, but he wouldn't come forward. He even knew he could get help for his heart condition. Heck, he was only sixty-three and something could have been done for him. He did the standard stupid man stuff: you don't say anything. It was that *keep stuff to yourself* crap... I know he even skipped doctors' appointments. I could just smack him.

What I got from him that I value is tenacity and a strong work ethic. He didn't have a high-paying job, but you know, he showed up every day, on time, and worked his ass off. He hawked his golf clubs every fall to buy us Christmas presents, then he'd work like a bastard to buy them back by spring. He could love deeply—I like to think I got that, too. I can actually love deeply.

Cherished memories with my dad, I have a few. One-on-one time with him, it was precious, like getting woken up to go fishing with him. It was dark outside, we stopped on the way to the lake to pick up smokes and get some dew worms. It stands out in my memory, the feeling of closeness, the sounds, the smells and all. It's like I have rooms in my brain—there's one room that is my dad's. I wish

I had a bunch more memories to fill that room. The space is there, but it never got filled up. Sad to say, but I think that's what my sons would say they wanted more of too. I didn't do as much as I would have liked with them.

What would I say to my dad if he was around now? "I love you Dad. Let's work on shit. Let's be the best we can be."

"Tell me about yourself."

"How'd you get here?"

"I forgive you."

It doesn't change anything, but now I understand how hard it is to be a good dad—that there is no better job in the world. There is no more fulfilling thing you can do with your life than to be a good father. The state of the world is such that we need more good dads. We've got lots of bad ones. If you want to end violence in the world, start with fathers.

My fathering abilities—it doesn't feel like I took a lot away from my dad. I guess like everything else in my life, I was going to be better at it than him, but it wasn't true, I totally sucked at it for a while, for sure. Not being where I needed to be as a human being and taking it out on people around me. Thinking all along what I was *supposed* to be doing as a man—having a job, family, house, all that stuff—telling myself *you should get a real job, you can't do all of that as a sculptor or a painter*; then you wind up with a real job that you hate, and a trap that you can't get out of. I was young and stupid when I became a father. Not knowingly reluctant, but reluctant. Jules's birth was pretty darned amazing.

My biggest problem? I was twenty-three years old! I let Kathryn do the lion's share. I was working, I used that as an excuse. I worked in a bar, I was drinking, coming home late at night. I was participating but not at the level I could have. If only life gave you second chances. I just don't think I had the maturity to understand the scope of what I needed to do, who I needed to be.

I was a weed-smoking, globe-trotting musician-artist dude... with a kid. The lifestyle I was embracing just wasn't compatible with being a dad. I held back. I didn't throw myself at it. Mothers, they're physically bound, but a man can be a father and walk away.

Jeff, 2016

Maybe because of my own dad not really connecting, I gave myself permission not to connect. The framework was wrong: I focused on making money and buying my family shiny new things, living on painkillers... I was trying to manage a life I didn't really want to be in.

I wish I had pursued my art earlier and got myself into a happier place. I wish I'd become more whole, done more of my own healing, become more of a person, and put that part of my life—being a father—later. You are the mentor when you're the father. If you're fucking up, you are not doing the world or your kids any favours. You have to be "on" all the time; they've got eyes and ears. I can remember after a fight realizing that my daughter was downstairs and heard it all. She was so little but missed nothing.

All of that was incredibly challenging, but getting through it has created an amazing family. I am pretty proud of my family—could it have been what it is without all of that? That struggle? I don't know. I really don't know. It's how you survive that stuff—you have got to love them.

Kathryn saved our family in 1985 when she removed my self-imposed obligation to go out and earn the money. She took it all on and I was able to begin to focus on my art. In 1995 Kathryn started her own business. I took on a much bigger parenting role, walked the kids to school, did all the cooking. I started to turn things around. I gave up being who I was trying to be and became who I was. I made a conscious choice to be more present. I didn't always do it—of course it went on, off, on, off... I had a loving and supportive wife—I'd never have made it otherwise. I dedicated myself to my family in those years.

Understanding that you are going to have to make sacrifices for your family and getting on with it, not balking at every step, I think that's essential. Otherwise you'll run out of energy, you won't perform. You have to make it happen. Don't think about the distinction between quantity time and quality time with your kids: it's all quality time! I renovated houses with a child strapped to me. It doesn't have to be all about indulging them, it's about doing whatever it is you do—with love. If you asked my daughter, Kate, about her favourite memories, the simple act of me walking her to school would be one of the highlights for her.

Model what you want to see: curiosity, empathy, gentleness. Help your kids be the kinds of custodians the planet needs. We need some pretty strong people coming down the pike. You know, we are leaving a mess.

My children were my art. What have I given them? Honesty, integrity, authenticity...the ability to use their hands, to play music, to make art! To have had all five of us performing together musically, that's rare. You don't realize that when you are in it. At what point do you know, *It's happening*—or is the beauty of it in not knowing? To have been present at the birth of all three of my granddaughters, that's even more rare. That was a gift from my daughter, she knows how much that meant to me. My dad would be so proud. He'd be saying to me, "Good job!"

Scott Moe
Shellbrook, Saskatchewan
Premier of Saskatchewan, 46

|||||||||||||||||||||||||||||||||||||||||||||||||||||||||||||||||||||||||||||||||||||||||||||||||||||||||||

Scott Moe grew up in Shellbrook, Saskatchewan as the eldest of five children. He worked in the agricultural equipment industry for several years before starting a political career in 2011. He began as a Saskatchewan Party MLA and eventually served several posts in government, including minister of advanced education and minister of environment. He won the leadership of the Saskatchewan Party and was sworn in as premier in February 2018, taking over from Brad Wall. Scott has been married to Krista for twenty-six years and they have two children: Carter, born in 1993, and Taryn, born in 1998.

|||||||||||||||||||||||||||||||||||||||||||||||||||||||||||||||||||||||||||||||||||||||||||||||||||

My dad's a man of huge integrity, a man I admire a great deal who has always been there for me. When a challenge comes up in my life and I look for and lean on him, he is always able to provide a listening ear. I'll get some sound advice, but he is a man of few words. He'll listen more than he'll talk. He's solid and I trust him 100 per cent; he is like a vault.

All my life I have aspired to be more like him. With five of us kids to juggle in his life, I respect the way he did it. He supported us all but never tried to take over. He let us follow our individual passions and got involved wherever he could in his own quiet manner. I was into hockey in a big way, same as a few of my brothers—but hockey was never his game. He didn't play or take an interest, but he would get us there and find a way to be useful behind the scenes, such as scheduling ice time. He never projected his own wishes onto us. That's hard for parents to do, harder than you realize until you are in those shoes. Lots of people are living through their children.

Dad was a farmer. Growing up I remember him as a very hands-on father. He was the one who got to deal with discipline but that was never an issue for us kids; we could rely on him being calm and compassionate, yet firm. And real. There was an awful, sad accident when I was a child of about six years old. My dog Laddie got killed when Dad was using a piece of farm equipment. He came in to break the news to me. I wasn't used to seeing him cry, so it was a surprise to me to see him in tears. I think he was more upset than I was. What he showed me, thankfully, at that early age was that even men cry. As a father, I have remembered his example so that I am able to readily express emotion in front of my kids.

When I became a dad at twenty (my wife was nineteen), we were still in university. Our main worry was how were we going to get through, and how were we going to cope from a financial perspective. It wasn't easy, but we finished our education. The financial piece? When I think back, that wasn't the important part at all. Those early years, I just loved them. I think about them as the *quantity years*. Children will spend as much time with you during these years as you are willing to spend with them. I loved being with my children, getting involved with their activities and introducing them to new things. I got to be there for a lot of their memorable firsts.

Then later, at thirteen, fourteen and beyond, I call those the *quality years*, when kids get to pick when to spend time with you. They are asserting their independence and individuality, so you have to be ready for them when they come to you, and make the most of your time together. I found that I needed to be flexible, meeting them on their terms and not expecting them to want to do the same things with me as they had when they were smaller.

If you are lucky, your kids will come to you with challenges in their lives, but the questions they ask might not be precisely what they want to know the answer to. I had to get good at reading between the lines. Our children, the next generation, they're smarter

Scott with wife Krista and children Carter and Taryn

than us, and they have access to more information than us. The only thing we have the edge on is a bit of experience, that's it. Give them everything you've got in the quantity years before they get to adolescence. When they are having a tough day, they pull back; you can see it in their eyes. Like my dad, you need to listen and not say much.

What kids are going through now with social media, all the usual stresses of peers and fitting in are very much amplified. Bullying, etc., I think it's brutal. You have to hope you have given them enough to get through. The highs are not as high as they appear at the time, and the lows are not as low as they think. But it's their reality, and you have to be there for them—bring the facts into the conversation and be a conscious parent.

Mental health—it's not "some" people, it's everyone who has to work to maintain it. I am not afraid to lean when I need to, and I am a lucky guy to have been able to find the right support close by, within my family—especially from my dad. He's shown resilience and is a great role model for me. I show my kids that it's okay to talk about the tough stuff. I also try to show my kids that I can let my guard down, and I think it helps them open up to me.

There's no manual for this stuff; you fly by the seat of your pants. You rely on perseverance, resilience and lots of love. For me, the work ethic, the moral ethic, character—it's so important to instill those early. When your kids hit the teenage years, you're not there when decisions come up for them. The calmness with which my father handled things was a source of inspiration to me. If I went to him with a problem one of my children was experiencing, he'd give me perspective. "This too shall pass," he helped me to recognize.

I was nowhere near ready at twenty to be a dad, nor at twenty-five. When I think back to those early days of parenting, I know I wasn't always the best example for my children. I'd lose my temper, say the wrong thing, sometimes offend them. I could have "walked the walk" more often, done a better job. I have grown into it, it's not something anyone could give me, I have learned from other people's examples. I started to get good at it, and then the kids were up and gone.

I definitely relied on friends for moral support as a parent. Not everyone has those; my close friends and I had lots of conversations about being dads. This was particularly helpful when we were raising teenagers. Especially the girls—we dads could support each other but had to admit we didn't understand what was going on in their lives. I loved every minute of it—I smiled, but I didn't understand. It felt like it was just that male-female thing; it was harder for me to relate.

It was easier with my son; I've kind of been there myself. There were some times he needed to lean on me during those quality years—a hockey injury, trouble with a teacher, an altercation at school, trying to map out his career. He might have been smarter, but I could relate to him and draw from my own similar experiences.

Life is full of choices. You can't have it all! For years I was able to coach hockey and softball, I had flexible hours so I could arrange my schedule accordingly. That all changed when I was elected as an MLA in 2011, and later as premier. The legislature sits right through until the end of May, clashing with softball season, so I had to give up the coaching of my daughter's team, which I had loved. Also, the hockey nights with my male friends went by the wayside.

It has been interesting for me watching my children make decisions. I had an "aha" moment when my son was considering career choices. He came up with two possibilities, architecture or engineering, then systematically researched where he might study. When we discussed the options and he asked, "Where do you think I could work, say, as an engineer, Dad?" I basically said, "The sky's the limit," reeling off a list of the major cities in the world.

Then he looked at me and said, "But Dad, could I live and work here in Shellbrook?" It hit me, this little community north of Saskatoon with 1,500 people was good enough for me, my parents and all my siblings and here I was anticipating my son would want to be anywhere else *but* here. "This is where I'm connected," he said. "This is my community, Dad. It's where I want to live." This was a reminder to me as a parent not to project my thoughts or dreams onto my kids, that this is their life. I told myself, *Get out of the way, Dad!*

Carter now has a job as an engineer in Saskatoon. He's back in Shellbrook frequently. I daresay one day he'll be back living here. My daughter Taryn is an independent soul. I admire her a great deal for handling a dilemma at the end of high school, when her final dance company performance fell on the same day as high school grad. She deliberated on it with a clear head and chose to dance. It was my pleasure to clear my schedule so that I could be the taxi service to get Taryn back to Shellbrook ninety minutes away so that she could enjoy as much of grad as possible after she performed. I brought her grad dress and she managed to get changed in the car. After high school, she thought about dancing professionally but decided to get started on her education as a speech pathologist—after checking that the university she wanted to attend had a recreational dance club.

I am inclined to be spontaneous, sometimes impetuous, which can get me into trouble. Now I have my own children's examples to follow, of making choices more methodically and rationally. If I was to give my younger self advice, it would be *Settle down! Just relax, take a breath. Don't fret. Things are not as bad as they seem.* While I know I have made mistakes, the kids have probably learned more from me than I realize—as much from the mistakes I made as from all the things I did right. They might have left home, but the job's not over. Neither are the pleasures.

Lorimer Shenher

Burnaby, British Columbia

Retired police officer, author, 54

‖‖

Lorimer was born in 1964 and was raised in Calgary as
Lorraine Shenher. Lorimer joined the Vancouver Police
Department in the early nineties, and was the first
detective assigned to the missing women investigation.
In late 2015, Lorimer began transitioning to male. After
taking leave from the VPD, he achieved significant acclaim
for his book *That Lonely Section of Hell: The Botched
Investigation of a Serial Killer Who Almost Got Away*, a
memoir of his experiences investigating the missing
women in Vancouver. His second book, *This One Looks
Like a Boy*, was published in spring 2019. He is married
to Jenn and they have three children, all in their teens.

‖‖

When I thought about becoming a parent, I pictured myself as a
dad, not a mom. I had known I was born in the wrong body since
I was about four years old. The first day of kindergarten we had
to line up to go to the washroom, and I lined up with the boys.
The teacher was gentle. "Lorraine," she asked, "how come you're
not with the girls?" When I told her I thought I was a boy she
said, "That's something you share only with good friends. I'm your
friend, I know how you feel. Keep it to yourself—but you do need
to go in the girls' lineup."

By all accounts I had a very functional, healthy and good
family, lots of support, but as a young transgender kid growing up

in Calgary in the seventies and eighties, I felt very alienated from everybody including my family. I wasn't a noticeably miserable kid; it was all on the inside. My mom says, "You seemed really happy," but I think she sensed there was something off, and I don't think she really knew what to do with me.

I felt very isolated. I acted like a typical tomboy, very into sports, not interested in playing with girls or the kinds of toys that girls were expected to like. All my friends were boys. My whole sense of self was male. I spent a lot of time with my dad. I was always more interested in what he was doing. He was a teacher and school principal, but in his spare time he was very handy—building, woodwork, repairs, roofing—and whenever possible I tagged along. I just wanted to learn from him.

Except for the clothing battles (my mom always trying to put me in dresses), I managed to feel quite free to be myself until puberty arrived. Puberty was hard. I wasn't a very feminine-looking girl, but I just got a sense from Dad that now our relationship had to change. I also think that he decided he had to work harder to pull my brother in. I don't really know all that was at play there, but it was tough for me. All of a sudden I wasn't able to participate. We didn't ever talk about that, but toward the end of his life we were able to talk about a lot of the important things.

He was a quiet, shy man and a great listener. He was always doing things for other people, didn't talk much about himself, was well read and liked opera. He was not a guy given to talking about his feelings. There were times I felt let down by my dad when I was growing up, when I wish he had gone to my defence. My mom... she's formidable; sometimes he'd let her steamroll over me. I could have used my dad's help, but I understand there would have been implications for him had he stepped in more.

You hear about disengaged fathers. "Checked out," so to speak. He was the opposite: tuned in, very family-oriented. You never got the impression there was anywhere else he'd prefer to be than *with us*. All through high school, he'd come to my basketball games and take me to my practices, get up at 5:30 a.m., make me oatmeal, come and cheer me on. That was our time. My mom's love always felt very conditional and contingent upon my behaviour, but my dad's love felt unconditional. Always.

I got myself into trouble as a teenager. I became really peer-oriented, then got into drinking, driving drunk; I was a bit of a nightmare. I never felt like anything I did impacted how much Dad cared for me, or made him love me any less. That was his gift, and is something I try to bring to my own parenting. I feel I can handle whatever happens. There were three hundred people at Dad's funeral when he died of cancer in 2016. He had great male friendships maintained over a lifetime. Three men spoke to me at his service and each told me Dad was his best friend.

I viewed transitioning as the worst thing I could do, I saw it as nothing but negative. For whatever relief it could give me, I was going to pay. Justifiably so, in the era in which I grew up in Calgary, I had a lot of concern about what transitioning would mean for my life and for the people around me. When I told my parents who I really was when I was twenty-five, my news met with their strong disapproval.

That's when I decided to move out west. I joined the police department. I started attending a group for gender dysphoric people and I met someone in the group who said, "I knew I was transgender and then I decided to be a lesbian," and I thought, *That's what I'm going to do.* So that's what I did. I started meeting women and didn't go back to the group.

Not long after that in 1998, Jenn and I got together as lesbians. We have been together ever since, twenty-one years. Meeting Jenn was so good for me. I got the sense that she was going to keep me from getting into deep trouble—either *loneliness* trouble or *transitioning* trouble. Jenn had already decided she wanted to have kids. She had always wanted children, even if she had to do it as a single parent. When I told her I didn't want kids, I asked, "Is that a deal breaker?"

"Well, you know... Let's see how it goes." Some of those things you need to have sorted out, but the issue was more my own. I very quickly had a level of trust with Jenn that I'd never had with anyone before, and the idea of children became a lot less frightening. She was so solid. Nevertheless, I couldn't imagine having kids; I was so

"It's all about me." Coping with being transgender, I didn't know how I could navigate the world with kids. I felt like my plate was already full, and I was really busy with policing.

Honestly, I didn't want to screw kids up. I guess that was my lack of self-confidence. I was thinking, *I'm too much of a disaster, I'm going to end up having disastrous children.* I saw myself as a father. I didn't know how I could be a mom. In addition, I'd always felt there was a certain inevitability to my transitioning at some point, and that made me think I would ruin my kids' lives. I told Jenn early on about myself, and told her, "I'm good now. I don't want to transition."

My parents really liked Jenn. They could see how good she was for me. We had a commitment ceremony in 1999 and both my parents came, but Dad wasn't willing to speak at our ceremony; he said he wouldn't feel comfortable. Even though he appeared quite progressive in his thinking, it seems that to speak at our service would condone same-sex relationships more completely than he was willing to do.

Perhaps some of this had to do with optics. He was very devoutly Catholic, a lay minister in the church. I felt like his faith was at odds with his personality—with what his heart really wanted to do. I think he could have embraced our relationship more wholeheartedly. There were a few times when I felt like saying, "This isn't really you, Dad." I never felt judged by my dad but neither did I feel I could discuss my gender dysphoria with him. I have a lot of space for his failings. I feel quite at peace with him and where our relationship ended up. I know that the man who embraced our family was his real, true self.

Long before I came into Jenn's life, she had made a deal with a male friend. As they were both pursuing same-sex relationships, and she wanted kids, he would help her by donating sperm. So that's what happened when we made the decision to go ahead and have a family. Jenn gave birth to our first child, a son, in 2001. I adopted him when he arrived. Our donor and his partner have always been in our lives. We see them regularly, on birthdays and so forth, and stay with them on Galiano Island three or four times a year. It's good.

Lorimer's children, 2019

Jenn's pregnancy had been hard on her, morning sickness right to the last moment, so I thought it should be my turn to carry our second child, or at least I should try... I felt male, so I wasn't sure it was going to work, but of course it did. Another son arrived in our lives in 2003. He's a little clone of me. Having him was a wonderful experience. He's my best project and I make sure he knows it. It's a bit surreal to me, kind of trippy. Next pregnancy, Jenn went up to bat again, and we had our daughter in 2005.

The kids are very secure; they know where they came from. I know what and who I am to them. I show up every day and I don't need to assert any ownership. It's felt very good for them to have more adults in their lives than fewer. I don't think the word *half* has ever been uttered—they see each other as full siblings and are more likely to see similarities among us than differences. We've had a great family life, and my father came around quickly after our children arrived. He was a very involved and happy grandfather, but my career was hard on me and my being transgender wasn't going away.

When I turned fifty in 2014, I noticed that things were changing, culturally. I began to feel more comfortable—being transgender was becoming a lot more talked about. You heard it every day, which gave me some confidence. The unravelling of my policing career was in some ways the best thing that could have happened to me, because it precipitated change. By going through a mental health crisis and subsequent therapy, and all the work I did with post-traumatic stress disorder, I resolved at the end of it all that I still had an issue to deal with, an issue that probably made me more susceptible to all the other things impacting me in the way they did.

By the time I was "ready" to transition I felt a little more trapped, scared about how it would impact my kids. It was one step forward, two steps back. I dipped my toe in to test the water. The kids have always been very open-minded. We have known lots of queer families and one of the kids' peers transitioned to female, so it wasn't a foreign concept to them. We also talked about identity and the struggles of adolescence. We let them know it didn't have to be a horror show. I explained to them how I'd felt as a teenager, how lonely I was, and why. We talked about it over weeks. Finally our oldest said to me, "Why don't you just transition?"

"It's a good question," I said. "I probably should."

"Yes," he said, "you'd be way happier."

We were able to talk about it some more. "Well, I'd worry about you guys… I haven't waited because of you, but I have fears. They might be based on how I grew up in the world, but there's still people out there that might judge you, might judge us, might say cruel things."

Our daughter said, "I don't care. They're not my friends if that's the case." Our oldest really likes to fly under the radar, but he said he was fine. Our middle guy said, "I'm totally good. You do what you need to do."

Eventually, we worked through a lot of issues. I tried to prepare them, because they just hadn't seen some of the awfulness out there in the world. The *what if*s, like "What if someone's parents tell them they shouldn't spend time with you anymore?" I wanted to reassure them, but also to let them know that I would be comfortable with the uncertainty, and that there might be challenging things for me to navigate with them. I also let them know it's okay for them to get angry with me. I was bringing a lot of complication into their lives. They could choose how "out" they were.

I have raised issues proactively. They are like, "Well, I don't care," but I reply, "But you might one day, so this is what I am thinking..." and they are like, "Well, okay." This choice I am making, it's me, not them; it doesn't define them or us as a family. I still need to be the person they know. They decided to call me "Lorm" when I changed my name to Lorimer—their choice (I used to be "Mummy"). Our donor is "Dada" and Jenn is "Mama." It would have been so much easier if I'd done it when they were toddlers. But work was really hard at the time and I don't think I had processed enough at that point to go into it in a solid mental state.

When you are transgender everything feels like a compromise. There was always something that didn't feel quite right to me. I got to be a quasi-mom, almost but not quite...or a quasi-dad, not a real one. It was more than what one would do as a mum or a dad—it was how I felt, my view of myself. I felt less of a nurturer and more of a doer. But if you were to take the roof off the house and look in, you wouldn't see a difference between what I would do as a dad and what I would do as a mom. It would be evidenced in my sense of self, in who I am. The whole process is strange; it's hard to explain.

When I finally told my parents I was transitioning, their reaction was so minimal I felt I'd wasted twenty-five years sparing them the difficulties. Their biggest worries were the kids and Jenn. They didn't want me to lose her and rightly so—she's the best thing that has ever happened to me. My dad was really supportive. At the time, he was getting treatment for cancer. I took him to one of his chemo appointments and he introduced me as his son, Lorimer. I was so proud of him.

Craig Lauzon

Ottawa, Ontario

Actor, writer, comedian, 48

||||||||||||||||||||||||||||||||||||||||||||||||||||||||||||||||||||||||||||||||||||||||

Craig Lauzon was born in Ottawa and is of Ojibway descent. He is a member of the CBC series *Royal Canadian Air Farce*, where his caricatures have included Donald Trump, George Stroumboulopoulos, Justin Trudeau and Stephen Harper. Craig was formerly an artistic associate at Native Earth Performing Arts, Canada's oldest First Nations performing arts company. He has two sons with his ex-wife, Tracy: Connor, born in 2001, and Jackson, born in 2006. He is now married to Erica.

||||||||||||||||||||||||||||||||||||||||||||||||||||||||||||||||||||||||||||||||||||||||

I've often joked about my combination of British and Native (French Canadian) parentage with the quip "I am Canada." My dad was a big Ojibway guy who had ten kids—nine with the same woman and me with my English mom, whom he was with for four years. She had already been married and had two daughters. I learned how to be a parent from my mom. Between the ages of four and eighteen, I only saw my dad a handful of times. I used to give cards to my mom on Father's Day. She could be loving and tender, yet stern and firm. As a single mom she had her plate full.

I knew about my father's other children, but they didn't know about me. I had this image of them in my mind when I was a child, sort of like the French Walton family living in this large house in Gatineau. At night they would be like, *"Bonne nuit, Jean Garçon."* I came to know much later in life that he was no more there for them than he was for me. I didn't meet my brothers and sisters until 2000. I was a secret, I guess.

I didn't want to be the kind of father that I'd had. When I was getting married, I worried about having kids. Anyway, I got over it and I loved becoming a dad. You never know until you are a dad what it's like. Having my kids and loving them the way I do, I wondered, how could people be fathers and walk away from their kids? How come they didn't want to be with their children as much as they could? The way I felt about my dad's abandonment was almost worse after having kids. I went into an angry period. Before that, I had just thought it was shitty for me.

My father didn't have an easy life. He worked in lumber mills, married at sixteen (she was fourteen) and had kids right away, way too young. He was unfaithful, continued to be that way all his life. People would say, "Oh, he's such a charming man." I hate it when people say the same about me, as to me it implies something sleazy, manipulative. My father died in 2010. I was a pallbearer. There were lots of women at his funeral that no one knew. People kept saying what a great father he was and how much he loved his children. My younger brother was furious: "Well, not *these* children," he said. "He was never here for us."

I've spent such a long time in a negative headspace thinking about him, about how I didn't want to be like him, instead of thinking about how I *did want* to be as a father. Somehow, I fell into some of the same patterns. I was unfaithful to my first wife and couldn't believe I was doing it while it was happening. I was like, *Who am I? I don't even know myself.* I destroyed my marriage. It was horrible.

We broke up when the kids were four and seven. It was hard to take. I drank a lot, becoming more like my dad. I was not the kind of person I like to be. It went on for about four years until about the time I met my current wife. I was still a bit of a mess. I'd dated, had a few girlfriends in between. They were great people, but I had messed it up. I'd get into the same pattern. It took a while for me to realize I was going to lose Erica if I didn't change. I asked myself, *How can I fix this?*

I'd done some counselling with my ex-wife before we split up, but I'd only done it because she wanted me to. I was going through the motions, not really buying in to it. This time I went to counselling on my own initiative, with Anishnawbe Health on Queen Street in Toronto. It helped a lot. Something shifted; I felt like a lot of stuff got lifted off me. I should have done it sooner. This is when I started to think more about what I wanted to be and less about what I didn't want to be.

I focused on positives. I made a conscious effort to see myself in a positive light and to think about how I want the boys to experience me. I want my wife to know that she can depend on me. I want her to know that when the chips are down I have her back. Same for my boys: I'll always be there for them no matter what.

Raising kids is harder than I thought. I want them to be strong and thoughtful at the same time. I want them to be men, I don't want them to be wishy-washy. It doesn't mean that they can't be in touch with their feelings; I cry at the drop of a hat. I don't even know what that means—*being a man*. Being responsible for your actions for sure: when you say you are going to do something, do it. Really, it's just being a good person. That's what I want for them. That's what I want for me.

Our first baby, Connor, was a dream, sleeping six to seven hours right off the bat—so then we were tricked into having a second one. Jackson didn't sleep more than two hours at a time so when he was about eight months old my wife was suffering big time with sleep deprivation. I had some time off, so I took Jackson and had him with me downstairs in the basement for the weekend, giving my wife time to sleep. I'm a heavy sleeper, so unless he was really crying, I didn't wake up. Somehow, I managed to get him over his sleep problems. I was primary caregiver for Connor for nine months; I just loved those days when they were little.

My boys are both funny and stubborn, but otherwise they couldn't be more different than each other. One is quite cerebral, into music with a dry sense of humour, the other into rugby, fishing and camping. We bond over music, comic books and superheroes.

It was tense to begin with when Tracy and I split up. I was the one who ended the relationship. To my ex-wife's credit, she's never spoken negatively to the boys about me. She's always been able to put the boys first and make sure they're okay. One of the reasons I thought we needed to split up was because of them—thinking about what they were learning by seeing their mom and I having problems. Since we split, we have always kept things cordial.

Nevertheless, it was still brutal for the boys. I came to hate the thing that people said all the time: "*Kids are so resilient.*" Well, they shouldn't have to be. I won't forget the tears when I left the boys, the pleas for me to stay. I'd drop them off and then bawl my eyes out all the way back on the 401. It made me wish I had taken counselling more seriously, and done it way sooner. The things that were wrong in our marriage were inside; it was me, not an external thing. Although sometimes you have to go through things to learn about yourself. Maybe I needed that.

It's not easy being a part-time dad. I get them every other weekend. It's truncated. It's hard to be disciplining when all you want is to have a good time with them. However, if they're in trouble with their mom, they're in trouble with me. I can't always be their buddy. We recently went to see an animated *Spider-Man* movie together. In one scene a police officer is dropping his son off at school. The kid exits the car and Dad says, "I love you, Son." The boy ignores Dad, who then uses his car megaphone to boom out, "I said I love you, Son. You have to say it back." Both sons leaned into me at the same time and said, "That's what you would do, Dad."

When I think back to my early years, I don't remember much about my father being around when my mother and father were "steadies." One powerful memory that almost makes me choke up is the smell of his cologne. Another is when Dad showed up at my mom's house when I was about four years old. It was one a.m. They woke me up out of bed. I was very excited to see him, and this young guy he had with him. I was the "dancing monkey" for them, doing my Elvis impression.

I found out later that it was my brother Luke who was with him. My dad brought him over after he called my father *le vieux* [old man],

Craig, 2013

and they got into a scuffle. "See that kid?" he said, pointing at me. "He's your brother." I was supposed to be the proof that Dad wasn't *le vieux*. "How old am I now?" Dad asked Luke. At the time I loved it, it seemed so cool. My dad was there and I was getting to do my

Elvis, but after they left it was another ten years before I would see my dad again.

I was in shock. *What happened? Did I bomb?* I wondered. I knew I must have done something wrong. I was still hoping things would work out because I had this collection of Father's Day gifts under my bed that I had bought and wrapped for him. But below the surface, anger was building. My mom must have tried to get a hold of him, but in those days if you changed your phone number, you disappeared. And she would never portray him in a negative light. "Oh, your dad's a great guy," she'd say. And I'd be like, "How can you say that? He's never around! How is he a good guy?" I went through phases where I was angry with her, too.

When I was about nineteen I called him and said, "I want to see you." We had dinner together that night, and I gave it to him. He barely said a word. "Yeah, yeah, you're right." No apology, but then his defence: "Well, you know, I didn't want to distract you," "I didn't want to interfere," and "You know, you never called me either."

Well, you know what I wanted? I wanted a dad. That's what I wanted. Whatever you think wasn't good for me, what I *did* want was my dad around. I was the kid, you were the adult. When I told him I was moving to Toronto to be an actor, he said, "A lot of gays do that."

"So?" I said.

"Just saying," he replied. That was his only comment. He didn't have an easy life, but a lot of people don't have easy lives. He couldn't cope, he couldn't love. As much as it felt impossible, I decided that I was going to forgive and forget, and bring fresh energy to the relationship. He never offered anything, no *"Sorry I wasn't there for you, buddy."*

I think it was a relief for him when he finally introduced me to his family, so they could all meet his secret son. I think he felt glad we were seeing each other. If I could say something more to him, it would be, "GET HELP!" He really needed therapy, but that's seen as the opposite of being a man and there was no way he'd ever do that. There was no way.

It was an unbelievable stroke of luck in my early years that my mom signed me up with the Big Brothers Big Sisters program. From the time I was eleven to sixteen I was matched with the greatest guy, Rollin. He taught me all the things my mom couldn't: camping, canoeing, chess, sports. He would have been an incredible father. Never got married, never had kids. He dated a lot—it seemed he had a new girlfriend every three months. He was an engineer, but quit engineering to become a shop teacher. He loved being with kids so much, everybody loved him. Very liberal, very accepting. He was playful, like a big kid.

Rolly had requested to be paired with a French-speaking child, but they didn't have a match for him at the time. My paperwork was all in English, so it was great when we met and I spoke French to him. Our relationship was an immediate success. I was the only "little" he ever had. Although we drifted a bit after I aged out of the program at sixteen, we were still close and he came to my high school grad. He died of a massive heart attack at the age of fifty-two, after getting back from a week of moose hunting, something he loved. Just recently my ex-wife sent me a box of photos of mine she had found, and there I am at my high school grad with Rolly at my side.

Wade Davis

Bowen Island, British Columbia

Anthropologist, author, photographer, 65

||||||||||||||||||||||||||||||||||||||||||||||||||||||||||||||||||||||||||||||||||||||||

Wade Davis was born in Montreal in 1953. He holds degrees in anthropology, biology and ethnobotany from Harvard University. Wade teaches in the Department of Anthropology at the University of British Columbia. He is an explorer-in-residence of the National Geographic Society and in 2009 had the distinction of delivering the CBC Massey Lectures. In 2015 he became a member of the Order of Canada. He lives on Bowen Island with his wife, Gail, and spends much of the summer in the Stikine Valley of northern British Columbia. He has two daughters, Tara and Raina, who are in their twenties.

||||||||||||||||||||||||||||||||||||||||||||||||||||||||||||||||||||||||||||||||||||||||

My father—he's the reason I became who I am. I think that if we were to look at five hundred character traits of your mum or dad, 95 per cent of the time you are either going to have the exact same traits or the polar opposites. For me, everything goes back to my father. He was an incredibly decent, ethical, wonderful, stunningly handsome man—an incredibly beautiful person. He was studying medicine at St. Mary's in London when Hitler's war broke out. He dropped out of school and disappeared mysteriously for three years. After his death I found a large pack of letters from my grandfather to various authorities in England, all of them seeking information as to the whereabouts of my father. The answers came back with various possibilities but no answers.

I believe my father was just a very confused young man. Perhaps something happened to him during the Blitz when he served in the Home Guard; perhaps he was suffering from some form of PTSD, or simply ashamed at having left medical school. He did not resurface until 1943 when word reached him that both his parents had been killed in a car accident, struck by a drunk driver on the Malahat highway on Vancouver Island. My father returned to Canada on compassionate leave, and in some sense never really got over it. He hardly mentioned a word about his parents, even in the presence of his one brother, and I know very little about them. He was part of a generation unprepared to speak about their emotions.

When he came back to Canada his life took a twist. He got a job in the corporate world, giving investment advice: grey flannel suit, boss who was a tyrant—I think it was brutal for him. He never spoke about what he did, or what he had planned to do, and I think he felt trapped. He could not—or would not—make changes, for fear of disrupting his family.

My father was the nicest guy, the antithesis of these fathers that children learn to fear. He was so approachable, in the here and now—but not accessible emotionally. His generation had yet to yield their feelings to analysis, a generation that had the utmost discretion and decorum. I admired that. Their language was different. You didn't ask, "*Do you feel like...?*" It was "*Do you want...?*" or "*Should we...?*" This was all compounded by the whole bourgeois miasma of where I grew up in a suburb of Montreal. Work was something that was abstracted from daily life. You go to work, you come home, have a few drinks, watch the telly, and you go back the next day and do it all over again. You putter in the garden, you play a little golf, but you don't talk about what you feel, who you are or what you believe in.

My parents were bourgeois in the classic economic sense. They had enough money to be comfortable, but they had to be careful. And as stolid middle-class people they spent what they earned in their white-collar endeavours to hire all services—be it a carpenter, plumber or mechanic. That created an odd world for me as a young kid as I never had any direct sense of my father doing anything.

He just disappeared in the morning, returned exhausted at night. He called it "the daily grind." I used to think as a young boy that he went into the city every day and returned a little smaller. The services they paid for, no proper middle-class person would deem appropriate to do. One gets the sense that doing stuff, making things, creativity itself is something that other people have and you don't.

It took me a long time to realize that creativity is a consequence of action, not its motivation. Believe it or not, I have struggled all my life with inertia. The only way I overcame this was to say yes to everything and to leap over every cliff. Had I not adopted an almost manic attitude, I would never have been able to overcome that inertia. My father was fine with his circumstances, for he was not an ambitious man. But I was, thanks to my mother, and had I not broken out, as it were, I don't think I would have been a very happy guy.

My father was infinitely kind and understanding. I think at some level he understood that he was not going to be able to provide the mentorship I needed, and he was never anything but delighted to know that I had found guidance in someone else. It was as if he understood from the start that there was only so much he could teach me. We never spoke about this, so I don't know if it's true—but if he did feel any resentment toward the amazing men who guided me, it never became apparent. He sacrificed a great deal to send me to Harvard, for example, knowing full well that every day I spent there widened the social chasm between us. It took me some years to appreciate what an amazing thing this was and how different my experience was from that of my more polished peers, with their burdens of family pressure and expectations. I never had any pressure to be anything or to follow in anyone's footsteps. I was never told that there were limits to what I could do or become.

I was very independent, commuting to Lower Canada College from the time I was eleven, and then once I was at Brentwood College on Vancouver Island I spent the summers working in the bush. There was a window of opportunity in my late teens where my father—*a* father—could have provided guidance, but instead this gap formed between us. By the time I was in my early twenties in the early seventies, the distance between us had increased.

While my father may not have taught me the practical skills I would have enjoyed, he inspired with his values and character, his kindness, decency, modesty and honour, and this was an astonishing gift, though something I only came to realize after his death. And it encouraged me to seek other mentors, the series of extraordinary men who have inspired my life. These have ranged from Harvard scholars to First Nations elders, from hunting guides to poets.

My father lived with a lot of stress. I think about how I handle stress. People are amazed at what I do and what I get done, but it's not bad when you do something you love. Hard is good, hard is what makes it good. Stress is when you are trapped in a world and you can't get out of it. My father had his first heart attack at fifty-eight and then another at sixty-eight that took his life. I was living in France when he died and made arrangements to return to Canada as quickly as I could.

When I reached the funeral home in Victoria, I was told by the director that time was of the essence and they could only allow me a few minutes with my father. As I entered the room where my father lay, I politely told this dreadful character, this merchant of death, that I had come a very long way to say goodbye to my father, and that if he or any of his staff interrupted me, they would be lying beside my father on the marble slab.

I went in. There was my father, stone cold, a bit of stubble from the morning's growth. I lay on him, I held him, I wanted so desperately that contact, that closeness with him that we'd never had in life. I cried, I wept—and then I wailed. I wanted to say all the things left unsaid. This is the thing when someone dies suddenly: if Dad had lived another twenty years, there could have been some reconciliation. We would have found peace.

Becoming a father was the most amazing moment in my life. When my first daughter, Tara, was born, I simply stared at her in bliss for about six months. I had never before experienced true selfless love. When my second daughter, Raina, came along, I wondered how I would possibly love her as I did Tara. Then of course the moment she appeared, slipping out of her mother's body with

Tara (LEFT), Raina and Wade, 2015

an ease and grace that she carries to this day, I learned—and really for the first time—that love is indeed infinite.

In general, I'd have to say that the biggest surprise was how easy it was to be a *good* dad. I feel for my parents' generation—all that they endured, all that they wanted to insulate their children from, all the challenges of raising families in a time of total social and political upheaval, civil rights, women's rights, Vietnam, drugs, the environment. We have had it much easier, for the social chasm and generational gap that divided us from our folks simply does not exist with our kids. My girls have always turned to me for support, and when they reached puberty, I had the privilege of being the one they sought for guidance. Those adolescent years were rich; we had such open, strong relationships.

One way to guarantee your children don't have drug problems is to be known as the parent who has experienced all these drugs. But my girls didn't grow up with parents who used drugs; they came of age in a home knowing about the nature of the use of these substances, both in our culture and the traditional societies of the world. They knew that there were no *good* and *bad* drugs, only good and bad ways of using drugs. I remember once Tara called me up from a music festival, having taken LSD for the first and, as it turned out, the only time. I was a bit taken aback, but I didn't scold her. I asked about the experience, where she had sourced the acid and if she felt okay in the wake of the experience. I think this relationship between us, and our family relationship if you will, with the entire drug challenge—which is around all of our kids whether we like it or not—may account for why neither of my daughters use any drugs today. Tara only very occasionally drinks a beer.

I travelled a great deal when my kids were growing up. I took them with me whenever possible. And more importantly, when I was home I was really *there*, welcoming them and their friends after school, helping with homework, reading to them every night. One year, Raina and I went through the entire collected works of P.G. Wodehouse! And every summer we spent a couple of months at our lodge, a remote fishing camp in northern Canada. It was off-grid, seven hours by road from the nearest town, no phones, internet or electricity. So that became the well we all drank from during the rest of the year. My father, by contrast, never travelled, but in a sense even though he was home he was never really there. We didn't have a great deal of what I would describe as "real time" together. That's just how it was.

We take it for granted nowadays that both men and women work. This is not only a reflection of the legitimate aspirations of women; it is an economic necessity for the middle class in today's economy. And the family has been redefined, embracing all sorts of configurations, all of which is great, for there is no such thing as "normal" when it comes to such a complex dynamic, and there are no limits to love. That said, I really do believe that boys in particular need a man in their lives, a mentor both strong and loving, a constant—like a mountain the wind cannot shake. In matrilineal societies it was the mother's brother. In our patrilineal tradition it has been the father. Such men are needed to provide a living embodiment of all that is honourable and true, as they wrap the young boy in a protective and life-sustaining cloak of moral and ethical values.

If I have one regret in life, it's the timing of my father's death. It was so sudden and unexpected, denying him the chance to know my daughters and leaving us no chance to find the true peace that I know would have come had he lived longer. Knowing how death can surprise us, I do try to share my thoughts with my daughters, offering advice, words of wisdom that they will be able to carry with them whenever the time comes for me to check out.

When each of my daughters turned twenty-one, I shared with them a story from long ago, when at that age, living in the mountains of Colombia, I met a Kamsa shaman who told me something I have never forgotten. "In the first years of your life," Pedro said, "you live beneath the shadow of the past, too young to know what to do. In your last years you find that you are too old to understand the world coming at you from behind. In between there is a small and narrow beam of light that illuminates your life."

Perhaps the most important lesson I've shared with my daughters—the words that more than any others I would want them to pass on to their children should I not be around—is the lesson I learned as a son, witnessing the disappointments of my own father. If you can look back over a long life and see that you have owned your choices, then there is little ground for resentment. Bitterness comes to those who look back with regret on the choices imposed upon them. The greatest creative challenge is the struggle to be the architect of your own life.

So be patient. Do not compromise. And give your destiny time to find you. My father died with a review of my first book in his pocket. What I would later accomplish, I know, would have made him very proud, allowing him perhaps to open up in new ways. At the very least, I would have had a chance to thank him for all that he did to make my life possible.

Don Evans

Victoria, British Columbia

Executive director, 57

||||||||||||||||||||||||||||||||||||||||||||||||||||||||||||||||||||||||||||||||||||||||||||

Don Evans is chief executive officer of Our Place Society in Victoria, BC, a non-profit social service agency that provides front-line service to Victoria's most vulnerable people. Previously, he was a co-executive director at First United Church in Vancouver. Don is father to a thirty-three-year-old daughter, and he has three grandchildren who live in Alberta and visit him regularly.

||||||||||||||||||||||||||||||||||||||||||||||||||||||||||||||||||||||||||||||||||||||||||||

I was given up for adoption at birth, but just three months later I was diagnosed with hydrocephalus, or fluid in the brain. I wasn't expected to live—and if I did live, it was anticipated that I'd have mental challenges. The adoption failed, leaving me alone in the hospital for four months. My next phase of life was almost four years of foster care. My foster parents had five children in their care, and taking children into their home was their source of income. When I was four and a half years old and deemed "fit for adoption," a new family adopted me and my foster family disappeared from my life forever.

My adoptive parents—who are wonderful—had a beautiful family of three girls and badly wanted a boy. I know it should not have mattered that my dad was not my birth father, but it did. From the outset, I struggled with belonging. I was a very fearful child: afraid of not being good enough, of not being liked, of being alone, of being in crowds. All of these emotions were rooted in the trauma I experienced in very early childhood. My adoptive parents tried.

They were very loving and caring, but I could never trust anyone, as I never felt that I belonged. At my core I felt different and could not allow myself to be vulnerable, to trust, to allow myself to attach to people.

I have very few memories of my life before the age of twelve, but over time I became very close with my mum and my grandmother. I still struggled to form a relationship with my dad. With other men, too. I have always found it easier to connect with women.

I became a chameleon, getting along with everybody, becoming what they wanted me to be, but inside there was this deep discomfort because I knew I didn't fit in. Because of my feelings of being unworthy, I was always trying to prove myself. I became a high achiever, doing well in school and later in business. But my feelings of being alone in the world didn't change. All of these feelings were internalized. I never expressed them—I didn't act out. My parents knew I looked at the world differently, but I was busy, appeared successful and never shared what was going on inside.

I was terrified to talk about my emptiness. I'd want to be around people, but when I was, I felt very separate. My dad tried so hard to connect with me and make time for me, but the things he was interested in didn't appeal to me. I don't think he knew what my interests really were. When my sisters got boyfriends, I'd see them connecting with him on things like sports, fishing, hunting—the sort of things that he liked but didn't interest me.

It was obvious to me that I wasn't like him. We were so different in our interests. He's a conservative guy, a man's man. I'm more liberal, a risk-taker, and I felt that I wasn't the son my father wanted. I didn't feel that I lived up to his expectations. I also didn't feel worthy as a male. Looking back at it now, I know I *did* live up to his expectations. My father adores me for who I am, as I am. We now have a much stronger bond. But at the time I was consumed by my feelings of fear, unworthiness and shame, and by my version of what and who a man was supposed to be. My whole life has been focused on shame. For a long time I was not able to identify it or to know what caused it, but I now know it's connected to my early abandonment.

I struggled with my sexuality in my early teens, wondering if maybe I was gay—yet I just wanted to grow up to be a straight male with a wife and kids. When I left home at eighteen, I continued to question my sexual orientation. Being gay was the last thing I wanted. I thought maybe this was a phase I was going through. In my early twenties I was in a relationship with my high school sweetheart, and I started thinking that perhaps starting a family with her would help to sort things out.

Our daughter arrived when I was twenty-three. Being her father was complete bliss for me. It was the first time I ever really had a connection with someone—this little person who was dependent upon me, was vulnerable. With her is where I learned how to love. There was a bond I'd never felt with anyone else in my whole life. She was and is my pride and joy, and I cherish our times together.

The struggle with my sexual orientation ended at age twenty-five when I knew for sure that I was gay. I also knew this wasn't at all fair to my partner. We split up when our daughter was three years old and my partner decided that our daughter would be better off living with me. I owned a restaurant at the time. We'd open for lunch and then I'd take my daughter to various places and to do activities like swimming, skiing and skating. Our bond grew stronger, especially when I took a couple of years off to devote myself to raising her full-time.

In those days, there were hardly any men raising children on their own, especially gay men. I felt extremely blessed and fortunate to have the opportunity to raise my daughter. It was difficult at times, but people were so supportive. When my daughter was preparing for a dance competition, it wasn't appropriate for me to accompany her into the dressing room, so all the mothers helped with her hair and makeup.

When my daughter was five, I met someone and moved to Vancouver to be with him. One day, my parents had arranged to come for a visit. I was so worried about my father finding out I was gay. They met Daryl, whom I introduced to them as my friend. Afterwards, my dad told my mum, "I think Daryl is gay," and she replied, "Well you know what that probably means..." And so I was out! Dad was very supportive. In fact, my whole family was.

My dad is loving and very compassionate, but I didn't see it back then. I continued to bury and mask my emotions, and only found a way out of all the fear and shame through substances. I could have blown it all. I got into recovery for addictions in 1998, and that's when things truly started to get better for me. I plan to continue my journey of healing and recovery all my life.

As I have healed, my relationship with my father has also improved—not because he's any different, but because I am. As I get to be more of my true self, and as my spirituality grows, I am able to trust, be vulnerable, accept myself and interact differently. Fear isn't getting in the way and I am no longer repeating the old theme of not being good enough.

Part of my fear, I now realize, was that I didn't allow my dad to get to know me, and I didn't allow myself to know him. At the time I didn't feel like he was trying hard enough; but he didn't know what to do. I can't blame him for that! What I realize now is that as a child I needed professional help. I wish there had been more awareness to get me started toward healing earlier. My dad didn't do anything wrong—he did what he could with what he knew. The same is true for me with my daughter, so I have lots of regrets there.

My dad is an emotional person, but in the past he was guarded. He had been raised by a single mum in the days when that didn't happen very often, and when boys weren't taught to show their feelings. Things have changed for him, too, and he now expresses himself better than he did before.

As for me, I was so afraid to show my feelings; I went through my whole life keeping them inside. What I learned about people with the disease of addiction is that *we* don't show emotion. It wasn't until I'd spent years in recovery that those walls started to come down. I'd spent those earlier years in my head. I'd think my way through everything; I was a problem-solver, very analytical. Also thrill-seeking, pushing myself into dangerous situations: racing cars, skydiving, even seeking pain and self-harming, punishing myself. I could have ended it all many times, but in spite of it all

Don with father Ray, daughter, and grandchildren, 2018

I didn't want to end my life; it was always about finding a way to escape and change my consciousness. It's been so hard for me to actually *notice* what I am feeling *when* I am feeling it.

My father is loving, understanding and generous. There were many special times when he gave me one-on-one attention and I didn't have to compete with my sisters or their boyfriends. He's an outgoing guy with lots of friends; he sings in a choir, is very active in his church and in political stuff. He is very positive and kind.

I sacrificed who I was to try to be who I thought my dad wanted me to be, but I lost myself. In fact, I lost myself in other significant relationships too. These were always very codependent; it was about their needs, not mine. I was always trying to please my partner, please my friends and please my dad.

Now that I can be myself with my father, my relationship with my daughter has improved as well. Even though we had a very close bond, she's grown up with me having very high expectations of her and she had a hard time trying to live up to them. I passed my high expectations on without knowing what I was doing. My daughter thought she had to be perfect as that was the facade I was showing her—no sign of any vulnerability on my part. Now we can both express our struggles, and we are much closer.

Our relationship as father and child was strained while I was active in my addiction. Thank goodness we had a strong foundation from those early years. When the addiction hit, I wasn't there for her emotionally or physically. There was also fear and paranoia on my part, along with a manic spontaneity. I'd often wake her up and take her somewhere, like to the airport, and off we went to some faraway destination without knowing what I was pursuing or what I was trying to get away from.

When my daughter was in grade eight, she found out that I was an addict. I sent her to be with her mum and a lot of things changed in her mind about who I was. She started doing poorly at school, sunk low and attempted suicide. Halfway through that year, her mum sent her back to me. I was in early recovery, a tenuous time, and I made the best decision ever by putting her into a private school in Victoria. I was lucky I had the resources to do it. My daughter thrived in that environment and I did what I needed to do, which was get clean and begin to find myself—through recovery.

Now I can receive the love my father gives. I can see the connection between him and his generosity in the community. It's what has helped me do the work I do. I have a passion for social justice, and my contribution to the community has given meaning to my life. My own brokenness and challenges have helped me connect with other people who are fearful or who feel they don't belong. I work way too much: I still have a constant voice that plays in the background—*not doing enough, not good enough*—but I am getting better at noticing it and silencing it. I also love my work, so it's impossible not to pour myself into it!

Today, my daughter is doing wonderfully, in spite of all the mistakes I made. She's a great mum to my beautiful grandchildren, whom I completely adore. It was through my dad's kindness that I began to know I was worthy of being loved. I had erected so many barriers that I just couldn't allow myself to notice there was so much love there all along. I haven't said a lot to my dad about how I felt as a little boy, and that was one of the reasons I had to give some thought to telling this story. I'm closer to my dad today than I have ever been in my whole life. He's a wonderful father.

Nowadays my dad and I read some of the same books. We chat about them, and we share our (different) world views and our interest in theology. I wasn't so interested in his life before, but today I have a strong desire to have this relationship grow and thrive. I want to learn everything I can from him that I turned my back on before. There's a real opportunity here to build a connection on a much deeper level. As I learn more about myself, I am sharing it with him. I am not afraid anymore because I value who I am.

Niigaan Sinclair

Winnipeg, Manitoba

Associate professor, 42

‖‖

Niigaanwewidam James Sinclair is Anishinaabe and originally from St. Peter's (Little Peguis) near Selkirk, Manitoba. He is an award-winning writer, editor and activist whose written work has appeared in *The Guardian*, *The Globe and Mail* and the *Winnipeg Free Press*. He trains educators across Canada, having written curricula for organizations like the Assembly of First Nations. Currently an associate professor and formerly head of the Department of Native Studies at the University of Manitoba, Niigaan teaches courses in Indigenous literature, culture, history and politics. He and his first partner have a daughter, Sarah, born in 2006. Niigaan is the son of Senator Murray Sinclair, who was chair of the Truth and Reconciliation Commission of Canada from 2009 to 2015.

‖‖

Sarah was born when I was thirty, at the exact time I started my PhD. I was at home with her for the first six years of her life and really, that was my *real* PhD. In fact, I can't remember what I was like as a human being before she arrived. Everything else I have done in life pales in comparison to being a father.

I was primarily raised in a single-parent family by my mother. My parents split up when I was five. My father was off doing really important things for the country—he was the first Indigenous judge in Manitoba, a senator and in many ways an "uncle" to the rest of

Canada. It wasn't that we didn't want to be with each other—I could always phone him, for example—but he was constantly being called upon by the rest of the world. I'd see him usually two weekends a month.

Our visits would often be interrupted, like at the mall: people would come up and ask him for things, seeking advice or to see if he could deal with something they were going through. This was the 1980s and Indigenous peoples were still suffering a lot of racism—with police, with the justice system, with whatever else. When I would go with him to work, grandmothers would bring in their grandsons, trying to get him to represent them in court, as he was the only Indigenous lawyer around.

I don't say this to mean *woe is me*, but we've always had a distance between us. I've always felt love and he's always been there when I needed him, but then there's been the work, the things that come from him dealing with so many big issues in the country: colonialism, violence, injustice. I've had to share my growing up with a man helping the country to grow up—and I'd be lying if I didn't say that's been frustrating. I wish we'd had more time together. But I understand. He's been busy.

It's also taken me a long time to realize that we have both been impacted by the history of this country, and to realize how much Indigenous people have gone through. My grandfather, my dad's dad, went through a lot—residential school, abuse, the war—and he brought a lot of that violence home. He became an alcoholic, likely self-medicating for the things he went through. When he drank he fought and hurt those around him—including his children.

My father saw first-hand the impacts of violence and it's been hard for him to talk about it. The result is we don't talk about it much, and that's okay. This silence, though, has led to other silences. The fact that my father went through such a hard time in his life and was still a great dad is amazing. One of the things he has done with me is always show me unconditional love, yet I still find I miss him.

Some of the best parts of me I got from my mom. She worked very hard to help me develop empathy, kindness, critical thinking and awareness of social issues, and as a social worker she taught me how to show care and concern for other human beings. For my emotional strengths, I have to thank my mom.

My father gave me a sense of spirit. When I was born, he began a journey into learning what it means to be an Anishinaabe and a man. He felt he didn't know enough as a young father to be able to give much to a son, so he began to attend ceremonies at the Midewiwin lodge. He spent time with elders and learned teachings—and finally, introduced me to this life. He met his second wife, my other mother, who helped him and also me on this journey. We still attend these ceremonies today and I have found answers to all of the questions I have ever asked about who I am, why I am here, who can help me and where I am going. I found meaning. For this, I thank my father.

My parental motto came from my mom: "*Whatever works.*" She was and still is the most practical person I know. When we couldn't afford much when I was a kid, dinner would be "whatever works." When I decided to not go to university and travel internationally, she said, "Whatever works." When I told her I wanted to give up being a high school teacher—a career I had worked to achieve for ten years—and try to become a writer, she said, "Whatever works!" Mom really made anything work. She made sure I had the opportunity to participate in anything—for example, in hockey. She'd borrow hockey equipment, used hand-me-downs, and I wore my dad's old skates. *Whatever works.*

This parental motto is serving me well with Sarah. It's allowed me to be adaptable and flexible. I have listened to her, I have paid attention to her needs and rhythms. When Sarah was a baby, I tried to always encourage whatever she was interested in that day. One day she stopped napping and I said, "Whatever works!" and then she started sleeping for fifteen hours straight at night instead. My partner and I were very happy. Now, Sarah is almost a teenager. "*Whatever works*" is guiding me through potentially difficult topics of conversation such as sex, puberty and dating. But like my dad, I'll talk about the time we spend at the lodge and ceremonies to try and tie it all together for her.

She's not a wallflower. Sarah is developing a public persona of her own. She's stepping into this a little early, but because I do so much public and political work in the media, she comes to my speaking engagements and sometimes she even speaks. At these times I love seeing her self-assurance and confidence, and remember how my parents have contributed to this moment, too. One time she met Justin Trudeau and engaged him in conversation like an old friend.

Now in my forties, I realize how imperfect I am. I don't like talking about myself, especially about my fears of rejection that led to difficulty in relationships and other issues going all the way back to my grandfather. I've made lots of mistakes. I'm human, too. I don't fault my family—or my grandfather—for anything. I am who I am because of him and I appreciate his incredible resilience. His childhood didn't give him what he needed and that led to legacies of silence I now want to undo. Every day is a struggle—some struggles I win, some I lose.

Of course, the legacy of residential schools impacts the lives of Indigenous people in various ways, but every Canadian is affected by it. My grandfather wasn't an alcoholic because he wanted to be; he was an alcoholic because he was physically and sexually abused as a young boy in residential school. He learned violence and brought that into his own life. People don't ever choose to become alcoholics; they are self-medicating the pain they live with and endure. Not everyone chooses alcohol either—some people lose themselves in shopping, gambling, their career...whatever it takes to create numbness.

If my father hadn't taken the journey of rejecting the violence my grandfather introduced into his life, and had not found our lodge and ceremonies, I'd be very lost. I don't know where I would be—I think I would have become an alcoholic and a very angry person. Being Anishinaabe plays a central role in my life and in my identity. Being Indigenous is something Canadian society still rejects, demeans and ostracizes whether it be in Parliament, movies or in the media. Things are changing, but too slowly.

Without the lodge, without those ceremonies and my beliefs, I would not be the father I am today. I am very proud of everything the lodge has made me. In our ceremonies we say, "*Ni minwendam omaa ayaan,*" which means "I am happy for all the things that have

Niigaan and Sarah, 2006

brought us together." It means that everything that has brought me here—the good, the bad, the great, the ugly—has made me who I am, standing here right now. We shouldn't run from those things, as they have all created us. And I am happy for all the things that have created those around me, too.

So I'm here because of my dad's uphill journey, and because of what I have experienced since I was a little boy. I'm here because of my mother and my dad's second wife—my other mother—too. I've taught my daughter that she comes from all of these places, ending up in the lodge today. She may choose to make that a part of her own life, too. Whatever works.

I think about the time before Sarah arrived, who I was then, and it's like watching a TV show—I can see it, but I can't feel it. I had a gaping hole inside of me that I was trying to fill in various ways: drinking, career, dating. Her birth was so beautiful; she was the first baby born on her mother's reserve for sixty years. Her mother is an incredible woman who insisted Sarah be introduced to her community from the first moment she entered this world. Her grandmother spoke to her only in Cree during her first moments. Being born at home is also a profound political act in this country, as childbirth has been taken from First Nations communities and the hands of women, medicalized by doctors and missionaries who considered midwifery a threat.

Her arrival had a powerful effect on me, but not right away. I had to earn it. When Sarah was only a day old, we were trying to keep her hydrated. I was dipping my finger into water and letting her suck on it and I had to stay up all night while she went in and out of sleep. In that time I attended to this little baby, I became profoundly changed; I felt a gravitational pull between the two of us that operates every second of my life.

Going through the split with Sarah's mother, that was rotten; I don't wish that on anyone. The worst part was telling Sarah we were going to split up. I didn't want to give her that kind of burden, but her mother and I are very good co-parents. It took us a while, but I consider her a good friend.

One of my biggest challenges has been intimacy. Because of the tension in the relationship between my father and my grandfather, my dad shied away from physical contact with me. He didn't hit me but he also didn't hold me much. I only remember a few hugs before I was about thirty-five, and my dad doesn't express love often. This is a bit of a "guy thing," but it's very much a "my dad" thing. Now he's changing, but for a long time I read on Twitter how much my dad loves me as many times as he had actually told me.

A generation later, the effect of this has shown up in my relationship with my daughter—as a need to keep her close. Frankly, I'm smothering her. She's actually said to me, "Dad, that's enough hugs for one day." I still hold her hand even though she's really too old for that. It's as if I'm trying to get back, to reclaim, what I missed out on. For so many of us, just touching our parents was something illegal and forbidden, as most of us would have been gone by the time we were five or six. This story is the intergenerational legacy of residential schools.

Another of the worst legacies to come from violence is silence: withdrawal, questioning feelings, not trusting yourself. Pain that you don't talk about that shows up in other places. Avoidance. When faced with conflict, there are two likely responses: fight or flight. My dad found ways to both fight with and flee from his father, but between my father and I there was no fight because he was usually not there. So for me, my response to conflict has most often been flight. When conflict comes up, I want to run to my computer, to social media, my work, television... I'll avoid it however I can.

Even with my daughter I struggle to talk about difficult things I am feeling. I'd rather just talk about the good stuff. It takes a lot of courage to overcome this sense of impending doom, this sense that if I share something that makes me feel vulnerable, the world is going to come crashing down. It's hard for me to talk about this. I hope to break the cycle. I hope to achieve more balance. I hope to be able to teach my children that our ceremonies, our languages are just as relevant as ever. There is no better means of understanding the world than with the ceremonies we've always had.

The world our kids are growing up in is so different. I was reminded of this watching the movie *Eighth Grade*: the peer pressure, the bullying, the need for approval, the stress. Being a kid and trying to get "likes" on a social media page? Talk about anxiety-provoking. I also worry about the increasingly poor state of the world. I worry about what Sarah will face in terms of the economy, pollution, changes to ecology; I worry that it won't be safe to trust things like your food source, and how we are not changing our habits despite all the knowledge and evidence that we should.

Growing up as an Indigenous person in Canada is to be continually under assault every day of your life. When I was a kid I tried covering up all the parts of me that were Indigenous, even telling people I was Spanish, which was ridiculous because I have the most Indigenous name in Manitoba. Despite all the amazing people around me, I had little pride. I was very ashamed. The world around me told me every day that I was worthless, that I didn't deserve to live.

Being a young Indigenous person in Canada is to be in a world that wants you to disappear. Whether they want you to die in prison or in a river, it's all still there. Indigenous people are still viewed by many the same way they were five decades ago. It just looks different—it may be less aggressive, but it's every bit as devastating. We still have movies that portray us in a dismal light, we still have politicians who say appalling things, we still have draconian legislation that is attacking us all the time, and a federal law and department that keeps us under control in Canada.

I can't pretend it doesn't exist; I have to prepare my child for that, but I don't want it to define her. I hope she won't inherit the narrative. I used to think it was resiliency I wanted for her, but now I see that being resilient means she is always responding to something negative, a struggle. I want something more for her, to have a sense of limitlessness for herself, a sense of constant and endless possibility. Every once in a while, I watch my daughter and I have confidence in her. I can see it's all there and I can see that she can rise above it. She's awesome and I'm pretty proud of the job I've done in raising her. I'm proud my family made it. I'm proud my family and I made her. *Ni minwendam omaa ayaan.*

Walter J. Natynczyk

Ottawa, Ontario

General (retired), public servant, 61

||||||||||||||||||||||||||||||||||||||||||||||||||||||||||||||||||||||||||||||||||||||||||||||||

Walt Natynczyk was born and raised in Winnipeg. He joined the Canadian Armed Forces in 1975, attending Royal Roads Military College and Royal Military College Saint-Jean. He went on to become chief of defence staff of the Canadian Armed Forces from 2008 to 2012, president of the Canadian Space Agency until 2014 and is now current deputy minister of veterans affairs. Walt is married to Leslie. Their three grown children are John, Will and Margaret, and their five grandchildren are Charlotte, Anna, Josephine, Benjamin and Charles.

||||||||||||||||||||||||||||||||||||||||||||||||||||||||||||||||||||||||||||||||||||||||||||||||

I can hardly wait to spend time with my grandchildren. When my own kids were growing up, I missed long periods with family due to operational deployments and training. So when we did have time together, we made the most of it! As a young officer, many of my friends were sleeping in, drinking with the boys, out golfing. After all the time I had been away from home, I just could not do any of that stuff. When we could spend time as a family, we were out together: hiking in the woods of Petawawa, fishing and canoeing. When I was a boy, I didn't have those opportunities with my own dad. I was determined to make time for my kids.

Now that our kids are grown and serving in the Canadian Armed Forces themselves, we seize whatever time we can to be with them and their families. We are so determined to have time together that we built a retirement home on the lake where our children and their families can be comfortable and can spend quality time with their children and their friends. This particular lake was a bit of a constant for our family, as relatives previously lived there. We camped and fished at their place when our kids were quite young. Summer holidays at the lake were one of the few "normals" in our military family life. We were moving to different locations every couple of years. We moved fifteen times! That was, and is still, the rhythm of military life.

My dad was absent from my life for different reasons. He was a good man who loved my mom and his children. He was a hard worker. I understand now that he was dealing with a lot of mental health issues as a result of his experiences in the Second World War. He died before my tenth birthday.

I made an effort to understand my father's life. I learned more about him years after his death from his brothers who settled in the UK, and also through my research on the internet. Dad was a veteran of the Second World War, a member of the Free Polish Army and a survivor of the Gulag work camps of Soviet Siberia, where he spent eighteen months.

The internet allowed me to discover my father's debriefing records, which he wrote when he arrived in the British Army camps in Iraq in November 1941. In his own handwriting is a report of what he and his family experienced during the early stages of the war. Their harrowing saga still sends chills up my spine. In February 1940, my dad worked as a blacksmith in Pinsk, Poland. The Soviets were in the throes of ethnically cleansing eastern Poland and creating Belorussia. My father was the eldest of ten children and joined his mother and father to be herded aboard cattle cars for resettlement. They thought they were to be moved elsewhere in Poland, but instead they embarked on a thirteen-day journey with no food or water, on their way to a work camp, a gulag, near the city of Tashkent.

My grandfather died on the train. My grandmother and the two youngest, twin infants, died in the camps. Death, filth, disease and lice were all around my dad and his brothers. They were starving. They were compelled to work on unimaginable and unachievable tasks in

Walt, his grandson Benjamin and son Will

order to earn their daily rations. My dad spent eighteen months doing hard labour before the Soviets allowed the survivors to leave.

Unfortunately, the three youngest remaining siblings were too young to travel and were given to the Red Cross. The remaining five boys, with my dad as the eldest, made their way on foot, hanging off the sides of freight trains, and by ship to Iraq, and then to Palestine. The boys were trained to be soldiers in the Free Polish Army, part of the British Armed Forces. My dad was a Sherman tank driver and served in North Africa and Italy. He was wounded at the Battle of Monte Cassino and recovered in Britain.

I didn't have a clue about any of the details of how my father came to Canada. I recalled that he would often say he had lost his country and his parents, and that he had come to Canada with nothing. It wasn't until I was chief of defence staff and giving a speech at Pier 21 in Halifax that I was approached by the curator of the museum, who asked how my father arrived. "I don't know," I told her. "I frankly don't know."

After my speech she found me again. She had done some research. "This is where your father arrived," she said. "Here, at

Pier 21." She gave me a photo of the RMS *Aquitania* and a copy of the ship's manifest detailing that Private Aleksander Natynczyk arrived on May 16, 1946 as part of a contingent of five hundred displaced Polish soldiers. She also had a number of newspaper articles and letters to the editor of the *Halifax Chronicle Herald* conveying the message that these Polish soldiers were not welcome in Canada. They should return to Poland as they wouldn't amount to anything and would be a burden on Canadian society.

Since seeing these articles, it has been my great pleasure and pride to give a number of speeches to diverse ethnic groups across the country, when I could happily tell them, "I guess it all worked out! And our family wasn't a burden on society!"

I have pieced together an understanding of what my dad went through and what kind of man he was. After arriving in Manitoba where he had distant relatives, he worked on a farm shoeing horses and then started work in construction, operating a tractor. After driving Sherman tanks in the war, it was easy for him to drive a front-end loader.

Some of my favourite memories of him are when he took me for rides at the work sites. I recall smelling the diesel and the hydraulic fluid, and walking through the mud. The conditions in which he worked were extreme. He could be either sun-baked, constructing hydro towers in the Manitoba swamps amid the mosquitoes and blackflies, or working in frigid temperatures for weeks at a time. I recall visiting him while he worked on the foundations of the Richardson Building at the corner of Portage and Main. It was January and minus forty degrees Celsius—it was crazy cold!

None of my dad's brothers or chums would talk about their war-time experiences with anyone but each other. I have memories of my father with a whole bunch of his Free Polish Army chums in the kitchen of our house in Winnipeg, where they would be singing army songs and telling stories, crying and self-medicating with lots of hard liquor. I realize now they were "treating" each other. It was actually peer counselling, with a lot of alcohol.

He tried to be a good dad. Even though he was dealing with his own demons, he showed me how to be strong, to be of service and

Walt with son Will and grandson Benjamin

how to support a family through hard work. I came to appreciate his grit and resilience. When he knew he was going to die, he asked my mom's brother, Uncle Edie, to take me camping and fishing, to give me opportunities that he couldn't. He died of sclerosis of the liver and bleeding ulcers, the damage caused by taking a lot of Aspirin after his drinking binges so that he could go to work in the morning.

In 2014 I was in England visiting one of my uncles, my father's brother Peter. His wife Sylvia had never heard him talk about the war years and warned me, "You are not going to get anything out of him." But Uncle Peter opened up to me for the first time. Because of my service in the armed forces and in operations, I was someone who could understand his terrible experience and with whom he could share his memories.

I am my father's son, trying to learn from what he endured. When I commanded troops I made the effort to emphasize the importance of supporting our servicemen and women suffering from mental health injuries. I have seen the harm done to those who don't receive help. I have campaigned long and hard for military leaders to create safe working conditions so that folks struggling with mental health injuries can overcome the stigma, can feel safe to seek treatment. This is my dad's legacy.

In 2004 I served in Baghdad, Iraq on exchange with the US Army. It was the night of the ninth of April, Easter Sunday, and rockets were raining down on our camp. As I tried to take cover, I could hear them getting closer and closer. There was nowhere to run; I took cover under my bed. Two months later I arrived home in Kingston to a massive thunderstorm over Lake Ontario. There was an enormous clap of thunder and I screamed, "Take cover!" I threw my wife out of bed and ducked beneath the bed. She got up and started to laugh. "You old fool," she said, "it's a thunderstorm." Then I started to laugh with her.

It was only later that I realized how good that laughter was for me. It turns out that I managed to process those events in a healthy way, and thankfully, I know how to take care of myself. I've done a lot of talking and releasing. Running and sport have helped give me mindfulness.

After my dad died, my mum was deeply depressed, raising three children on her own. We were very poor and on social welfare. My uncles tried to support and encourage me. My uncle John, my dad's brother living in Canada, even bought me a bike. But he was dealing with his own struggles with PTSD and severe alcoholism. So I had to do a lot for myself. By the age of sixteen I was assistant manager at a fast food restaurant, a master warrant officer in air cadets and on the high school football team. I had also bought myself a car. Up to that point I'd never travelled, other than for cadet summer camp, and had not dined in a restaurant. I discovered I could apply to the Royal Military College to cover my education, and left home for the military at seventeen years of age.

By the time I was twenty-five I was married and becoming a father! I didn't know what kind of father I'd be, but I knew I was going to take the best of my dad's and my uncles' lessons. It turns out I also inherited an anger issue from my dad. I knew it was there and that it had the potential to derail me. I have worked hard to be totally focused, to be aware of my own emotions, to not lose my cool and to do whatever I do very deliberately. Just like in the forces—keep a clear head and bring consciousness to everything I do.

When I was home, I often had a baby strapped on me. I was a very hands-on dad, down on the floor, reading, playing and later supporting my children's involvement in hockey, ringette and soccer. Involvement in sports helped them settle in after each military move. The biggest challenge was our lifestyle—constantly moving every couple years and my wife coping with me parachuting in and out of the family when I was deployed. Whenever I hear the song "Cat's in the Cradle" I am reminded of how much of our children's upbringing I missed.

When the children were little, keeping in touch while I was deployed on a peacekeeping mission wasn't easy. Contact a couple of times over the six-month tour using a ham radio was a luxury. When I returned home after as much as a year away, I'd get sick once the flow of adrenalin had drained from my system. Meanwhile, my family would have changed. My wife Leslie and the children would have grown together; expectations and rules would have shifted. It took time, good communication skills and lots of patience to adjust to the new normal.

Parenting has felt like my real purpose in life; everything else is secondary. My advice to fathers is this: plan around your kids, be there 100 per cent and when it comes to grandchildren, drop everything for them. That's what I am relishing in this phase of life. I can be there for my grandchildren in a way I couldn't for my own children. What would I say to my dad now? I love you, Dad! Thank you for giving me the life I have. So much of who I am is due to the brief life lessons you gave me—a little has gone a long way.

Rick Hansen

Vancouver, British Columbia

Athlete, activist, 62

||||||||||||||||||||||||||||||||||||||||||||||||||||||||||||||||||||||||||||||||||||||||||

Rick Hansen was born in Port Alberni in 1957. At the age of fifteen he sustained a spinal cord injury and became paraplegic after being thrown from a pickup truck. His Man in Motion World Tour, a twenty-six-month, forty-thousand-kilometre wheelchair trek through thirty-four countries in 1985, raised twenty-six million dollars for spinal cord research, rehabilitation and sport, and changed the way people with disabilities are perceived. Over the last thirty years, his Rick Hansen Foundation has generated over 359 million dollars to raise awareness, change attitudes, and remove barriers for people with disabilities as well as fund spinal cord injury research and care. Rick is married to Amanda, who was his physiotherapist during his Man in Motion World Tour. They have three daughters, Emma, Alanna and Rebecca, and two grandsons, Reid (deceased) and Everett.

||||||||||||||||||||||||||||||||||||||||||||||||||||||||||||||||||||||||||||||||||||||||||

My dad was a great guy, and I had a complex, dynamic relationship with him. He was very committed to sport, his family and his community in positive ways, but he was a disciplinarian. I was made accountable in ways that would be considered harsh in today's world, but it caught my attention—and served its purpose. When I was six years old my dad had a work accident. He was working as a lineman for the telephone company. A telephone pole fell on him, trapping him and breaking his hip. It left him with a debilitating injury and disability, but watching him stay active and move on with his life after the accident had a very positive influence on me.

My dad assumed a very traditional role in our family—protector, provider. He was CEO of the home, but not a nurturer—that was my mum's role. My ideas of equality, absolute equality between men and women, are very different from his. My fatherhood has evolved significantly from where my dad's was. I have worked hard to achieve a partnership with my wife Amanda and equality of status within my marriage. It's very different from when I was growing up.

My accident destroyed my ideal view of what my life would be. I wondered if I could get married. I didn't think I'd ever be able to have a family. I had to let go of my dreams and rebuild my life. Amanda and I married in 1987. Emma ("bringer of life") was born in 1990, Alanna in 1992 and Rebecca in 1995. They are brilliant, beautiful and magnificent! I am so grateful. I am one of the luckiest guys on the planet.

From the beginning, Amanda and I were able to discuss our parenting as true partners. It was in my relationship with her that I realized I was not going to simply replicate my father's role and way of being. Our relationship became the bedrock of my journey, and with equality of voice we were able to set out and articulate the parameters of roles and responsibilities. These were not static, but ebbed and flowed with our children's lives; there was always a degree of consciousness that we brought to this.

I was determined not to miss the most important parts of my girls' lives. I had talked to a few guys, men in their sixties, about what they would do differently if they began fatherhood all over again. All of them said the same thing: they regretted "not being there." I decided I wouldn't let that happen for me. It's easy to say, but then you must have a personal covenant, and accountability to match your intent. The only way for me to do that was to set up continuity in the scheduling of my home time and my office time, and to include my wife.

We considered, for example, what was reasonable in terms of how many days I could be away from the family. We came up with

Rick with daughters (FROM LEFT) Emma, Alanna and Rebecca, and grandson Everett

some numbers and decided upon a limit of thirty sleeps over 365 days. It seemed like something tolerable for all concerned. In reality, it was sometimes only ten in 365; other years it might be thirty-three. Important events for my family got priority, and other competing needs got cast aside. I was able to make room for them, but I learned the hard way that I also had to make room for myself. I had to lose sight of that before I truly knew how essential it was.

Life was full. My children were very little. As a leader in my community, and coming from a world where my health and vitality and the activities I was engaged in took priority, it wasn't easy to change the bandwidth. I found myself in a deep, dark place, feeling frustrated, resentful and disconnected, losing energy, getting sick and wondering what on earth was the matter with me. I'd always give up something in the complexity of the schedule. "Me time" got lost: the chance to be in the wild, outdoors, alone—fishing, for example.

I had to get to a place where I could give myself permission to make time for myself. I had to find a way to navigate this central need that was otherwise being drowned out, and not have it perceived as some bizarre need for self-indulgence. To manifest it into reality, I had to share my goal with people close to me and gain their support. It was a truly difficult time, for sure. There are a few photos in the album from that time that I look back on. I see myself in the photo but I don't remember being there. In that window of time before I fully turned the ship around, I realized that I might have been present physically, but I wasn't really there. I was exhausted and running on vapours.

When the girls were really little, I would always have a girl on one knee. Then a girl on each knee. When two became three, a little step was made for the back of my wheelchair for Emma to stand on so I could carry all three. Beautiful memories. Between the ages of eight and eighteen, that was an intense decade, just a huge energy output, things were fast and furious. I wouldn't have traded it for the world. When I think back, some of the best moments came at routine times, like when we were in the car. The girls would be in the back, I'd turn the radio down and tune in to them instead. That's often when I got the best glimpse into their world—what they were really thinking, needing and feeling.

Sport has always played a critical role in my life. That's where I learned many of life's great lessons. My career aspiration was to be a phys. ed. teacher, so it was natural for me to become a coach for my daughters in soccer, volleyball and softball. Being there in their sports lives gave continuity to my experience of being a father, and a tremendous opportunity to nurture character. In the complex and uncertain world I brought them into, I think that contributed to their ability to be resilient, to self-regulate, to be critical thinkers, to be self-aware and to express themselves.

Fatherhood doesn't end. I am walking beside them as they have moved into adulthood. I have tried not to project my idealistic view or allow my judgement to skew in any way who they are or what they could be. My goal has been to honour their sovereignty to craft their own lives. It's not easy—I've had to catch myself many times when I found my hand leading my arm, tempted to meddle or impose. Of course you follow your natural instinct to protect your children, but you try not to put them in a bubble. It's a hard thing to find the

Rick with grandson Everett and daughters (FROM LEFT) Emma, Alanna and Rebecca

balance between nurturing and stifling their sense of adventure and journey. Love, hurt, pain, loss, trauma, setback—they need them all. There's no playbook, you have to craft your own journey.

The hardest part is when they suffer. My biggest challenge as a father was in 2015 when my eldest daughter gave birth to her first baby boy, Reid. Reid died just before his birth because of a knot in his umbilical cord. Nothing—not any or all of the loss and trauma I have experienced in my life—prepared me for the loss of this perfect baby who for forty weeks had received our greatest love. Protect my daughter? I couldn't do that. But the sorrow this loss hollowed out in me was ready to be filled with joy when Emma gave birth to her second baby, a healthy boy named Everett, on December 16, 2017.

The "art of fatherhood"—it's definitely an art, not a science. Our home is a hub where they can come and go; in fact right now I have the privilege of having Everett and his parents live with us. A surprise for me has been the depth of the bond between us, the emergence of it, layer after layer and the revelations that occur. It's a visceral thing that's hard to explain, the reciprocating love and the challenges they have given me. It would have been easy at times to say, "That's it, I'm done. This is who I am," but by putting myself in their shoes, in their hearts and minds, I have pushed myself to keep growing.

There are a few things I thought I'd never do as a parent. At one time I didn't think I'd be the kind of dad who imposed rules, but of course I did. I also didn't think I'd ever live vicariously through my children, but a few times I have caught myself doing that. I had to know the difference between holding my values and beliefs and projecting my wishes. I read a book when we were preparing Emma to sleep in her own bed, and followed the advice about overcoming your child's objections. We let her cry herself to sleep. It took forever. I ask Emma if she's been scarred by it and of course she doesn't remember. It seems I was more traumatized by it than her.

My girls have been a gift to me in terms of my personal development. A big thing for me as a father has been the realization that a problem doesn't automatically require a solution. Sometimes issues and challenges need to just be held. My learning was about who *not to be* as an intervenor and problem-solver. I had to get my butt kicked a few times to see the mistakes I was making. As a father with a disability there were obstacles, things I couldn't do and places I couldn't go with them. It's been important for me to not feel sorry for myself. It would have been all too easy for me to have been bitter, angry, resentful. I had to take my ego out of the equation.

Sometimes it wasn't me taking care of them, but them taking care of me. And there have been times where they have helped me find a way around something, like getting me on the slopes with a monoski, reclaiming a piece of my life that I thought was gone forever. Even breaking new ground, like when Rick Mercer called to ask me to do a bungee jump. After I told him it wasn't on my bucket list, he asked me to think about it. At home, my girls challenged me: "C'mon Dad, you've got to." With this kind of encouragement, I managed my fear. I got through a threshold and did it. They were so proud.

I could have been tripped up by my disability so many times. In fact, when the news that we were expecting our first baby reached the media in 1989, someone wrote an anonymous letter to the editor saying how sad it was that this disabled person was allowed to have children—who knew whether this child would be born disabled? They continued: *Didn't everyone know that disabled people were a burden on the state, and now here's a family who are going to be dependent? Shouldn't there be a law against this?* It stung. After all I had gone through to try to bring people to a place of inclusion, this was a shock. Naturally, I refused to buy in to it. I wondered: Should they have printed it? I think so—they exposed a part of the world that still existed, and it confirmed for me we still had work to do. And that I was going to be the best dad ever.

Dan Pontefract

Victoria, British Columbia

Author, speaker, 47

||||||||||||||||||||||||||||||||||||||||||||||||||||||||||||||||||||||||||||||||||||||

Dan Pontefract is the bestselling author of several books on organizational leadership: *Flat Army: Creating a Connected and Engaged Organization*; *The Purpose Effect: Building Meaning in Yourself, Your Role and Your Organization*; and most recently *Open to Think: Slow Down, Think Creatively, and Make Better Decisions*. Dan is the founder and CEO of The Pontefract Group. He also works as an adjunct professor in the Peter B. Gustavson School of Business at the University of Victoria and is the former "chief envisioner" and chief learning officer of Telus. He is married to Denise and is the father of three children, ages eleven, thirteen and fifteen.

||||||||||||||||||||||||||||||||||||||||||||||||||||||||||||||||||||||||||||||||||

When my children were little, zero to five, it was all pure joy. Somewhere around age eight it got way more challenging. I have had lots of epiphanies in my approach to parenting. I have flipped from thinking that technology gives us the edge, to realizing that it takes it away. I see that as our children are evolving, Pavlovian urgency has taken over. No one can wait. Gratification has to be short-term. I think of it as becoming prey to the "tyranny of the urgent." We think we are doing all the right things, but we are living in what Nicholas Carr terms "the shallows." You can't live life according to a fridge magnet, or in the six-second photo bites of Snapchat.

Our fifteen-year-old daughter has observed that no one much looks up anymore. The focus on a screen is all consuming. The "battle royal" has been happening at our house and we are using software called Circle with Disney to try and maintain order. The video games our son has become involved in are set up to become addictive. He gets fixated in a mind-boggling way. When we enforce the boundaries, he erupts. The urgency and need for belonging by way of these online encounters is huge for him: "What do you mean I can't play it today? I got eight comments, and a hundred and sixty likes." It becomes all that matters, that immediate hit of approval. They don't know what they are missing out on. They are craving that next hit, the likes, the gems you accumulate in the game.

I'm lamenting the absence of the ability to really pay attention, to dream, to have patience, to distill one's thoughts. Where, I wonder, is the deep resonance, the critical thinking and the inference? Can my kids still get that? We are trying to dig deeper at our house. I seek out reading material about being more human to put in front of them, something that will appeal, I hope, to their young minds. We recently bought our children books of poetry and classic literature. Thankfully, they are being read.

I don't really know if I am a good parent. Will they turn out okay? They don't exactly hate me, but it can be rough around our house. I make them do other things with their time, and they don't thank me—yet. I'm harder than their mum is on them. I'm not thinking about giving in to pressure today, I am trying to think about five to ten years down the road. I have tried to begin with the end in mind. I could certainly make the choice to have a peaceful life and just roll over, but I refuse to abdicate, I don't want to be that person.

We are a digital family, we always have been, but we are re-examining that as we go along, like families in Silicon Valley who move their kids from the tech schools to Montessori. We are smack dab in the "screenage years" dilemma. I never anticipated this. I pushed the children to write online, develop their own blogs, create their own identities. Would I do that again? Definitely, but I'd approach it differently.

FROM LEFT: Claire, Denise, Dan, Cole and Cate

I feel as though screen time became an issue only because I didn't know it would become an issue. Knowing what I know now, I most certainly would have discussed what constitutes healthy screen time much earlier than what occurred. Limits would be instituted much earlier in life. Consistent conversations would be had with the children when they were between the ages of five and ten on what constituted good and bad screen time. Good screen habits would have been fostered.

I still have so many parenting hurdles ahead of me. I'm doing far more active parenting than I ever imagined. I'm on them, in a loving way. I dread to think how I'll cope when they are older and the risks get bigger, be it alcohol, drugs, sex and all that. I'm trying to focus on what's good right now, what I am thankful for, what I can successfully do with and for my kids.

When I was a teenager, my phone privileges were taken away by my dad because I'd done something wrong. Back in the day it was a landline. At times, I have a Churchillian rigidity with my kids, a sense of caring so deeply that I am willing to be unpopular. It would be easier to not care. I hold on to the thought that these morsels of guidance I am providing are giving structure and that they will resurface in positive ways for them throughout life. I envision a deeper relationship with my children when they are older, and when they can eventually go for a beer with Dad.

Together, it feels like we are making a rich soup. They have seen me struggle. I had to do a rewrite on my second book in the summer of 2015 after writing ninety-four thousand words. They witnessed my complete existential crisis. I think it was revealing. Cate (then aged seven) said, "Daddy, I want you to know how proud I am of you for writing two books to get one." I think that if you are honest about your successes and failures as a father, you are teaching your kids humility.

Mine wasn't the easiest of childhoods. My mum was a raging alcoholic. I knew from the age of nine or ten what was going on. I think my empathy and sensitivity manifests from that time. I tuned in to my father. Between the ages of about twelve to sixteen he'd use me as a crutch, as a sounding board for "Project Mum." We took walks together, lots of walks, and I took my job as confidant seriously, thinking I could really help him figure it out. He tried so hard, for years, to help my mum, but she didn't want to be helped. They eventually decided to have a third baby to see if that would fix things. Instead, after my brother Adam arrived, things got way worse—when Adam was about thirteen years old my dad gave up. They split; he took Adam with him.

Meanwhile, my father had said I was "not to attend university anywhere in Ontario," my home, my province. I didn't really understand, but what he knew was that I was too busy trying to take care of him, and I needed to be more than a three-hour drive away. Montreal turned into the best place for me to grow into a man.

My dad was the rock in our family, the incredible salient philosopher. He was an electrical engineer who emigrated to southern Ontario from the UK. His own father was from a rough family in the north of England, but had become mayor of Blackburn and had airs about him. He treated himself like royalty. You had to walk ten paces behind him around town, so my dad tried to be the opposite with me, his son—so that we'd be really close. He's succeeded. He doesn't say "I love you," but he'll write it, send me his poems, and I sure feel it.

He was always present, with a *"take no prisoners"* kind of attitude. If you crossed him, he would use his intellect, his philosophical approach to prove there was a cost to this. In a relationship, you'll pay. I've had to learn to let some things go, because my dad never let anything go. I appreciate all he does to be a great father and granddad.

As a man in a testosterone-driven world, I'm working on who I am. I see myself as a metrosexual feminist. I push the gender limits. I am the one with the fashion flair, who does the interior decorating in our family. I wear things a lot of guys wouldn't be seen dead in. I wear hats from the 1920s. I'm emotional, I let it all hang out. I cry in front of my children. I don't want to hide any emotion, be it sadness, fear, anger, frustration. I can go to the deep end with my feelings but balance my behaviour. It's who I am, being open, maybe too open.

I quit a fraternity back in 1990 because I couldn't cope with the culture of guys behaving badly. I don't just believe in gender equality, I believe men need to lean back more. How do we elevate women? I'm so glad I have two daughters. Do you know how hard it is not to focus on male sport? It's what we are fed. I want my kids to know it's not all about the men. I am consciously bringing my son into things that he might otherwise opt out of. We go to women's soccer games. Inclusivity is important to me. *Feminism* is not a word to be scared of. My dad and I truly connected, but I don't think he succeeded at developing his relationship with my sister.

I want that with all my children, so I'm putting my money where my mouth is. We have weekends away, I get one-on-one time with each of my daughters and my son: kayaking, hiking, fishing, galleries, coffee shops, a movie or just talking. When I was growing up, my father was so preoccupied during my formative years with trying to rescue my mum from her alcoholism. I am determined not to miss these important years with my kids. Being a parent is the most exciting thing I have ever done! It's also the hardest.

Paul Sun-Hyung Lee

Toronto, Ontario

Actor, writer, comedian and TV host, 46

||||||||||||||||||||||||||||||||||||||||||||||||||||||||||||||||||||||||||||||||||||||||||||||||

Paul was born in Korea and came to Canada with his family as an infant. They settled in London, Ontario before moving to Calgary. He moved to Toronto in the summer of 1990. His film and television credits include *Shoot the Messenger*, *End of Days, Inc.*, *RoboCop* and *Train 48*. Paul has been characterized as Canada's favourite dad for his endearing role as Appa in the popular sitcom *Kim's Convenience*, which recently aired its third season on CBC Television. Paul is married to Anna and they have two sons: Noah, born in 2004, and Miles, born in 2009.

||||||||||||||||||||||||||||||||||||||||||||||||||||||||||||||||||||||||||||||||||||||||||||||||

Becoming a father for the first time, I had serious doubts about being able to cope. I was so terrified of doing something wrong, of killing the baby! I doubted myself all the time. I remember at one point my wife and I were wondering when this baby's real parents would show up and take him back. We felt like stand-ins! If he spat up a bit, he'd get a whole new outfit. We were so over-anxious, we turned him into a cautious child. By the time his brother arrived, we were in a different phase of parenting. If he threw up, we'd wipe up the barf and let him keep playing. He was better able to take risks. Of course we eventually relaxed, and the priority shifted from keeping our kids alive to making them into decent human beings.

I feel very privileged to have had the chance to be a stay-at-home father for my boys in their early years. It was one of the perks of being an out-of-work actor. My wife was the primary breadwinner at the time. Her maternity leave was ending when a TV show I was working on was winding up, so it worked out well. I took over at home with Noah, and then was able to be at home with Miles when he was born.

Those early years together gave us a very strong bond. It was an amazing opportunity to build a relationship with my sons. At the same time, however, I felt quite isolated as a parent. The days were long. There were support groups and many activities set up for moms, but nothing for men. I'd go to the park, for example, where it was all these women. It's not like we didn't talk; they were nice to me, but I felt like an outsider. People also made assumptions, like I was "babysitting" my kids. I took umbrage about that. I was the primary parent—I wasn't babysitting my kids, I was *raising* them.

Guys—we need to be given more of a break. It has always been women doing the lion's share of parenting, and I think that when men do try and get more involved, they're not taken seriously and even belittled. Assumptions get made about who you are and what you want, and you are on the receiving end of disapproving comments like "I'll bet you can't wait to be back at work," and "You watch you don't mess something up. Don't make a 'dumb dad' mistake." Little by little it felt like constant undermining—death by a thousand cuts.

Some guys can handle that feedback, some can't. Some are like, "I'm not even going to try." In media, dads are portrayed all too often as buffoons. I think that has quite a lot to do with why some men avoid hands-on parenting, because there's a built-in bias. I'm a lucky guy—fortunately I didn't take that stuff too seriously. I wouldn't trade those years with my boys for anything.

My wife and I are on the same page when it comes to parenting issues. We work really closely together to make it work for our boys. We don't take it for granted. Our style is cooperative, and we are very actively involved in our children's lives. My parents were more likely to stand back. It's more an Asian style. They are very religious; in fact, both are church ministers now.

My dad wasn't a stay-at-home dad, but our restaurant was just across the street from where we lived in Calgary and I'd go to work with him every morning. I didn't realize that my dad was actually looking after me. I loved it because it gave me a sense of purpose: I was helping my dad. I had very simple tasks, like sweeping and mopping the floor, helping with food preparation. It was a fish-and-chips restaurant and we served clam chowder. Dad would give me a dime for my work, and I'd go down to the 7-Eleven at the end of the street and buy myself a comic book.

Back at the restaurant, I'd sit with Dad. We had a routine. I'd read my comic book, eat crackers and have a Coke in a Styrofoam cup. Dad would read his paper and drink his super-sweet coffee. I loved it—these are my strongest and fondest memories of our time together. I grew up working there, from grade two through high school. As I got older he gave me more work and paid me more. I worked at my mom's store, too—she was manager at the Mac's store.

It's really typical in Asian families to use your kids for cheap (or free) labour. We weren't well off, we lived month to month, but I never felt like we lacked anything. My parents found a way to get my older sister and I what we needed. My parents wanted us to be Korean. They took us to Korean language school; they gave us piano lessons. They gave us Korean food to bring to school. I just wanted to fit in! I didn't want the rice, the seaweed, the fish, the kimchi... I wanted what everyone else was having. I actively pushed back. I didn't want to be Korean. I deeply regret that now.

Because my parents worked such long hours, holidays and recreation didn't happen much for us. But I remember once they took us on a camping trip into Kananaskis Country—the Asian immigrant family who had no idea about camping. We set off to hike around a lake, ill-equipped with no food or water. It was a huge lake that took us about four hours to get around.

I've got my dad's work ethic. Roll your sleeves up—talent and intelligence only take you so far. His sense of sacrifice made a deep impression on me; everything was for the family. He reused things, he never bought new clothes for himself. Both my parents sacrificed for us children. When we did get something little, unexpected, it meant a lot, because money was tight. Everything was for family. I feel that way about my kids; they mean the world to me. But I realize that if I act like love equals indulgence, it's a bit of a two-headed monster. Have I spoiled them? I wonder now about the right thing to do.

In the typical Asian style, my dad was stoic and didn't readily express emotions. He wasn't given to shows of affection, either. Although he wasn't open about his feelings toward me, I never felt unloved. I'd tell Dad I loved him, but I didn't expect to hear it back. Asian friends of mine have pointed out that their dads never speak about love either: "The only time he'd say he loved me was if he was dying." In Asian culture, talk is cheap. It's what you do that speaks volumes. I've always been very expressive about my feelings; whether that drove my dad insane, I don't know.

Dad rarely lost his temper, but when he was really upset, watch out—he'd blow if you crossed the line. My children don't have to guess what I am feeling; I don't keep it in or store it up. I'm expressive and when I'm mad, I'm a yeller. I got that from my mom. I'm also a hugger—I'm very physical with the boys. We kiss and hug freely and we are very open about our affection toward each other— I'll never change that. Dad's more private about that physical connection, but he's shown me in every other way that he loves me.

I am teaching my boys to be forthright with their emotions, to know it's okay to talk about how you feel. I want them to be able to take care of themselves emotionally. I see my older boy in his peer group: they are comfortable with each other and give hugs freely. I love that, but it reminds me that not everyone sees it as a positive. Christie Blatchford wrote an article railing against affectionate behaviour between boys, saying that she thought Toronto was becoming a "city of sissies" filled with girly men. She saw it as a sign that boys needed *toughening up* and speculated that if her dad were around, he'd have told them to "act like a man." It broke my heart to read this. Are you kidding me? Why on earth would anyone be uncomfortable with warmth and affection?

I love that Toronto is actually very open, multicultural and accepting of differences. My son has gay and trans friends; it's so normal. It's the older people who are making these differences a big deal. I want my boys to be kind, compassionate, thoughtful and

Paul with Noah (LEFT) and Miles, 2017

enlightened. I want them to be confident in their abilities, identities, sexualities, to know who they are. Males have to work to maintain their self-worth. The big pushback from the alt-right for white males is because they are so used to *being* the narrative and to everything being catered to them. When things shift they feel threatened, they feel they are worthless, when that's not the case at all. Sharing the power or the limelight that comes with male privilege doesn't mean they will have any less, it just means it's shared.

I think it's especially important nowadays to be aware of how you are raising boys because of the dangers of toxic masculinity. The depths of my disappointment with men in general have been tremendous. The amount of vitriol, spewing of hatred, misogyny that's perpetuated—it's awful. It's okay to be masculine, but there's no place for aggressive male behaviour. "Stop being an asshole" is what it comes down to—it shouldn't be hard.

Appa, whom I play on *Kim's Convenience*, is like an amalgam of the older Korean men I grew up around who are like part of your family but not really. They always want to be right and are used to being deferred to, calling the shots: "It's my way or the highway." I intrinsically understand that kind of male. I think that most of us understand it even if none of us would want to be that kind of father. He's very sheltered in the way he sees the world. His thinking is old-fashioned and outdated. He'll misread situations and doesn't realize he's the one who looks silly. He's passionate about things, and his love is big.

In real life there are ways that I am kind of like Appa, as well as like my own dad. Both of them have this complete love and absolute devotion. They'd do anything for their kids, and that's the kind of guy I am. As for Appa's stubbornness, I hate to say it, but my father and I are like that as well. And I love Appa's sense of humour—the way he teases his wife, his daughter—that playfulness, I've got that, too. In other ways we are very different. Fortunately, I'm not as opinionated as Appa, and I'm very much more of a peacemaker.

I haven't always handled stress well; I could have done a number on myself. I know it's not wise to try to micromanage. As a society we have taken parenting too far. I've learned that less is more. I'm standing back more as my elder son gets further into adolescence. I'm making myself available but not pushing or probing. I'm letting him know that there is nothing he can do that will shock me. As soon as I gave myself permission to step back, to intervene less, to trust more, the stress levels dropped all around.

There's some fear for every generation. We used to worry about kids' exposure to television. When I was a kid I had the TV on for company; it was my babysitter because my parents were out. Now, I still turn it on if I am home alone—I don't actually watch, but it's like a security blanket. I understand the lure of the screen, but I don't let it interfere with things I need to do.

Phone addiction these days is a big concern, and of course I worry about video games. The kids know how warped it all is— *Mortal Kombat*—it's so way over the top. Occasionally we happen upon something untoward when we are watching a film together. Although the instinct is to say, "Turn that off right now," we talk about the content instead. We turn it into a teachable moment and use it as an opportunity to discuss boundaries and appropriate behaviour.

Don't be intimidated by parenting. There's a new generation of dads on the horizon. It's a brave new world where dads don't have to feel like they have no place in raising their children. *Failure* is not a bad word—you learn way more from your mistakes. Appa might be a blowhard, but he notices the consequences of his awful mistakes and he grows. There's a constant evolution of learning to better himself, to be a better dad and a better husband.

Stuart Shanker
Rice Lake, Ontario
Psychologist, philosopher, author, 66

IIIIIIIIIIIIIIIIIIIIIIIIIIIIIIIIIIIIIIIIIIIIIIIIIIIIIIIIIIIIIIIIIIIIIIIIIIIIIIIIIIIIIIIIIIIIIIIIIIIIIIII

Dr. Stuart Shanker is a distinguished research professor emeritus of philosophy and psychology at York University and founder of The MEHRIT Centre. He is a successful author and speaker, and Canada's leading expert on the psychophysiological theory of self-regulation. In 2012 he published *Calm, Alert and Learning: Classroom Strategies for Self-Regulation*, which became one of Canada's bestselling educational publications, and in 2016 he followed with *Self-Reg: How to Help Your Child (and You) Break the Stress Cycle and Successfully Engage with Life*. Stuart has a son, Sasha, born in 2002 and a daughter, Sammi, born in 2005.

IIIIIIIIIIIIIIIIIIIIIIIIIIIIIIIIIIIIIIIIIIIIIIIIIIIIIIIIIIIIIIIIIIIIIIIIIIIIIIIIIIIIIIIIIIIIIIIIIIIIIIII

These are difficult times for children of all ages, and for their parents. I see tremendous anxiety in all the work I do with families, and also confusion for fathers about who they are and how they should be. There is a lot of interest from men's groups like Fathers of Ontario. It's an important time to support fathers, and elevate fatherhood, instead of the dumbing down we often witness in media. As a philosopher, I have become convinced that parenting is the secret to the meaning of life.

My own father was a Depression-era character in small-town Ontario—he had a very tough childhood. He was taken out of school during the Depression and worked from a very young age. He didn't get much of a childhood. Although I didn't have much of a childhood either, I got the education my father missed out on. I was a scholarship kid—I did well at the University of Toronto, then earned a place at Oxford where I did my doctoral degree. My father was enormously proud of me for my achievements.

The relationship I had with my father was complex. I know that I was an unusual child. Looking back, I know our relationship was a struggle for him. Our lives and experiences were so different. I was bookish, and he did not come from a world where one would read. In my early years my father did not disguise his disappointment in me. He was very hard on me and I was frightened of him. When I was ten they put me through some tests. I don't know exactly what it was—IQ or something—but I know the results came out very high. After that, my father seemed to understand me and we became incredibly close.

Then when I was twelve there was another significant shift. My father became very ill and I was the one to take over his building supply store. The whole dynamic between us changed as he became quite dependent upon me. However, I realize that the relationship between us was only great because I had the good fortune of being able to meet his expectations. He projected his own wishes onto me and I earned his approval. My sister, meanwhile, didn't make it in his eyes. Although she became a psychologist (and a very good one), he made a habit of denigrating her: "Well, you are not a *real* doctor."

As a father, I fell into a trap of constantly pushing my son. He got in to a really good prep school but it should have been obvious to me that it was not going to be a good fit for him. It all backfired and of course I should have known. I was seeing his character traits as if they were weaknesses and felt that if he were pushed harder, he'd rise to the challenge. This didn't happen, and I had to work very consciously at seeing who my son really was without me imposing some kind of idea on him. To actually see him, not my vision of who he should be.

I have tried to make sure that my children have a childhood, roughly compensating for the absence of mine. My father was an intensely moral man; the most important things for him—which I heard about over and over—were honour and integrity. I learned from him that I had to be a mensch, a person of noble character. That transcended anything else he wanted from me. He had a strong sense of serving society and loyalty to Canada. They [Canada] took us in, he felt—what can we give back? He was appalled with anyone who was driven by personal ambition. As a consequence, I have been heavily motivated to do things of benefit for my country.

I trained in psychiatry with the distinguished Dr. Stanley Greenspan. He made a video that I still show parents. In the film, Dr. Greenspan is meeting with a three-year-old child. He engages with the child while the father appears detached, sitting on the couch. He's invited to get down on the floor with his child and when he does his whole being changes. He blossoms in front of our eyes. When I am watching this with parents, I want to say, "This is what you'll get as a father—you have to be willing to get down and be in their world, but you will experience genuine joy, something you won't experience at the office every night, you're going to discover the meaning of life..."

Another training video we show is a dad and his nine-month-old baby. It's painful to watch because they just don't connect with each other. Dad is unable to read his baby's cues, feels rejected, becomes more intrusive and things spins out of control. Next, the father is given direction: to start changing and dressing the baby, to do the feeding, to sing to the baby, to play with him. Two months later, we see father and son together again. The father has got to know his baby, and what we witness instead is a lovely dance of reciprocity. Dad reads his son; they are not strangers anymore. It's very power-ful. Some men never discover what they are missing.

There's no doubt in my mind that even with all the work I have done in my field, I projected my own wishes onto my children as much as any parent, and lost sight of what this is all about. We live in small-town Ontario, we play hockey. My son, aged ten, was a pre-cocious little hockey player. But I made a big mistake as his father. I totally overlooked the joy that he experienced playing the game ("It feels like flying, Dad"), I lost sight of him, of the team, of the camaraderie, because I got hooked thinking about NHL potential. I came close, I suspect, to ruining hockey for him. I remember at one game he was playing, I could see he was missing opportunities. I was fuming and began challenging him: "Why didn't you try? You had all those breaks."

"Dad," he said, "I wasn't working on scoring." Another game they had got pounded by the other team. He was coming off the ice rosy-cheeked and beaming from ear to ear wondering, "Did we win, Dad?" I'd learned my lesson. I backed off, but it would have been better if I had done so earlier. My son got his first job this summer as an assistant hockey coach. Despite me, he still loves hockey.

I made a similar mistake with my daughter when she was showing so much promise as a swimmer. I pulled some strings and got her in to meet with the Canadian women's swimming team, who told me, "We'd like her to sign up for Swim Canada." I was all excited, and my wife said "Are you nuts? They train in Toronto. Are you going to get her there five to six times a week?" Sammi loves to swim; I could have destroyed that.

I became a father in my late forties. It began with heartbreak— when we lost our first child. It took a while, but my wife and I were able to nurture each other through it. I did a lot of personal work during that time, a big part of which had to do with my career and my identity. Until this time I was striving to be the best academic I could, writing for maybe a thousand people in the world. *So they can see how clever you are?* I asked myself. *Who cares?* I began to think. *If you are this smart, what can you do to actually make yourself useful?* I changed gears altogether. I wanted to be of service. I wanted my work to be used by average people, to be accessible, and I was no longer going to do it to inflate my own ego.

I was very much influenced by the work of John Bowlby (*Child Care and the Growth of Love*) and his theory of attachment in parenting. I have failed at many things in life, but I have been very successful in giving my children a safe and secure attachment where they can have complete reliance on me, and where the love between us flows naturally and reciprocally.

One of my early lessons as a parent was to take full responsibility for my own responses under stress. There were times when I would have an immediate and visceral reaction to something they'd done.

Stuart with daughter Sammi, 2017

I don't want to say I ever harmed my children, but I certainly didn't help them. If I think back on those moments, there has always been a reason for the behaviour that occurred. I don't believe they were "being bad." In fact, one of the things I preach across the country is that there's no such thing as a bad child. It's just a shame that I sometimes forget that with my own children. It's in those moments when I am flooded that I need to be able to give myself a moment of pause.

Recently, I did some interesting work, looking into why a child stops in an IQ test or a math test. What happens in the child's brain when they stop? What we learned as scientists, and what I have learned as a father is that it is enormously complicated, and that there isn't such a thing as a stupid child. When children stop, we found that their limbic brain has kicked in and you have to figure out why those brakes have been applied and how to release them. You realize that you never know what a child's potential is. We find out when testing that the brakes were applied, but what we don't find out is what is still available.

My son missed a lot of school last year because of chronic tonsillitis. After one absence he told me sheepishly that he'd failed a math test. I decided I could teach him the math. Bad idea for him, bad idea for me. He was giving up and I was so close to concluding that my child has limitations. What his math mark illustrated was not a lack of capacity but that this kid was on his own after missing so much while the rest of the class kept moving. With the help of a tutor we hired and some careful scaffolding on her behalf, he got caught up and regained his strength. The point is, you never know when it's a stress reaction. I wish I'd known this ten to fifteen years ago. I know it now because my son has taught me and I've been listening.

I love the lapses that occur during downtime together at home when everyone is relaxed. A few evenings ago, my hulking son comes home around 8:30 p.m. I'm lying on the bed with my daughter and my wife, giving my daughter a head massage with this little gizmo. My son leaves the room and returns with his gizmo and gives it to his sister, who massages his head. Shortly after she asks him, "Would you like me to make a ponytail with your hair?" He allows this, and I lie there breathing in the beautiful energy—the kinds of moments that are at the same time ridiculously banal and exquisitely heartwarming. It's not the cruises, the rock concerts, the fancy holidays. For me, these are the best of times as a father. The trick is to notice these moments, to know you are having them when they happen, not after!

The thing I miss the most about my dad is the conversations. We could go places. He never gave me advice but would ask me well-crafted questions that would make me think and lead me to deeper understanding. As my son gets older, it's so tempting to use my wisdom and give him advice, but I am following my father's example. A few days ago when he asked me about something, I was dying to say no and wield my authority. Instead, I asked him a question so he could think through the issue. I guess it worked because I haven't heard back. I think it's a stronger approach because I know his values are firmly planted. I can place my trust in his wisdom and the result is I have a child who thinks for himself instead of one who is simply obedient.

Robert (Lucky) Budd

Victoria, British Columbia

Author, oral historian, 43

‖‖

Lucky grew up in Toronto and moved to BC to study. After becoming involved with the digitization of CBC's audio archives, he became a host of CBC's *Voices of BC*. He is the author of *Voices of British Columbia: Stories from Our Frontier* and *Echoes of British Columbia: Voices from the Frontier*. Since 2013, Lucky has co-authored nine award-winning children's books, including eight with Roy Henry Vickers. Lucky is father of two children: Levi, born in 2011, and Emma, born in 2013. He and his partner, Jessy, have been together for eleven years.

‖‖

My dad was sixty-two and I was thirty-two when he died in 2008. Of course it was a tough time, but by that stage I had made my peace with him. Our relationship had been strained for years. A shift had occurred when I was about twenty-three. I had written to him about an ongoing source of difficulty between us—what I perceived as his stance as a "victim," always blaming others for what happened to him and unable to take responsibility for his choices and circumstances, including decisions he made which led to strains in our relationship.

He didn't get it. When he wrote back, the tenor of the letter was, *You don't understand. People always... I have had to...* It provided further confirmation of what I had been referring to. That's when I realized, *It's not my job to change this man.* Nor is it my job to hit him over the head until he understands my perspective. The word that popped into my mind, clear as day, was *respect*: if I'm going to have a relationship with my dad, I need to respect his limitations and expect nothing more.

I don't think he knew how to be his own best friend. Like many people, he had his demons and he lacked the confidence or fortitude to notice how he could help himself. I think he was very insecure, which led to stress. He looked good and presented well—but underneath that veneer there was a lot of turmoil. Although he had a good heart, he made a lot of poor decisions and got in his own way. He didn't use things that happened in his life as opportunities for introspection and growth to the degree that it would propel him forward. It's as if he didn't realize that he had the power to be different—though I know he wanted his life to be different than it was. He just kept getting in his own way.

I moved out west for university when I was nineteen and my dad said, "When you graduate I'm going to buy you a camera." But graduation came and went, the camera never materialized—and of course I never asked. This was a microcosm of our relationship. He was not present at my graduation and it didn't even occur to me that he should be. Our lives were that separate.

An epiphany came for me not only when I accepted that I couldn't ask him for anything, but when I realized I needed to not *want* anything. That's when I grew past the point of needing my father to be anything else other than what he was, limitations included. We were able to have a good relationship if all we ever talked about was sports and superficial aspects of our lives. I had no interest in fighting with him and I realized the onus was on me to not let our interactions go to that place, as we so easily could. I was determined to avoid a conflicted relationship that would serve neither of us. Instead, I found my peace with him.

In a way, a sad way, it's helped me in my life, not because he was a good role model, but because I've made choices to evolve past what he was able to be. I actually believe this is what a child is supposed to do. In order to do so, at various points in my life, I have become both my mother and my father, and then made very

Lucky with wife Jessy and children Levi and Emma, 2018

deliberate decisions to forge my own way. As my brother once pointed out, "I am who I am in spite of him, not because of him."

In the years since I have become a father, I feel I can relate to him a lot better, even though his life may not have been a "success." It's a pity: for all his shortcomings, I know he'd have had so much fun with my children, whom he never got to meet. In fact, I have a lot of questions I wish I could ask him. I recognize that we have more common ground now than we did when he was alive, and as I get older I have more compassion for his struggles as a parent. That being said, I can use his influence to avoid making the same mistakes as he did, making his influence a positive one.

My parents split up when I was four years old. We lived with my mom after that (and later my stepfather), but my three siblings and I had visits with my dad every second weekend, then a dinner date one-on-one with him once a month on a Tuesday. Everything around their divorce was handled so poorly. Things got really, really ugly. Lots of fighting, asking us to carry messages, putting us in loyalty binds. My father wasn't honest about some of his dealings and the whole thing ended up with him on the defensive with his tail between his legs. It must have been a terrible way to live.

What's more, interpersonal relationships were very difficult for him, which would have made his isolation even harder. He struggled with this till the end. Sadly, in one of our last conversations he told me how miserable he was. He confided in me for the first time about how hard he was trying to fix some of his most personal relationships. In that moment, I wasn't his estranged son, I was a helpful ear; we were speaking to each other as adults. I knew the history and felt compassion for him and his circumstances. In the moment and even now, I was thankful to be there for him. I really wanted to help.

I was the peacemaker in my family, a pretty easy child compared to my older siblings. Now that I'm a dad I have more empathy for my own father. He had a couple of really high-maintenance kids, and I can surely relate. I realize one of the huge differences between us was I was much more prepared to be a father than he was. One, I started parenting at thirty-four; he was only twenty-four. Two, I've got better communication skills. Three, I've got a good attitude. Four, I'm much more of a conscious person, I can take agency over my life and make changes. Five, I am able to meet my kids where they need to be met, as consciously as I can, and I'm not putting myself first.

I also have the best partner I could imagine. My wife, Jessy—I'd be hooped beyond hooped if it wasn't for her! We are a genuine *team*; we show up every day. We work together seamlessly. We are constantly assessing and adapting to the needs of our children. By the time my siblings were the age my kids are now, my parents weren't even speaking to each other and we were constantly caught in the middle.

My parents' relationship was dysfunctional from the beginning. My dad, there's no way he had the tools to be able to handle what his kids gave him. As much as he sabotaged and did so many things wrong, I can't even begin to say how much he was in over his head, he didn't even *know* he didn't have the tools. Who did he talk to? Who could he lean on? He didn't have a Jessy and he didn't have a friend to lean on in the way he finally did with me in that last bit of his life.

To make things worse, when my dad was pushed to the max he was physically abusive. He used to say, "Violence is the last recourse of an exhausted mind," so I guess he was often exhausted. I would never let myself go there, but I've seen red and I had never experienced that before I became a father. My son is incredible, but he's in this world to kick ass and take names. He's gutted me many times and I love him for it. Nothing else has taken me to that extreme place, so I do have some compassion for my father. Unlike him, I recognize that my children are the best teachers I will ever have. Hard as it may be, I am rising to the occasion to be a better father and person every day. It is the hardest work I have ever done.

That first year of my son's life was the worst year of mine. He came out screaming and didn't stop until he was about fourteen months old. We couldn't lead a normal life, like other people taking their babies out to restaurants and playgroups, and no one we knew was having these kinds of extreme experiences. Our own families were not particularly helpful (in fact, they either moved away or stopped coming to visit) and we were all alone with this unsettled, screaming baby. I really needed a mentor to show me that things would improve, to empathize with my experience. I did not have one. At the time I felt that all the effort I was putting in, twenty-four seven with no respite, was not good enough. What I have had to learn to parent this child is above and beyond what I ever could have imagined. It has been among the best experiences of my life, and definitely the most challenging.

Thankfully, with this trial by fire I have become a very different person than I was before my son was born. I could actually relate more to my dad now, if he were around, and I would love to share with him what I have learned. For example, before I became a father I could not have had empathy for or channelled the emotion for the character in *Orca Chief* (a children's book I co-authored with Roy Henry Vickers), who says "Who do you think you are that you can drop an anchor down on my house?" in a scolding, paternal way. Now, I possess that voice—it's my dad's voice.

I miss him. I'd like to ask his advice—and I wish he were around to teach my children how to skate, to play ball and board games with. I got a lot of very good things from him; one of those is how to play and have fun! Sport, he was all over it—baseball, hockey...

When I returned to Victoria after my dad died, I kept thinking about him as an old tree that used to be in my backyard. I used to play on it, and under it. It had a big rope swing on it and even when I didn't play on it anymore, it was always still there. My dad dying felt like the tree being ripped out of the ground and everything changing in the backyard. The light fell differently, the shade's not there, I can't ever go back out and swing in that tree anymore. Everything in my world is just *different*. Somewhere deep down I have understanding for my dad and I have reached a place where I am finally grateful for what he *did* give me rather than pissed off about what he *didn't*.

Kevin Newman

Toronto, Ontario

Journalist, author, 60

||||||||||||||||||||||||||||||||||||||||||||||||||||||||||||||||||||||||||||||||||||||||

Kevin Newman was born in Toronto in 1959. At CTV
he has been the host of *W5*, *Question Period* and *Kevin
Newman Live*. He was national correspondent for CBC
and CTV News before moving to the US to work as a news
anchor and correspondent for ABC News and co-host of
Good Morning America. After that, he was the founding
anchor and executive editor of *Global National*. Kevin
won two Gemini awards for best news anchor (2005 and
2006), Emmy awards for his breaking news coverage and
a Peabody award for ABC's millennium night coverage.
Kevin has been married to Cathy since 1985 and they have
two children: Alex, born in 1986, and Erica, born in 1989.

||||||||||||||||||||||||||||||||||||||||||||||||||||||||||||||||||||||||||||||||||||||||||

When they become fathers, why is it that dads are not willing to
talk about how awkward they are, how their lives have been turned
upside down and how some of the time they're completely overwhelmed? Women can talk about this, but for some reason men don't
like to admit it to each other, sometimes not even to themselves. They
fear being vulnerable. I talk to young fathers at any opportunity I get,
and I have yet to hear one begin with, "I don't know what I'm doing
and I'm afraid I'm going to hurt the baby." I want new dads to make
sure they get something out of it rather than just *provide*, to get in
there and have those intimate moments, put their babies to sleep
themselves, learn what each sound may mean and how to soothe.

The relationship I had with my dad wasn't the easiest. We were never that close. He just wasn't equipped to handle communication in the modern sense at all, as is true for so many men of his generation. There were handshakes instead of hugs, and although he was around, I never felt that he gave me the attention I wanted or needed. I know it sounds really harsh, but the example of a father that he set was definitely not the man or father I wanted to be. I knew that was *not* how I was going to raise my children, take care of my emotional health, all those things. I knew what I *didn't* want to be.

I knew he wished I was more athletic and outgoing. He was quick to point out what I had *not* done well and rarely praised what I *did* do well. I tried to avoid displeasing him, and fear of his rejection was a pretty strong motivator to achieve. I feared his disappointment and while attempting to avoid it, I became a bit of a perfectionist.

Married with two children, I had certainly set myself up for a fall. The demands I was making of myself were impossible. While driving my career path into higher and higher gear, I compromised my family life and ultimately my well-being and happiness. When I got dropped as host from *Good Morning America* in 1999, I sunk really low; I was numb and pretty depressed. I got in the car and drove up to Canada. I reached out to my dad and asked him to have lunch with me.

I needed to have a conversation with him; I guess I was desperate for reassurance. *Do you care about me? Do you love me?* I wanted to know. Dad thought it was weird that I had to ask these questions, but at the end of it, I didn't have any anger left for him anymore. There comes a time in a man's life when he thinks, *Stop blaming other people.* Instead I felt sorry, recognizing that as an adult my dad had such a limited emotional range and language. I was ready to move to a place of acceptance. After that, things were different between us. I didn't fear him the same way, I wasn't worrying about trying to get his approval. So many bad things had happened to me in such a short time, I was already at rock bottom; I had nothing left to fear. From that point forward, the sting was gone from our relationship.

It was 1986 when I became a dad. I had badly wanted to become a parent, but I didn't think through what it would mean to me, and how it would change my life. Men aren't encouraged to engage in discussions about becoming a father before they actually become one. It never occurred to me to talk to my wife about it, and certainly not to anyone else. Men, we can talk about sports or current events or our careers, but there was no meaningful discussion about fatherhood. It's probably the biggest role you'll fulfill in life, and to be so ill-prepared for it makes no sense. My whole life—it's been like a moving target without signposts and without a consistent, positive male influence. Mum and two sisters at home...even our dogs were female!

My generation of men were some of the first to be more involved in childbirth, to be in the delivery room. We were pushing the boundaries in that sense, but we were still outliers. It was still, "Isn't it cute that you want to be in there?" and, "Are you sure you can handle this stuff?" Cathy and I attended childbirth classes together, but it was only focused on the supporting role I would play for my wife. The classes prepared me to be a better husband while she gave birth, but nothing touched on who I was going to be as a father.

When we brought Alex home, Cathy and her mum were clearly the experts. I figured out that my role was to act as "perimeter defence," taking care of them so they could focus on the baby. In retrospect, I should have trusted myself more with Alex. I should have tried harder and I should have asked for more patience from them when I fumbled. But after your wife has given birth, you don't really want to ask for anything—it's humbling. I acquiesced.

It took a long time for me to be able to tune in to Alex, to understand his language, what the sounds and cries might mean and how to do something to soothe him. If I could do it all over again, we'd talk about it all and I'd step into more of a principal role. Younger men in their thirties becoming dads, they have much better emotional language than men my age, but they're still not communicating well about fatherhood.

We need more support for fathers. Too often men are viewed as hapless guys, ham-handed, not delicate enough, good for strength but not valued or respected for being able to attend to details—yet in all other aspects of men's lives, we know this isn't true. My advice to men would be to think about who you are, what kind of a dad you want to be, and talk to your partner ahead of time about your involvement and expectations. Find someone who can act as a mentor, another man you can talk to, a father you respect. I'd like to see men coming together and having real conversations considering the question "What's a dad for?"

The old model of fatherhood, it's still out there. A lot of men my age make the mistake of clinging to ego. They think, "I'm the man of the house, therefore it should be my way or the highway." You are supposed to be firm, clear and assertive.

But there's no manual with your kids: you fake it until you make it. At some point, I had to let down my defences and admit I didn't know what I was doing. The great lesson in life for me has been how much better life gets when you relinquish the alpha in your own family, allow your kids to challenge you so you can learn about yourself and develop mutual respect, especially as your kids mature. It takes a conscious effort to let the children take their turns. You have to let go of the idea that your children are a reflection of you. When the hard times hit, it's just hard times, not *What have I done wrong?*

When the kids were little, I had thought about the obvious expectations of being a good provider and role model, and besides that I expected to be all the things I wished my dad had been: affectionate, approving, attentive, emotionally connected and present in every way. I did lots of things right: I was tender and caring, I played and danced with my kids, had dinner with them, I was physically affectionate... But increasingly I just wasn't there.

I had put my career first and continued to tell myself the story that I was doing it for my family, even when it was obvious that I was becoming a visitor in my own home. I had terrible work shifts. I uprooted our family several times. I remember on one occasion coming in the door and Erica screaming because she didn't recognize me. I felt terrible, but when the boss called with even greater demands, I somehow couldn't say no. After growing up looking for my father's approval, my adult life was being defined by my own quest for approval through my career.

Kevin with daughter Erica, wife Cathy and son Alex, 2018

It seemed impossible to be the man I wanted to be as well as the father I wanted to be. Cathy did most of the parenting and reaped most of the benefits. She was the one who had her finger on the pulse of the kids' daily lives. They were very connected to her, and seemed to do just fine without me. Erica and I were close, but things between Alex and I were strained. He had a really rough childhood. I tried to get him involved in things like sports. At one time I became his Scout leader, but any direction I tried to turn him, he was determined to resist. I failed him in those early years—and Erica, too. I could have been less ambitious, but there's no perfect answer.

The teen years, they're disorienting. The darker times come from a feeling of powerlessness. It's supposed to be your job as a father to prevent harm, and you simply can't do that. I was a more relaxed parent with my daughter. I was able to stand back and watch her personality emerge. She was lovable and easygoing, affectionate. As it turns out, I should have spent as much time worrying about her as I did my son.

Erica was victimized by her peer group and internalized the negativity. She needed all the help I could provide to build up her sense of self so that she could defend her emotional boundaries. I became softer with her, more questioning, listening, encouraging, and very cautious to not be too critical. Now, she's all grown up in the best possible way, getting married in a few weeks to a fabulous guy. Pure pleasure.

With Alex it was a whole different story. I feel sorrow about his early years. I was the one conveying to him that strength, toughness and self-confidence were the defining characteristics of being male. He was shy, confused, angry, insecure and unable to talk to me about what was going on inside him. Much like I had been with my dad, Alex was feeling misunderstood and he was desperately trying to win my approval.

In 2004, when he was seventeen, Alex told us that he was gay. I became afraid for him. I had feelings of loss for a life I had told myself would be his, and I worried about what his life would now be like. I had work to do in order to accept his truth. I wondered if this meant I had failed as a father, and worried what people would think about me. I thought perhaps things would become easier between Alex and me after he came out, but it was the opposite. I wanted to show him nothing but support and acceptance; meanwhile he kept testing me for the smallest hint of censorship.

Three years ago, Alex and I co-wrote the book *All Out* about our relationship. We wrote our chapters independently of each other, Alex writing half the book and me writing the other half. We had an amazing writer and editor to work with, Kate Fillion, and when she read our material she said to me, "Well, your son's gone deep, but it's an uneven book, because you haven't gone as deep or dug as hard." *Oh fuck*, I thought.

I started over. The book became the main conduit for re-examination of every pain point in my life. Just to remind myself of some of them, I'd return to the places I'd been, see the same people again, relive the moments. In the process, I reached a new level of self-awareness and certain aspects of painful memories shrunk in my life. A lot of the garbage I'd carried as a father turned to dust and it was easier to blow away.

When the book came out, my father and I ran into trouble again when he read how I described my feelings of abandonment when he left my mum and our family when I was fourteen. He was furious with me, and felt blamed, angry and embarrassed. The book became a wedge between us, but after six weeks of silence he was willing to talk. We had a more direct conversation and unravelled some of the past. We got over the impasse. This led to greater understanding and a more open and honest relationship—so helpful and healthy as he was approaching the end of his life. He trusted me to be an influence, man to man, in a way that could never have happened before. We had found a vehicle for healing between us.

He died six weeks ago. At the end, there was nothing left for me to say. I had still never heard him say he loved me in my whole life, but I had learned to stop expecting it. My dad's generation were totally bottled up; men's lives were so stifled, how did they live in those tiny little boxes? My generation, we've been half-bottled up. I am encouraged and hopeful for the generation of men becoming fathers today—they are more emotionally engaged and are challenging the template for fatherhood.

As for me, I think I'm calmer. I see myself with more humour. I'm a good dad, I'm the dad I always wanted to be. Baring my vulnerability helped me get it out there—being open and honest about what I didn't know. I haven't fully forgiven myself for the errors and omissions of fatherhood, but I'm a lot less harsh on myself. I'm improving.

James Charlie
Penelakut Island, British Columbia
Activist, retired health centre director, 68

||||||||||||||||||||||||||||||||||||||||||||||||||||||||||||||||||||||||||||||||||||||||||

James was born in 1952. He has been married to Lexi for
almost fifty years. They have three sons: Jim, Clayton and
Clinton, all in their forties. At the time of our interview
James was working as the director of the health centre on
Penelakut Island (formerly Kuper Island), BC. James was
featured in a 1995 film by Gumboot Productions about
the Kuper Island Residential School. He and his sons were
featured in the 2017 film *Leave It on the Water* as they
trained to represent their community in the world's largest
outrigger canoe race. Carrying on a tradition of using
canoe racing as a form of healing, they entered the biggest
canoe race in the world, taking them all the way to Hawaii.

||||||||||||||||||||||||||||||||||||||||||||||||||||||||||||||||||||||||||||||||||||||||||

My earliest memories are of working in the fields, harvesting fruit in
the summer, vegetables in the winter. Following the crops, it wasn't
uncommon for us to live in twelve different places in a year. Child
labour without proper clothing and rain gear. Not much food for us,
either—we were a family of seven, I was the third born. My older
brother was our babysitter.

One summer we were in Washington State, near Mount Vernon,
and it was way too hot for picking at two in the afternoon. The pick-
ers would play games, and one of the games was to make boys fight
each other, the fathers forming a circle around them. At age five my
father bet a dollar on me and put me up against a ten-year-old. I got

beaten up pretty bad. My father discarded me like a rag doll because I had shamed him. I learned that for my father to love me, I had to win fights. That was my first loss in a fight, but it was also the last; I never lost a fight again after that.

My dad was so hard on us, it was almost impossible to please him. There was hardly any compassion, love, direction or communication. When he was sober, he managed to teach us a few things, like honesty and a strong work ethic. On one occasion my brother and I stole some erasers and pencils from a store. Why we did, I don't know—maybe we thought we could go to school one day. When my father found out, he made us take them back.

When Dad was drunk there was nothing to learn from him. He'd drink any time he had the money; it could go on for three to four days, and during that time he'd be very abusive to us children and my mother. She'd get a beating frequently and had many black eyes. His behaviour was sickening and it broke my heart. If I interfered, I'd get beaten up, too.

I ran away from my parents when I was twelve and ended up back on Kuper Island living with my grandmother's sister and brother. They put me in the residential school in grade four. I'd only ever attended school sporadically before then. I knew nothing about reading, writing or math. At school I got three square meals a day, a warm bed to sleep in and hot showers, but I had left one place of abuse to arrive in another.

The mental and physical abuse I had suffered at home happened at school as well. But worse still, in the residential school I was sexually abused, which took my suffering to a whole different level. I had run away from home to escape the abuse—now I didn't know where to turn. I asked myself, *Why was I born? Why am I here?* and *What's the point in me continuing to live?*

My mother died not long after I went to Kuper Island. She was murdered in Seattle and for some reason members of her family on Kuper Island blamed me. Now my burden was bigger—with grief, loss and a whole pile of guilt. It was a few years later, when I was about eighteen, that I was watching news on television and they

LEFT TO RIGHT: James with sons Clinton, Jim and Clay, 2018

were interviewing this homeless person in Seattle. It was my dad, and I knew then that he was drinking himself to death.

In all those years he'd phoned a few times, written me a couple of letters. He had always wanted to reconnect, but neither of us had a place to make it happen; there was no place for us to be together. During those teenage years when I was in a bleak, black space, I could have really used my dad, and I was still craving the connection. However, at the same time I was experiencing such inner conflict. I loved him, but I hated him, too, and felt overwhelming anger toward him.

It wasn't long after seeing him on TV that I found out he was sick in hospital. I went to visit him. I wanted him to smarten up. I tried to focus on my love for him, I tried to awaken his spirit. He knew who I was but he couldn't open his eyes or speak. He'd already made up his mind—he was going to be with my mom. I still crave that fatherly love and guidance; I yearn to lean on him. Or is what I am craving just the idea of a dad?

I became a dad to Jim when I was only nineteen, then Clayton and Clinton before I was twenty-five. There were some amazingly happy times, but sadly I knew nothing about disciplining effectively.

I didn't know how to communicate with my boys. *Why am I such a disaster of a dad?* I asked myself. Alcohol was a problem. I had begun drinking when I was a little boy in the harvest fields with my parents, when they would bring cheap wine called Apple Jack or Apple Andy and it would help us stay warm and survive the cold weather.

I don't think my boys would paint a pretty picture of me as a young father. I tried to give them some of the things I missed as a child, like soccer, baseball and football, except then I took the fun out of it because of the pressure I put on them. I provided for them during the week and made work my priority, but the weekends, when the kids were home, the drinking took over. I know they did not trust me. I didn't talk to them, I didn't explain things, I would just snap. Then I'd retreat into my own shell, emotionally unavailable to my whole family.

All those demons of the past—I hadn't begun to address what had happened to me. Here I was, perpetuating the harm done to me. I'd rant on at them: "As long as you live here, you have to do what I say, and if you don't like it there's the door." And two sons took it; they were gone by the time they were sixteen. It wasn't until I was in my late thirties that I began to realize the harm that I was doing. By that time, the boys were all gone. Still, I asked for their forgiveness. Two of them said, "Okay," but the third said, "I have to see you change first."

I worry: all of the abuse I inflicted, how are those scars going to heal? They are good boys—I initiated them into the longhouse when they were fourteen. They have many fine qualities, but they've had their own battles with alcohol. They have made positive changes, they are growing. Emotionally they are in a good place. Actually, they've left me behind in a lot of ways.

I am trying to be a better father and grandfather. Till the day I die I'll be working to improve my relationships with my sons. I don't expect the harm to be erased, but we'll do the best we can. I have to work on myself constantly. It's all too easy for me to resort to put-downs; I learned it all so well. I am learning to deal with my feelings: even when I am mad I find ways to express myself positively.

I grew up with so much confusion about what it means to be a man. As a young man I had many work opportunities to be a provider: fishing, sawmills, logging. Where do we go when all that disappears? What happens to the proud warrior? I was abusive, that's how I acquired my power. But it wasn't really me. Now I don't need to try to make myself a hero. I accept my role and understand who I am. I want to build a safe and healthy community. And that begins at home.

That's the advice I'd give to any new father: you have to know yourself. You have to be ready to take on the job of Dad on day one! So many First Nations men, they don't think their life should change just because they are a father... Well, it has to! Learn to play! A lot of men my age, we never learned to do it and we missed out on so much. Bond with your child, play, sing and read to them. I can't think of a single time my dad ever played with me. When I have flashbacks, they are never of us playing together and having fun. None of us laughing together, just a few of my dad laughing *at* me.

I didn't learn about my cultural identity from my family and in residential school I was taught to reject my roots. I didn't want anything to do with Indians. I am so lucky I found a strong mentor who became like a dad to me on Kuper Island when I was in my twenties. He taught me about my culture and introduced me to the longhouse. "You have to know this history," he told me. "It's your island." I adopted him like he adopted me. It's the best thing that he came into my life; I was very lucky. He's gone now but he left me all the richer in heart, mind and spirit. I think in many ways he was similar to my dad, but he wasn't drinking himself to death and he wasn't abusive. He took the time to teach me and he called me out on my behaviour.

Dad and I missed out on so much. If he were alive, I'd tell him that I forgive him. I would say, "Let's move on, Dad. Let's learn how to be a father and son, let's learn to play, let's learn to talk, to get to know each other, let's learn to laugh, let's learn to value each other and learn to LOVE!"

Vikram Vij
Vancouver, British Columbia
Chef, restaurateur, 54

||||||||||||||||||||||||||||||||||||||||||||||||||||||||||||||||||||||||||||||||||||||

Vikram Vij grew up in India. He left in 1984 to study
hotel management in Austria and came to Canada in
1989, taking a job at the Banff Springs Hotel. He opened
his first restaurant in Vancouver in 1994. Vikram is a
widely celebrated chef, sommelier, TV personality and
co-author of three bestselling cookbooks. He and his
ex-wife Meeru's restaurants in Vancouver and area include
Vij's and Rangoli. Vikram is also head chef of My Shanti
restaurant in South Surrey. Vikram and Meeru have two
daughters: Nanaki and Shanik, both in their twenties.

||||||||||||||||||||||||||||||||||||||||||||||||||||||||||||||||||||||||||||||||||||||

My father had a vision for how and who I was going to be. He held up
shining examples of the men he admired: Gandhi, Nelson Mandela,
Martin Luther King. He believed that smart men look a certain way,
and have military-style haircuts. Of course I realized that the length
of their hair had nothing to do with their intelligence; these men had
a focus, a calling in life. Yes, I wanted a focus—also called a *drishti* in
Hindi—and wanted my own calling, but they had to be from my own
thinking and ideas. The examples my father gave actually pushed
me to want the opposite—like really long hair.

The length of my hair became a central feature of the dynamic
between us, my need to assert autonomy and his need to demonstrate power and control. "Why does the length of my hair matter
so much?" I'd say. "Leave me alone, I'll make my own mistakes. If

I fall down, I'll wake up some day! You don't need to mollycoddle me!" Before I left to study hotel management in Austria at the age of nineteen, Dad and I had a huge fight, sparked once again by him wanting me to get a haircut. "If you don't get it cut, you are not going to Austria," he said. I got it cut, of course, and was on my way to a new phase of life, to be able to express myself in ways not possible with my father in India.

I'm the one who carries the Vij name, the only son, and I feel lots of pressure. My father would say things like "I know you are going to make us proud one day" (*but obviously not right now*). I was not an outstanding student, but my people skills were strong. I've always loved people, and thankfully I had a subtle cuteness that people enjoyed. People liked me, and I liked them back. So with my dad, even though there was constant bickering, we had a tight bond. The relationship with him was not one of stress, because there was affection and genuine love and lots of respect for each other.

He wanted to provide a level of containment, a white picket fence in my life. "You can't let a bushtit go wild," he reasoned. "You have to clip its wings." For him, my life needed to be a well-mani-cured garden and for me, it needed to be the jungle. I thought I was a lion and I knew I could survive. He was controlling in many ways. He loved me so deeply, he didn't want anything to go wrong for me. Even today, he loves me so much that if something were to happen to me, I think he would die.

When I got to Austria, I let my hair grow. On my first visit home to India, after almost a year away, we fought about my hair again. "Go get it cut—your hair. Go, go!" He couldn't stand it. He was paying for my education, and eventually my respect for him became bigger than my need to demonstrate autonomy. Since then I have avoided creating issues. I have great respect for him and what he's done for me.

He is influenced by the class system in India. It is terrible, but so normal. This means that he's very judgemental. I've got the name and the fame, he's very proud of that... "Yes," he says, "you're famous, but you haven't made a shitload of money." I did not get his conscientiousness. My father spends nothing on himself and

Vikram with Nanaki and Shanik, 2016

knows where every penny goes, whereas I spend lots on myself, and drive the poor man crazy by spending a hundred dollars on a bottle of wine. In his mind I should have amassed great wealth by now.

My first daughter's birth was the most touching experience of my life. I fed her, I cradled her, I bathed her; her exquisiteness made me weep. I was hesitant, even paranoid that I'd do the wrong thing, but I learned to trust myself.

My relationship with my girls is central to who I am. I have truly never doubted myself as a father. I've doubted myself as a man, and as a husband, but never as a father. It's my pillar of strength. I know there are some people in this world who actually don't like their kids—hard to believe, but someone said it to me the other day. Some of my proudest moments are when people approach them in public and make comments about who I am and what I've done, and they'll say, "He's just my dad." That's truly the only way in which I want to be distinguished, for the reason of who I am *to them*.

What shadows we can cast as parents. My father had so much power to influence me. When I was little someone came up to him and said, "Oh, your son is so cute," and he said, "God gave him the looks, but not the brains." I immediately asked, "Why did you say that, Dad?" He said, "Oh, I was just joking," but the wound from that small dagger was already there.

I am sure I have done some of those things with my girls, yes, trying to be funny. I think that in some ways I'm the same kind of dad. Many of the qualities my father emphasized are exactly what I want my girls to have, like integrity, honesty, tenacity to work hard, to handle adversity, to not lose it, to remain focused—my dad taught me all that. He thrives on trying to be the best dad; it comes from a very strong place culturally. Despite my resistance and crankiness—the strong father in me? That came from Dad. He also chose the best mum in the world, she is a pillar of strength for him and for us. I truly love my mother as a human being. She is gentle, understanding and most of all, a very good soul.

For me, food is the entrance to the heart. Love of food equals love of life, making good food is the essence of caring. When Meeru and I split up, my girls were so mad at me. They were twelve and fifteen, and bitterly upset with what was happening. They thought it was all my fault. I knew I couldn't tell them anything different, and it would be so wrong to try. For a long time, they viewed me as the villain.

The adjustment to being single was brutal. It would break my heart to leave them on a Sunday evening, to go back alone to my apartment. I'd stay in the driveway, smoke a cigarette, two, delay the moment when the sad truth of being single would hit me all over again. I'm the first one to admit I screwed up my marriage: it was my ego. Admitting this was my first step to taking a good look at myself in the mirror, and to recovery.

Now Meeru is managing the kitchens at Vij's and Rangoli and she has been a pillar of strength to the staff and, most importantly, she and I are still very good friends and we respect and talk about our kids with a lot of love and affection. We have been able to reinvent our relationship and yes, we do disagree still on some things, but a lot of times I fully support her and she fully supports me.

My way to handle the difficult times with the girls was to show my love the best way I know how: by making them delicious food, pouring my love into cooking. I was also patient, and I worked hard at rebuilding trust. I kept thinking that eventually, it is my actions that will speak the loudest. Cooking is my language of love. I believe I cooked my way back into my girls' hearts.

So many people lick their wounds, take offence with their children. I like that my girls challenge me. I hate it when fathers say, "She doesn't reach out to me." *You* are the one who must reach out, it's your job as a father. I have heard men say they have given up on their child: "Well, I tried five times to call her, and she never phoned me back." My response is, "Well, try fifty times, try one hundred and fifty times. *Don't give up.*" I send text messages to my girls every morning. I call, I go out of my way to connect wherever and whenever. I will be the first one to reach out. I am so passionate about them, and our love.

My focus is my fatherhood, not my cooking, not my restaurant, not my TV shows, not that stuff. I want to be remembered as Vikram Vij the great father. I want my kids to say, "My dad's crazy, my dad's nuts, but fuck, I love him."

Show your feelings and be open with your children. Listen to them and ask how they feel. I wear my heart on the outside. I cry at movies, weddings. I cry all the time, I sob, I melt like butter. No one has to guess what I am feeling. Except I can't show my father, or tell him how I am feeling; I've never been able to do that. And there are things he can't talk to me about or ask me, like whether I have a girlfriend, whether I am having sex. Our relationship is wired differently, but now I accept him. I can't change him. I don't want to change him.

I may be emotional, but I am practical and bring full awareness to my role as a father. I am guided by a conscious, methodical approach and know that I am planting seeds for the future. Being a dad is the best thing I ever did.

Brett Kissel
Flat Lake, Alberta
Country music singer and songwriter, 29

‖‖

Brett Kissel grew up on a cattle ranch in the region of Flat Lake, Alberta, about two hundred kilometres northeast of Edmonton. At age twenty-two, he was signed to Warner Music. Brett has been honoured with a Juno Award and multiple Canadian Country Music Association Awards. He is the only Canadian who has ever toured with superstar Garth Brooks. Brett is married to Cecilia and they have three children: Mila, born in 2016; Aria, born in 2017; and Leo, born in 2019.

‖‖

Dad is the most important title I'll ever have. Being a husband is huge, too—it's tied. Being an entertainer and performer is certainly great but it's so irrelevant in the grand scheme of things when the job I have is to raise human beings.

I was married at twenty-one. Very young—and of course it was a steep learning curve. What I originally thought was being passionate and assertive in my marriage, I soon came to realize was becoming aggressive. I went into counselling alone, and soon after my wife and I started marriage counselling with a great counsellor we found in Edmonton, and we have been seeing him for eight years. Mostly, it's a quarterly "top-up," but when we need him it's a lot more, and at times we use Skype to see each other. He's a guy I give a lot of credit to; he's helped us gain the tools to be very aware, close and clear in our communication.

I know some people can't bring themselves to reach out, but I've always thought if we can take guitar lessons or voice lessons, why can't we take marriage lessons? If I can go to the gym and be more physically fit, why can't I learn to be more fit mentally or emotionally? Cecilia and I encourage other couples: fuck your pride—just do it. To guys I'd say, "Don't go to a bar and down six beers when things aren't going right in your marriage and think that's going to solve something."

A healthy relationship with my wife leads into why I'm able to be a good dad. Nothing has made me happier than becoming a dad. I don't think I have had a bad day yet! When we first got pregnant, we had warnings from every corner about how awful certain things were going to be, dire warnings from random people who told us we would disconnect as a couple, we would not understand each other anymore, we wouldn't get any sleep, we'd go grey. Oh, and good luck going to another hockey game or having fun with the boys!

What's with all the negativity? "Terrible twos"? How could you create that kind of orientation to a child's second year of life? It's such a privilege to have kids; I cherish what are often perceived as the tough times. I have some friends who can't have kids—or have had such difficult times starting their families. So, we do everything we can to embrace the crazy and to love the chaos of parenting.

Sure we have had sleepless nights, but they don't last forever, and babies change so quickly. They'll be eighteen and moving out before we know it. So I have taken the sleepless nights in stride. I can cope with this little baby; it's their "normal" and they want some frigging love! I always got up with my wife for night feedings, changed the diaper, coddled, swaddled, burped—we did it together. Some dads I know say, "I let my wife do all that stuff—when they are walking, talking, that's when I'll be there." I think, *Oh my gosh, you will have missed everything*. The surprise for me is how good it has all been. The day Mila arrived was the best day of my life, and all that I give to her I get back a million times.

I had a great relationship with my parents growing up on a cattle ranch in the Flat Lake region of Alberta, northeast of St. Paul, which is northeast of Edmonton. My grandfather was a big positive

Brett with wife Cecilia and daughters Mila (LEFT) and Aria, 2018

influence on me—we lived in the same yard, ran the farm together. He would teach me to check myself, to think about how important an issue was—which things to bring forward and which things to let go of.

My parents did everything to encourage and support me. Dad and I always got along. He didn't tell me he loved me, and I didn't say it to him, but I knew he was there for me and cherished me because I could feel it and see it in his eyes. He trusted me to make good choices for myself, which was a wonderful vote of confidence. When my brother and I were teenagers, going to the rodeo, graduation parties, that kind of stuff, he didn't tell us not to go, and he didn't say, "Don't you be drinking." He'd meet us in the garage with a six-pack and tell us, "Here's my cell phone, call me—I don't care if it's three in the morning. I'll pick you up and I'll never be mad at you." We could trust him, we were safe. And if we ever did call on him to pick us up, he'd take us to McDonald's on the way home. No shame, no blame.

Dad wasn't so good at handling his feelings. He's a farmer, a quiet, unassuming guy. He's meek and mild. If he was upset he'd disappear—he always had a project: gone to the garage, to the shop, out on the quad chasing cattle. If there was a confrontation at home, if I was in an argument with my mom, I'd turn around and Dad would be gone. Gone. You'd find him ten miles away. He just didn't know how to deal with conflict.

As I got older, things at home got more challenging. When I got involved with Cecilia, my mom was very much against the relationship. There was also a family dispute going on. The family farm operation broke up and my grandparents and parents, who were once close, were in serious conflict. When my mom directed her anger toward me, and her problems got worse, I looked to my dad to take a stand, to give me his blessing with Cecilia, but he didn't, couldn't or wouldn't. He'd prefer to let things go rather than rock the boat, always. He'd talk with me about hockey and music, and leave all the important things out. Our relationship is as good as it can be, but we could go so much deeper. I know I am missing out, and so is my dad. I have learned to love my dad through this and not to expect anything different because I would be constantly disappointed. I've got great male mentors, but they aren't my dad. I can't expect them to show up for me, to offer that consistency and constancy. But I crave that deeper connection with him—let's hope we get there.

Growing up in the country, I got a lot of great lessons from Dad. Although he's a quiet farmer, he's also a jock, a man's man. I'm thankful he taught me to move in a man's world, with some good-old-boy, legit manly things like butchering meat, operating any kind of machinery, fixing just about anything, going on road trips, eating steak and drinking beer! A big part of who I am embraces what are thought of as feminine characteristics, so what he taught me helps me achieve a healthy balance.

When we were expecting Mila, the turmoil in our family was having a significant effect on us. Cecilia had some health challenges that were dangerous for the baby, and that were induced by the outside stress in our lives—from my mother and my family war. We recognized that whatever shit was happening in our families—hers

Brett and Cecilia with their children (FROM LEFT) Mila, Aria and Leo, 2019

or mine—we were not going to take it forward with us. We made a decision to focus on ourselves and the new generation, and we put up a "force field" that has stayed with us from that moment forward. As much as I would like all of my relationships to improve, it is most important that we make our own happiness, and our place of comfort and safety, within our own nuclear family.

My first instinct in many situations is still anger. However, I've learned I can accomplish what I need to without going that route. Brett Kissel now is very different from Brett Kissel in 2011. The calmest I was then is the most aggressive I am now—I've come a long way. I'm still learning, I'm growing, and I think that's essential to becoming the father I want to be.

When I look to the future, I want to cultivate a relationship with my children based on trust, openness and honesty. I want to build a friendship while still remaining a parent first and foremost. I see those memes on Pinterest, on fridge magnets, that say, *I'm not your friend, I'm your parent*. I genuinely want to be both and I believe it's possible. I worry about the world I have brought my kids into; there are so many risks associated with growing up in this complex world. I think the greatest protection against the potential emotional harm that may reach my kids is making sure that they love themselves. That is the best armour against any troll on social media.

Right now, living in the US, a fear I have for my children is for their physical safety. Sure, the US is an independent and "free" country, but with so many school shootings it's so hard to watch the news. When a tragedy occurs, such as a mass shooting, the effect it has is amplified because it gets replayed time and time again by the media. I think the fear this generates prevents us from setting our kids free. I want to be overly protective—yet at the same time I want my kids to be independent like I was. In Alberta there was lots of opportunity to stand on your own two feet. You got your learner's licence at fourteen and could drive on your own at sixteen. Plus, I was a kid from the country so I had freedom, lots of freedom. Striking the best balance between being overprotective and being too lenient is going to be tough.

All in all, like I do with my career, it's important to know where you've been to know where you're going. And I've learned a lot of lessons from my parents—the things they did right and the things I didn't agree with. My upbringing was great in many ways, but my transition to adulthood led to being estranged from my own mom.

Parenting is hard. It's emotional. And it's so difficult at times. But still, it's so worth it—every minute of it. And if Cecilia and I can do right by our kids, and work toward building great human beings, then I believe we can look back on these days with pride and fond memories—knowing we did a good job. And honestly, I don't need to win a Grammy. What I want is for my kids both now and when they're older to say, "You know what? My dad was great. I love him." That's the kind of Grammy I want: the "Best Dad Grammy."

Ian Brown

Toronto, Ontario

Author, journalist, 65

||||||||||||||||||||||||||||||||||||||||||||||||||||||||||||||||||||||||||||

Ian Brown is an award-winning author and a feature writer for *The Globe and Mail*. Ian is also a freelance journalist for magazines such as *Saturday Night*. He was for many years the host of CBC Radio's *Talking Books*, as well as the anchor of TVOntario's *Human Edge* and *The View from Here*. Ian is married to Johanna and they have two children: Hayley, born in 1993, and Walker, born in 1996.

||||||||||||||||||||||||||||||||||||||||||||||||||||||||||||||||||||||||||||

How do you measure your success as a father? Do your children do well, do they go to a good school, are they engaged in the world, do they read, contribute, create? Are they good conservators, stewards? Are they responsible, do they have a good sense of humour, are they dashing? Are they married well, producing grandchildren, etc.? These are the standards by which we often feel compelled to measure our success as parents. They have nothing to do with the actual relationship between the father and the child; they're mostly concerns about status. And yet, although my children are vastly different from each other, my identity as a father is the same with each of them.

Walker looks about twelve and has the mind of an eighteen-month-old. He can't speak, he can't tell me what's bothering him. He's mobile, but he has to be fed by tubes—he can't swallow. He still has seizures. But he has a personality, he can communicate, he can have an emotional relationship with you.

Hayley's the opposite in terms of capability: very smart, competent, thoughtful, reads a lot, and she's very organized. Nothing about them is similar on the surface, obviously. But Hayley is probably my favourite companion in the whole world, in part because she is so alert to the value of relationships. Maybe having to live and communicate with Walker taught her that: she isn't hierarchical in the way she relates to people. She is never ashamed to reach out, or to be open to the possibility of love.

While there are a million ways to measure the success of my paternal influence with expectations that are imposed from without, I am freed from that with my son Walker. The success of our relationship is the quality of our connecting *in the moment*. Is it fun, is it deep, is it meaningful, can you feel it? You might say that's subjective, made up in my mind. To that I would say most parents' ideas of their relationships with their totally normal children are completely made up as well, such as mine with my daughter. I can talk to her about anything. She's insightful, calm, original. I hope I am the same to her, at least sometimes. But ultimately, the success of our relationship can only truly be measured by how we relate, how we connect, what we learn from one another.

I just loved being with my children, the physical proximity. With Hayley, just sitting with her, looking at her, feeling her little body, looking into her eyes. The same with Walker, this bumpy little strange guy, giving him baths, noticing how it would calm him down—and how that, in turn, would calm me down.

One of the things I had to figure out was how to have a relationship with Walker without words. A lot of our relationship is intuitive, reacting or responding in the moment on a physical or emotional plane as opposed to an intellectual one. If Walker were here now, he'd stand up and visit with us. He'd be attracted to the shiny things on the table; he'd probably make a grab for this shiny pot and try to knock it to the ground to make noise, to make light, to create havoc. The moment we became distracted, that's when he'd take aim. He's good at that, he likes to do it. Enact maximum chaos. His behaviour has a sociopathic feel to it. I used to watch him and wonder, *Why is he so weird? Why is he such a freak? Is he a psychopath?* There were no good answers.

I would ruminate on this at length, trying to figure out what was wrong with him and how I could fix it and make it right. It was so exhausting. And so, after many years I stopped asking how I could make him stop and simply tried to better understand why he might be doing what he was doing. I began to realize that he had an awareness of his own incapacity. He knows he can't do what other people do. For instance, he loves it if you engage him in a conversation and treat him as if he's responding—it brings him to life.

It was only at that point when I began to take him more seriously, as having something to offer even if it was offered in an unconventional or subtle way, that I began to understand him a little better. Every once in a while, by outsmarting me, he was trying to show me that he could be my equal. I used to think that must feel great for him. But then I realized it also felt great to me—that what he was truly trying to show me was that *I* could be *his* equal. In his company, I am as disabled as him: I can't speak his language, I can't figure out his meaning, I can't make myself understood. In a way, that's his great gift to me—showing me that I can be his equal. It frees us from the usual hierarchical expectations of the parent-child relationship. I could finally stop caring about the usual conventions and get along with him as best I could.

Once you stop trying to make your children into something valued by our culture, once you start understanding who they are *as they are*, you are both incredibly freed. That's my experience, in any event.

The late psychologist Donald Winnicott wrote that for a father to be successful, the first thing he must do is ensure he lives long enough to get his children on their feet. This is a reminder to men to stop habitually putting themselves in the way of peril as they are typically prone to do.

The second thing Winnicott says that you must do in order to be a successful father is to fail your children: you must disappoint them. In a *natural* way, he says, not by dropping them off an emotional cliff by having incestuous relationships or by being violent or beating the shit out of their mother—just the unavoidable human failings and inevitable disappointments of everyday life. This idea of perfection that we are bandying about these days—it's impossible! You know it from your own life: the career may be a huge success, but it's peppered with disappointments. Relationships have their natural ebb and flow. People know this about themselves and yet don't apply it to their children. They somehow think it's their job to rescue their children and keep all problems away from them.

Perfectionism is a pathology. It's a disease. This is in part a problem of not reading things deeply: you don't know about life's failures, people's failures. If you are focused on social media, for example, you think everyone except you is a perfect parent. I'm not suggesting we lower our standards, but failure is very instructive and illuminating. If you pretend failure can't exist, you take away the opportunity to look inside yourself.

I think that's what Walker did—removed any whiff of attaining perfection. He thereby showed me that judgement is precipitous and always stupid. For that reason, I'm relieved there was no genetic test in utero that would have presented the ethical dilemma of whether to end his life.

A lot of parents I've encountered seem to think that anxiety and imperfection should not be part of a child's life. We could go over to the school near my place, a very good school with educated parents, and watch them drop off their children. We'd see them totally occupied with their cell phones, checking messages, social media or whatever they do. They're not interacting with their children: they're managing their kids as they simultaneously manage their information intake. They aren't paying attention. And if it's a problem there, it's a problem everywhere. For instance, the constant babbling you do to a baby who gazes at you; the continuous commentary that you provide to a child on what you see around you and what's happening. It's the kind of banter you keep up with the dog. When Walker was a little boy, we developed a private language of tongue clicks that only he and I could speak. Very funny and a source of abundant pleasure.

That's where language comes from, from which understanding emerges—the process by which we develop shared meaning and interpret our environment for our children. If we are totally preoccupied by our devices, how can this happen? Doesn't it put it all at risk?

My dad was a great guy. He liked people, and he loved his kids as companions. Our relationship was deep and comfortable, very solid. He was born in north London into a rather cold English middle-class family, a simple guy in many ways. Not a risk-taker, a bit mild, a bit too conservative for his own good, but he was a very good father. We were never afraid of him. To us, he was great.

A very calm guy, he didn't lose his cool. He had vast supplies of patience; he was long-suffering when it came to his marriage, and unfortunately neurotic enough to believe that constituted a relationship. My mother constantly picked fights with him. I think she wished he'd fight back, but he only ever did on one occasion: mostly she ran over him. Dad would tell me stories, a bit about the war, his childhood, but he kept quiet about his feelings. He might have been a more conscious, reflective type, but my mother made it quite clear that she didn't approve of holding anything up for analysis.

He thought about things a lot, and he was patient and open enough to change his mind. Every now and then he'd turn thoughtful. When he knew that he was dying of congestive heart failure and only had six months to live, I asked him, "What do you think will happen when you die?" He said, "I'll go to heaven and meet your mother and she'll be upset because I have kept her waiting so long." The next day he called and said, "I've been thinking about what you asked me. It's a bit presumptuous of me to say what's going to happen." I wondered if he meant whether he'd been good enough to get into heaven; believe me, if my father didn't deserve to get in, then no one does. But it had made him think. Like other people who made it through the war, he'd judge his behaviour and that of others according to well-known pillars: kindness, patience, cleanliness, loyalty and sense of humour, especially in a fix.

The American poet Robert Hayden once referred to the "austere and lonely offices" of being a father. My father sought warmth;

I remember kissing him once when I was a boy and my mother chastising me, saying, "What on earth are you doing, kissing your father?" I felt like saying, "Why don't you go fuck yourself?" To this day, it still infuriates me.

I miss my dad; I miss his physical presence. He acted as a guide for me, a companion, and a model. I'd have a Scotch with him, then get back to my work—which is what I always did. It's like hiking with a dog: they zoom ahead, then they come back, check on you, and off they go again. And now I'm kind of isolated, like I'm hiking alone. I wish I had told him I loved him more often, but I think he knew all the same.

There is something appealing about being a father when you get it right. It's a calm place, a great place to be. It provides the opportunity to be close, but also to be observant, objective, not pulled into the vortex as the mother who bears the child often is, but able to fully reap all the same benefits.

The great revelation for me is that it's what you do, not what you say, that speaks most clearly to your children. It is enough that you are kind, that you listen, that you try your best at what you do, whatever you do. If you keep trying with enthusiasm despite the outcome, your children see the pleasure you get, rather than just the terrible disappointment they might also pick up on. My father wasn't emotionally articulate enough to say that, but he was able to show me.

The only time my father ever struck me was after my mother had struck me, and I'd grabbed her hands—I was sixteen at the time—and said, "Don't do that again." My mother responded by asking my father if he was going to let me treat her like that. I don't remember the actual blow; I just remember suddenly being on the other side of the room. He said, "I'm sorry," and I said the same. I repeated my apology when I was about fifty and he was ninety. "I'm sorry," I said, "that I was such an arsehole back then."

"No, no, no," he said. "You don't have to apologize. You were fighting for both of us. I was not strong enough to stand up to her."

At the end of Dad's life, my brother and I took him on a journey to Boston. We were at the airport with him, having our photo taken, before my brother caught a plane. You can see in the photo that my

Ian and son Walker, 2007

brother had been crying; I look bewildered. But my father, who is in the middle, has a look in his eye of full existential crisis: he knows he's going to die, he knows this may be it, he's here with his sons, he knows they love him, he doesn't want to leave, but he knows he has to. It's all there in that instant. I'm so glad to have captured that moment. We didn't know it was the last time we'd all be together. It's hard to look at the image, but I am forever grateful that we took the time and had that experience together. You have to face the truth of life, dark as it sometimes is. We helped each other do that. We were allies.

At the end of my book *The Boy in the Moon*, I describe Walker having a seizure. It was the first seizure I had ever seen him have, and he fell over like a stack of plates into my arms. Someone asked if I needed help. I said, "No, it's okay." I knew what to do. Walker's eyes were going like metronomes, his body was shaking from its core; it was as if he were dying. I thought to myself, *All I can do is be here to receive him when he comes back, so he's not scared.* In that moment, another truth crystallized for me: I knew that he loved me, and that I loved him—and that this was sufficient. The truth of that love was in our companionship: he knew it, I knew it. It was the most important thing that we needed from each other.

Walker is strong, lively, he's got a great sense of humour, but there are many things I have wished for him that he didn't get—that he could be handsome, smart, talented. Those things didn't happen. A lot of his life hasn't worked out so great. But what I ultimately have gained from Walker is a finely distilled essence of togetherness, of companionship, of going through this incredible experience of being in the world with this astonishing boy. You can be afraid of the experience, you can think that it's trying to destroy you, that you have to fight it and defend yourself. Or you can say, "It's there, it's unavoidable." You can try to revel in whatever beauty and pleasure are there, and maybe you can help each other out. There are lessons to be learned on both sides, and as the father, you are perfectly positioned to make this work.

Hayley was talking to a friend not that long ago, a friend who'd had all the privileges of great wealth while growing up, including the best education that money can buy. Unlike Hayley, she had attended a very good, very expensive boarding school. They were discussing their different paths and where they are in life now—and that despite those very different paths, they now find themselves in about the same place. The only difference, Hayley's friend pointed out, is that Hayley has a relationship with her father.

And a relationship can't be bought. However many other things I have fucked up—and they are legion—Hayley and I have our relationship and a wonderful closeness. I didn't send her away to school; I wanted to be near her. I wanted the gift of her company, of watching her come into her life. My wife, Johanna, is very good at appreciating the presence of people. Somehow, we have raised an observant, bright, empathic, generous daughter.

Being around Walker must have been hard at times for Hayley. I think it made her life a lot lonelier, and sometimes sadder—kind of like being an only child, except that she wasn't an only child on the face of it. But having a brother with a disability may also have given her something, as it has given us all something. He adores Hayley, and when we are both with him I'm like, "Here I am, Walker. It's Dad!" but he only has eyes for her. He's like, "My sister's here. Fuck you, Pops."

Intellectually disabled people reveal more to us of ourselves than we might otherwise encounter. I know it's a controversial point of view, but in terms of one's ethical evolution, I think the disabled are the world's teachers. In fact, when I think about it, most of the biggest pleasures in my life have centred around doing things with my children, together, in proximity. New things, fresh things, dangerous, risky things: going out in choppy waters, into the mountains, out to the sea; teaching my girl to swim in Georgian Bay, off the rocks! I'm not wildly fond of changing a diaper, but even that brought me closer to my kids. It's just shit, not nuclear waste.

With kids you can conjure up the most immense pleasure in simple ways. Lying next to my daughter on her bed prior to reading her a story, looking up at the ceiling, then looking over at her, then looking away and then making sure she sees me, then looking back away, making this fantastic game of it—it's not Disneyland, but it's exquisite. Or you are reading a book for the fiftieth time, you know it so well, it's so fucking boring you can feel your brain dribbling out of your ear as you read, but you know that you're participating in an ancient ritual, an honourable feat to nurture your child, and one you and she will always remember as something you did together, free of distraction. What would you rather be doing? Smoking a joint?

You don't have that much time in life, you don't have that much opportunity to connect emotionally with anybody, never mind your children. These opportunities to be human, to be successful but also to fail, they are all we have. Grab the chance to be with your kids in a real way. I would say that 95 per cent of what I worried about while I was raising my kids—*I have to do this deal or this story, it's more important*—was complete and utter bullshit. I should have said, "Let's go and count the trees again and see if we can get to a hundred." Time with them has been the best and most satisfying experience in my life. I feel connected to the world, and more alive because of them.

After growing up witnessing the spectacle of my mother arguing all the time with my father, badgering him and shaming him to manipulate him and keep him within her orbit, I promised myself I wasn't going to live that way. I am not sure I succeeded entirely, but I made some progress away from living that way. I'm as affected as anyone else by the models that are held up to boys as examples: the strong, silent, buttoned-up, wealthy, successful, but cold model of success. That was a vision I tried to fight off, though the mirage lures me to this day. You see its effects everywhere, especially in the number of men who still cannot talk or even write about the crazy delicacies of human interaction, who refuse to talk about their feelings, who have been raised *not* to talk about their feelings—by their fathers.

When my dad died I was on a backcountry motorcycle trip in Chile. One day, after getting separated from the other guys, I was in this huge sandstone arroyo, where for some reason I built an inuksuk. It's not the sort of thing I normally do. Later, reunited with my pals and sitting down for lunch, my phone went off. I had to stand on a chair at the foot of the restaurant's garden to get reception. That was where I heard the message from my brother Tim telling me that Dad had died.

Back home about a week later, adjusting to life without Dad, a robin showed up in our backyard. My dad was a well-dressed man, English tailoring and so forth. Dapper. I'm not prone to this kind of make-believe sentimental thinking; I knew the robin with its reddish waistcoat was not my father. That robin comes back. I know it's not Dad. But I wish it could be; I wish I could believe it was my father. This robin has stayed, and it returns every spring to our backyard in Toronto with its family, and every year I think, *There he is again, checking in.*

When I was in university, I had a girlfriend who lived down the street from my apartment. I'd sometimes stay the night with her and at about six a.m. I'd go back to my place. One morning my dad passed me by on the street in his car and asked, "Where've you been?" I just said, "Round and about." Of course he knew what was going on, but he wasn't critical or judgemental. He just let me know that he knew that I knew that he knew.

He had a habit of calling me at 6:30 a.m. and saying, brightly, "Come on, aren't you up yet?" as I groggily picked up the phone. That was his way of imparting discipline: by showing me what the habit of an early riser was, by making me see the benefits of a routine. And so when this robin shows up, it's like one of my father's early morning roustings: *Are you awake? Are you alert? Are you paying attention, even at this early moment in the day? Because there's lots to see, my boy.* Maybe it's an idealized version of him. But I need to maintain an idealized version of my dad: it's the one he tried to present, and the one I have held on to.

Shea Emry

Whistler, British Columbia

Speaker, activist, retired CFL player, 33

||||||||||||||||||||||||||||||||||||||||||||||||||||||||||||||||||||||||||||||||||||||||||||||||||||||

Shea Emry is an award-winning all-star middle linebacker
and two-time Grey Cup champion. He played eight
seasons in the Canadian Football League, most of them
with the Montreal Alouettes. In 2011 Shea suffered a
concussion that derailed his football season. He found
himself battling mental health difficulties; the depression
he had experienced during adolescence returned to
him. Shea has been using his platform as a professional
athlete to share his story with youth, fostering awareness
about wellness and mental health. He is married to
Devon Brooks and they have two children: Rozen, who
was born in 2014, and Clooney, who arrived in 2016.

||||||||||||||||||||||||||||||||||||||||||||||||||||||||||||||||||||||||||||||||||||||||

I'm a Canadian through and through, and I come from a strong
family. My parents have been together for forty-five years, and my
grandparents just celebrated their seventy-fifth wedding anniver-
sary! I have a great relationship with the male role models in my
life. I've always looked up to my grandfather, my uncles and my old
man. He travelled a lot for work when I was growing up. He'd be
gone for stretches of two or three weeks, but when he was home he
was really present, made an effort to participate and coached a lot
of sports. My pops is stoic—he rarely has a lot to say until something
needs to be said.

I get asked a lot about the men in my life. Who were the men who raised me? What they all looked like to me was big, strong and powerful. They worked in what were then male-dominated or exclusively male occupations. Dad worked in the forest firefighting and disaster response business. My mom's dad was in the pulp and paper industry and a few of my uncles were in the timber, forestry, and fishing industries. They were coaches in hockey and rugby; they were fishermen and hunters. My family, the world around me and the movies I watched all reinforced the same image of how to be a man. Men are tough, stoic, strong and courageous. They don't make mistakes and they're not vulnerable. That's for damn sure. Over and over again, that's what I picked up on.

I had a really rough time in my high school years because of how some early childhood traumatic experiences had created an internal torment in my mind. These experiences changed how I viewed myself, and I shut down. I was scared to take risks and felt like I would be betrayed and hurt if I put myself out there. My fight or flight sensors were going off at all times.

It wasn't just what happened to me, but the spin I put on it. I kept repeating the negative story and reliving the experiences. I couldn't escape my limiting negative thoughts. Because of the messages I had internalized about masculinity, I gave myself nowhere to lean. I kept it all bottled up inside me and became buried under the armour I felt I needed to put on to defend myself. All this changed who I inevitably became, changed my identity. I was depressed but I was not going to admit it to anyone, not even myself.

I stopped doing the other things I enjoyed in my life like piano and guitar. I lost myself in football, as it gave me the outlet for the one emotion I wanted to express—anger. I was good at putting on a mask, hiding what was going on inside me. I was a handsome and fit bloke, a quarterback, had a great social life and beautiful girlfriends: it all looked like something out of the movies. I was an expert at giving people what I thought they wanted.

It was easier to be busy than it was to be reflective. I covered everything up so well I had no idea who I was. Sometimes with the way I acted, I knew I was the one being mean, but then I'd tell myself, *That doesn't matter; I need to stand up for my ego.* I've gone back years later to a couple of people I treated that way, and said, "Remember that time when..." They knew exactly what I meant, so I was able to apologize.

All of this of course was so exhausting. But it wasn't until 2011 that things really changed for me, when I was in the middle of the CFL football season. Playing for the Alouettes, I got a bad concussion that put me out for the remainder of the season. I learned that I was not a machine. Having to reckon with my vulnerability brought on a big identity crisis. This is when the depression I had experienced in my adolescence came back to visit me. I had to dig deep to get better.

I continued to play football—with the Montreal Alouettes, then the Toronto Argonauts. I met the most amazing woman, my life partner Devon Brooks, and we welcomed our first child Rozen into the world in 2014. Rozen and I developed a strong connection from the get-go. I didn't really know a lot about babies; I had no clue what I was doing, but I was determined to make it work, and out of that I got this beautiful relationship.

When Rozen was still quite tiny, Devon had work to do in Mexico City. We all went together and while Devon worked, Rozen and I spent upwards of eight hours a day together. I had this backpack loaded with everything we needed and away we'd go. I built up so much self-confidence during that time. Now if Devon's away for a week, I'm totally fine; with a good stroller and my adventure backpack, there is no aspect of being a hands-on father that I am not completely comfortable with after four plus years of fatherhood.

In 2015, I got halfway through my first game with the Saskatchewan Roughriders before another concussion ended my football career right in its prime. Transitioning out of football has been hard. I had to figure out who I was and what was next. At first, I was spinning. My darkest moments were inside my own head. I drank too much—hard liquor—and hit bottom in 2016 after watching the awards for the Grey Cup in Vancouver.

Rozen was just a little guy and I wasn't taking care of what I needed to take care of—procrastinating, not communicating. Even if I was physically there, I wasn't present. I wasn't just a disengaged father; I was a disengaged husband and I was putting my relationship with Devon at risk. I went into therapy and did some hard work on what was going on in my head. The dark times helped me reach out for help and grow, gain confidence as a man, as a father, as a husband and as a businessperson. This process has not stopped.

Fatherhood exceeds any expectations I had for it. I'm getting more because I'm giving more. I'm anticipating better communication between me and my children than I had with the adults in my life. When I grew up it felt like there were socially ingrained ways of showing respect: "Yes sir. No sir." I'm taking a holistic approach to nurturing my kids in the hopes that they learn how to really respect others and themselves. This goes for both my kids, but especially my son—I am going to support him in knowing who he is, expressing himself, understanding his emotions and being his true self. For me everything was so tense. My dad was there for me; I could have talked to him, but I just didn't do it. I tied myself in knots instead.

In alpha-male environments, a lot of "peacocking" goes on. I think about the "dude" culture. As guys, we amplify some very negative aspects of being male that are one-dimensional, and that cut us off from who we really are. I do a large portion of the household chores and I don't worry at all about being judged for that—but I know in some circles it would be frowned upon. There's this outdated notion that men shouldn't care, that it's not cool to be a caretaker.

Devon and I have worked closely together and she has helped me on the path toward optimal health and happiness. That path wasn't always clear, nor was it in just one direction. I sure don't feel that I have all the answers, but Devon and I support and lean on each other and do our best to find the answers together.

I know that social conditioning is going to mean different things for my son than for my daughter. I'm aware that I have to counter the enormous influence of the media. I am tuned in to the messages directed at boys, but I am also scared about what the multimedia platforms are telling little girls. I didn't tell my two-year-old daughter to say, "Me princess," but that's what she's picking up.

I am aware of technology and its potential effects on my children. I've seen some really negatively affected kids, especially when

Shea with wife Devon, and sons Clooney (LEFT) and Rozen, 2017

it comes to video games and their content. The desensitization to weapons, sex, drugs and violence against women is grotesque and I don't envision it getting any better. We won't have video games in the house, but it's going to be hard to run interference and protect my kids from this out there in the world. Censorship? It's gone out the window. I was away for a weekend on an island getaway and there were these six- to-ten-year-old kids stuck in front of video games on a gorgeous summer day. They were like zombies—killing zombies. It's non-stop violence: *boom, boom, boom.* Guns, rape, violence—*Merry Christmas, Johnny, here's a video game to further stew the toxic media infiltrating your mind.*

It was never for me, but when I've worked with boys in groups—sometimes upwards of 75 per cent of them list video games as their main source of passion or entertainment. On the one hand we have the Me Too movement empowering women and challenging men to take responsibility for their actions, yet on the other hand boys are immersing themselves in these misogynist, violent worlds. Where's this all going?

I was at a friend's place and he was playing *Grand Theft Auto*. He's like, "Watch this." He drives this car in the game, he proceeds to pick up a prostitute, and there is literally a drop-down list of all the things she'll do with him and all the prices—this is all in a "game" that kids play. They perform the chosen sex act and he kicks her out of his car—then he shoots her in the back of the head. How does this "game" exist? How can it be legal? That was five years ago, and that version has been superseded as the consumer seemingly wants it faster, more furious and more violent. And we talk about gun control?

I am so glad we live in a community that's very outdoor-oriented. I see being in nature as an antidote to the negatives children can get sucked into. My kids are going to be active because we are active. They're not going to be couch potatoes. I also appreciate the shared approach to raising children. We have surrounded ourselves with great people we trust who will play a big role in raising our children. Most importantly, I want to raise my kids to make decisions for themselves. We can guide, nudge, but they'll create their own wisdom and happiness.

As a husband and father I have had to cast off a number of assumptions about being a provider. For example, we can't afford our own place yet, and for a while I was really hard on myself about that. I allowed myself to feel bad that we had to live at my in-laws'. I've got over that now. I've reframed my unhealthy ideas and the unnecessary pressure I was putting on myself. Another big surprise for me has been allowing myself to become domesticated. I had to get my male ego out of the way, and now I get great satisfaction from taking care of the house and being able to handle multiple projects at the same time. I have spent so much of my life frozen in my tracks, worried about what people might think, afraid to take risks, to be vulnerable, and with an intense fear of failure. Now I am in the flow, being real, able to be gregarious, telling my story and loving life.

Shea and Devon with their sons Rozen and baby Clooney, 2017

David McLean

Vancouver, British Columbia

Lawyer, businessman, 81

||||||||||||||||||||||||||||||||||||||||||||||||||||||||||||||||||||||||||||||||||||||||

David McLean was born in Calgary in 1938. His father was a CN employee and union leader, and David's early years were spent living in a prairie station house. David started his career as a lawyer, and later became involved in real estate investment, film production and aviation. In 1994 David was appointed to the CN board by Prime Minister Jean Chrétien. He became the longest-serving chair in the history of the company, and also chaired the Canadian Chamber of Commerce, the Greater Vancouver Board of Trade and the board of governors of the University of British Columbia. David was president and CEO of the McLean Group until his son Jason succeeded him. David has been the chairman of the McLean Group since his son, Jason, succeeded him as CEO. He is the father of Sasha, forty-three, as well as Jason, forty-five. He and his wife Brenda have been married for forty-six years, and they have five grandchildren.

||||||||||||||||||||||||||||||||||||||||||||||||||||||||||||||||||||||||||||||||

I've dodged a few bullets in my time: heart surgery, prostate cancer and now managing to rehabilitate my two new knees which were replaced in January 2017. I think I'm twenty-four, and why shouldn't I? My father lived until he was ninety-five! Maybe I am trying to reclaim my youth. I bought a new car this year, a convertible. My wife said I was being frivolous, but I decided I was going to do it anyway (and no, it's not red).

Both Brenda and I had first marriages before finding each other. I hadn't remotely considered being a father before, but once we were together, I knew it was different. Becoming a father was the best thing I ever did. I was very excited to be a dad. I was thirty-four years old, and 100 per cent ready. There are no words to adequately describe the experience of participating in the arrival of a baby. It changes your life completely. Pure joy, and it's been great ever since.

My father was an older dad. He'd already had six children by the time I came along. He worked shifts for CN, awkward hours that meant our lives slipped past each other for a lot of my childhood. He worked the three-to-midnight shift, he'd come home and sleep until nine or ten a.m., long after I had left for school, and he would be gone again when I got home. His days off were Wednesday and Thursday, days when I'd be busy at school. I played on many teams—basketball, football—but I don't remember him ever coming to a single game.

I liked my father a lot, but we were not close. I didn't want that to be the case with my children. I wanted them to know me, to talk to me, to trust me. My focus was to be around, to show up. I made that decision when I decided to be a parent. I tried to find a balance between the two extremes I had witnessed: under-parenting and over-parenting.

My boys were always happy to have me actively participate. I was prepared for that not to be the case, as I knew some children painted their parents out of the picture. That didn't happen with my boys; there was always room for me. I have wanted them to be and feel included, to be involved in my life. If we had people over for dinner, the boys were part of the occasion and joined us at the table.

In fact, a lot happened at the dinner table. That's where they became involved in the family business. It all came out around the table: the good, the bad and the ugly. One day I got a call from a reporter asking me, "At what age did you get the boys involved in the business?" When I said two and four he said, "C'mon..."

David with wife Brenda, and sons Sasha (LEFT) and Jason, 2018

Communication was critical between me and the boys; there was nothing we couldn't or didn't talk about. This was a distinct change from what I grew up with. Perhaps it would have been different if I hadn't been at the tail end of the family. During the last thirty years of my dad's life, though, after Mum died, communication between us improved and we were really close. He remarried at the age of seventy and then outlived his second wife.

One thing I could never understand is people encouraging their children to go off to get educated a long way from home. Then so often they would meet someone there, get married, settle down and never come back. I gave my boys a role, getting them involved in the business, and they tended to stay around. This would never have happened if they hadn't wanted it. I never had to persuade the boys; they loved what we were doing and took on key roles. We were doing exciting things in the company.

When they were twenty-two and twenty-four years old, I did something that's quite unusual: I handed them effective control of the business by giving them 55 per cent ownership, while Brenda and I retained 45 per cent. Together, we have Vancouver Film

Studios, Blackcomb Helicopters and various real estate investments. We would like to educate our grandchildren so that they can participate as much as they wish, as soon as it is practical.

There are not many dark moments for me as a dad, but there are a few times when I have stuck my neck out. Some people believe you should just stand back and let your kids exercise their own free will. I don't believe in that. If my child is about to jump off a bridge, do you think I'm going to stand there and watch it happen? No, I'm an interventionist. Everyone I talked to, all my friends, said, "You can't get involved, you can't interfere." I said, "If my son is about to do something crazy, it'll have to be a frosty Friday in July for me not to say something."

As a father, you have to wear your heart outside of your body. Jason got into climbing in a big way. He went with an adventure group to Everest's base camp at 5,380 metres. I know he was in his element, and very courageous. Another climb was Mount McKinley in Alaska, North America's highest peak. Jason climbed with two others to the summit at 6,190 metres. Three in his group got altitude sickness and couldn't complete the climb. It took twenty-three days to get up and back. That trip was in mid-July. It was minus forty degrees Celsius with eighty-kilometre-per-hour winds. I was terrified.

I was in a CN committee meeting when he was doing that climb, and my assistant came into the meeting. She said, "Your wife is on the phone." It is a moment that will forever be seized in my memory. As I stood up, my legs were weak and my heart skipped. When I heard Brenda's voice at the other end of the phone, she was expressing elation: "They are down!" The year after his ascent of Everest, another group of six went up and were caught in a terrible storm. Three died. This event really changed Jason's view of life. I think it made clear to him that it doesn't matter how good you are, how well planned your trip is, if conditions turn against you, you are in trouble. After that I finally said to him, "Please keep your climbing to levels below 3,000 metres!"

I worked a lot harder with my own kids than my dad did. He didn't do what he needed to do to make fatherhood important. He was a great man, I loved him, I only wish I could have had a deeper relationship with him. I often say he did the best he could with what he had. My dad had a grade four education and both his parents had died when he was young. He had no strong guiding light, so I value what he was able to do with his life. He was a basic man with basic values. Responsibility was the foundation of his life and a huge part of what he gave to me. At the age of ninety-three he decided to file his own tax return, and sent the tax department several thousand dollars "just in case" he owed something. It took me months to get it back.

I've been lucky. I've been able to do well in my career, but I never had any illusions that making money was more important than my family. They are my reason for being.

Stephen Reid
Haida Gwaii, British Columbia
Author, bank robber (deceased)

||||||||||||||||||||||||||||||||||||||||||||||||||||||||||||||||||||||||||||||||||||||||

Stephen Reid was born on March 13, 1950, in Massey, Ontario. He began writing in 1984 while serving a twenty-one-year prison sentence for bank robberies undertaken with the Stopwatch Gang. His first book, *Jackrabbit Parole*, was published in 1986. Stephen married his writing mentor, poet Susan Musgrave, at Kent Institution in Agassiz, BC in 1986. After being released on full parole in June 1987, he lived with Susan and daughters Charlotte and Sophie on Vancouver Island and Haida Gwaii. On December 21, 1999, he was sentenced to eighteen years in prison for another bank robbery. While in prison Stephen wrote his second book, *A Crowbar in the Buddhist Garden*, which won the City of Victoria Butler Book Prize in 2013. Stephen died on Haida Gwaii in June 2018.

||||||||||||||||||||||||||||||||||||||||||||||||||||||||||||||||||||||||||||||||||||||||

Men—we have given ourselves a lot of trouble, pursuing an artificial standard of "being a man," hiding and burying our emotions, then covering them with addictions. I love it when I see a guy who can go flamenco dancing one night, get his fingernails dirty, cook a meal, braid a child's hair, chop wood—men can do it all, but there's a lot holding them back from aspects of their lives; they can't get over themselves...so much joy available that many guys are missing out on! I believe that most men hold on to this unflagging belief in their manly self-will: we act like we know it all, we don't ask for directions and we don't ask for help in our lives even when we are desperate.

My dad was a really interesting, really sensitive guy. He had a poem published in the *Sudbury Star* when he was in high school. But he was an intellectual trapped inside a working man's life. He had to live with lots of contradictions. I don't think that he really fit in with the other guys.

Money was tight. Family life was stressful: nothing going on, one communal knife, not much food. As a child, that kind of poverty is debilitating—you're always hiding it from other kids, hiding that your underwear is ripped and that you don't have much for your lunch at school. We had those awful shows like *Father Knows Best*. I thought other people's families were like that and I felt ashamed. I'm the second child and I had nine siblings. One died early but the others are all still alive.

I adored my dad, but he never expressed love. Back then children were supposed to be seen and not heard, and *A man's got to do what a man's got to do*. I don't think he lived up to his own image at the time, and he couldn't face his own fears. One of the enduring images I have of my father is of him sitting at the end of the table with that thousand-yard stare. He wasn't available, always somewhere deep in his head, not really there eating a meal with his family at all.

My dad was never really abusive, but he drank far too much. He could blow a paycheque buying rounds down at the hotel. It seemed anger was the only emotion that he showed with ease. If we did something wrong it was instant rage, no middle ground where we could talk about our mistakes. And when things went right, like if I got 97 per cent on a science test, he'd say, "Where's the other 3 per cent?" I knew he was just joking—but I *didn't* know, I was just kind of wounded. When I got older I just laughed it off.

I was a touchier, feelier kind of kid and if I displayed an emotion, my dad couldn't handle it; it was a sign of weakness. When things were troubling me, my dad was not the person I could go to. I wish he could have shared who he was, what he was, so that I could have been who *I was*.

I felt a lot of pressure to be perfect, to not disappoint him. I wish he'd encouraged that zany side—he didn't see that in me, or if he did he didn't value it. If I ever got full of myself or put on airs he'd deflate me in a flash with "Who do you think you are?" and "You are too big for your britches." This built in me a sense of insecurity, a hypercritical voice that is always there playing in the background. You're fearful and insecure, but then you'll overplay your hand, be narcissistic and egotistical.

When I began to be abused at the age of eleven, I kept it all inside. Especially because of the homosexual nature of what was going on—my father would have gone through the roof. I felt complicit; Paul (my abuser) didn't hold a gun to my head. I had a choice but I wanted the things he was giving me: the alcohol, the drugs. Hell, I was eleven, I was so vulnerable, he took advantage of me. The shame and guilt I felt were overpowering for me. I was so conflicted and had no real way of understanding my own emotions.

I just knew my dad wouldn't be able to cope. If he found out what was happening, he would have killed Paul—but it was the rage he would have saved for me that kept me silent. To stay out of trouble I learned to lie, a lot, but also because I wanted so much to look good in my dad's eyes.

Paul and I got stopped once by an Ontario Provincial Police officer. There I am, twelve years old, driving a grown man's car, we've got an open bottle of booze with us and we're on some tiny back road. All that happened is Paul got out, chatted with the cop, then got back in behind the wheel and I slid over the console to the passenger side. I kept that all inside until I was in my fifties. No one knew about that, including my wife. No one.

My huge secret. Small town, big attitudes, smutty, clumsy references to sex in jokes, but no real conversation about meaningful or intimate topics with Dad—or anyone else. Nowhere I could lean. There were times I would walk around that small town, snowbanked sidewalks, so separate from the world. No one to say anything to, my whole life so dismal. I can think back to my first panic attacks. I was a little bit older then and if I'd only known what was going on

I could have sorted it out. I didn't own my feelings, just like my dad hadn't owned his.

Special memories of Dad? We had a one-week canoe trip up through these Ontario lakes—lovely, lovely. My brother David and I: swimming, hunting, fishing, having so much fun. Sleeping in trappers' cabins. Dad shone for me that week; he was in his element. He represented someone who knew how to survive in the woods, navigate, keep us dry, fed and safe from wolves. It's a time that has stood out for me all my life.

One quality I am grateful for that my father instilled in me is dignity when it comes to accepting consequences, that old *Take it like a man,* so to speak, to face what I have done wrong with as much dignity as I can muster. I don't actually see it so much as a masculine trait but as a human trait. Men have given themselves a lot of trouble, relying on brute strength or force. Men are evolving as we speak, but the messages they get are so confusing—*Be sensitive,* but *lace up your boots*—and don't own those feelings.

Somehow the idea that prevailed for my dad was that if we just don't talk about stuff everything will be okay. He could not face conflict. Before he died, we had some time when he could finally talk about things close to the heart, things he'd kept inside, like about his own father, whom he told me "was a mean piece of work." I saw tears well up and then he turned away.

Parenting, it's the biggest job we ever have. Do what's best for them, not what's best for you! Let them make mistakes and don't be devastated by them! They need to know that no matter how impossibly bad things are, you can cope and you will get through it.

Of course it's an altogether different story if it's your own mistakes that are devastating them. Addiction and crime got me into the most hopeless, helpless and humble of places. I sucked so much out of my family—my wife Susan and these two incredible pieces of magic, Charlotte and Sophie. When I was first in prison Charlotte seemed the strongest of all four of us, but the sad thing is she shouldn't have needed to be at the age of seventeen. Sophie learned to separate who I am from what I had done, which is quite a skill—something that I can still learn to do.

Stephen with his grandchildren, 2016

The secret self-loathing that pools in the heart of every junkie was magnified so much for me after what I'd done. Sophie was a casualty of my behaviour. I was on the brink of taking my own life when my psychiatrist told me, "This isn't about you anymore—you have had your life, and you're going to prison for a long time. This is about a ten-year-old girl. You have to show her that no matter how badly you screw up your life you can still survive, maybe even have a chance at redemption. That's the one gift you have left to give."

It was while I was in prison that I began to reclaim the "heart place" of a parent. I started to re-enter the realm of selflessness in small and ordinary ways. One way I have been a capable parent is in my ability to talk to my children about things, anything, and not hold them to an artificial standard of perfection. I am proud of the early parenting I provided for Sophie when I was clean and sober. I could really be present, and I was a full-time dad wearing her on me in a backpack.

I recognize the noble instinct to make life easy for our children—also to protect them and help them avoid making mistakes. My advice: back off and let them make them, and don't be devastated by the results. Easy words, right? Of course we know this, but putting it into practice is really hard.

My dad's propensity for overindulgence—I know that I inherited that from him. Could I put my family's needs before my own? No. But that's what you have to do as a parent. It's a huge lifestyle shift for men. You can't just continue your old lifestyle. You can't push this parenting role to the side and not engage. Pay attention and keep connected without interfering as they move into the teen years. Have fun. Know that it's a difficult job but keep doing it anyway, as best you can, forgiving yourself along the way. It's a lot of work to teach children not *what to think* but *how to think for themselves*, and when they do—it's exasperating!

What would I like to say to my dad now? "I would have loved to know more about who you were and what was in your heart. You robbed me of that, or I robbed myself in my complicity in the relationship." Quite a while ago I decided to love my father, and care about him for who he is. I love him. I love him no matter what happened. He is who he is, I love him for his imperfections—but I wish he had loved me for mine. He was a product of his past just as I became a product of mine. I made a mistake much different but far more devastating than my father's. I took myself out of my children's lives with crime and heroin. I lost my family, but really I lost myself.

This is the best time in my life right now and my kids are doing wonderfully well. Now both my daughters are mothers, and I'm a grandfather. The love between us never went away. They love me to death! My grandchildren will never see me loaded. My relationship with my wife Susan is the best it's been in thirty years. Go figure, we finally did what we needed, we have achieved *absolute grace*. I'm such a fortunate guy to have it end up this way. I am learning to honour myself.

Ben (TOP) and Mark Mulroney

Ben & Mark Mulroney

Toronto, Ontario

TV show host, 43; investment banker, 40

||||||||||||||||||||||||||||||||||||||||||||||||||||||||||||||||||||||||||||||||||||||

Ben Mulroney, born in 1976, is the eldest son of Brian and Mila Mulroney. His father was prime minister from 1984 to 1993. Ben completed a law degree at Université Laval in 2001. He is host of the daily entertainment news show *etalk* as well as CTV's morning show *Your Morning*. Ben previously hosted *Canadian Idol* and has written a regular column for the *Toronto Sun*. He has been married to Jessica since 2008 and they have three children: identical twins Brian and John, born in 2010, and Isabel ("Ivy"), born in 2013.

Born in 1979 in Montreal, Ben's brother Mark has spent his entire career working in financial markets, spending time in New York, Toronto and London. Mark currently serves as a managing director with Scotiabank's global banking and markets team. He is a graduate of Duke University and is married to Vanessa, whom he met while working for RBC in the UK. They have three boys and a girl: Maximilian, born in 2010; Dylan, born in 2011; Ronan, born in 2013; and Mila, born in 2016. Mark and Vanessa are very active in their community and support causes such as mental health, children at risk, the arts and public policy.

||||||||||||||||||||||||||||||||||||||||||||||||||||||||||||||||||||||||||||||||||||||

Ben: My relationship with my father is wholly positive. The older I get, the more connected I feel to him. As a father myself, I remember an incident that brought me closer to my dad. It was that first time I read the Riot Act to my children. We had some friends over and the kids were playing upstairs and making too much noise. I'd asked them to keep it down a couple of times, and when that still hadn't happened, I put on my "big dad" voice, wanting to instill a bit of fear. I went up there sounding like I was very, very angry, when in fact I wasn't angry at all. I got the result I wanted: they settled down right away. On the way back downstairs I had this "aha" moment when I realized, *This is what he had to do all the time when we were growing up*—those times I thought my dad was angry with me, he was actually doing what I had just done.

I saw what just occurred in a whole new light. I had fresh insight into what kind of a father my dad was. I achieved a new recognition and appreciation for him, for his willingness to do the dirty work and to be a strong father. He was doing the right thing and so was I. Parents are *supposed* to use their authority.

That "aha" moment on the stairs was significant for Dad and me. Now I was able to access a whole part of our relationship that only became available to me as a parent. Up until then, I felt like I was a child speaking to my dad, but now I was a new parent speaking to an experienced parent. I find I am reaching out to him more as I get older, and we spend more time together talking about things that matter. Now the stuff we share is infinitely valuable and with the passage of time it's deeper, richer and more meaningful to me.

Mark: Dad calls me on a regular basis with no particular mandate or agenda. I'll tell him what's going on with me and I hear him laughing, chuckling—not at me—and I know he's thinking about himself when he was my age, forty. It's a release for me. It settles me down. It puts everything into perspective. In my mind, it's what a father should be.

His wisdom as a father has permeated our relationship, although he never makes it sound like he's giving advice. He might say to me, "I am not exactly sure what you're talking about, but this is what I think..." He's a labour negotiator, so he'll soften me up and then get to the point after disarming me. A few years ago, our conversations changed: there was no "thing," no reason for the call except to be in each other's lives. He might say, "I was just thinking about you," or "I want to say I am so proud of you..." It's uplifting. Right away, I want to tell my wife, "I just got the best call from my dad."

Even when he might be telling me something that is hard to hear, or that I don't agree with—I always know he's got my best interests in mind. If I think back to when I was four years old, for example, he could be fiercely proud of me, but if he was disappointed, he didn't hold back. It was never a threat, but the thought of Dad being disappointed, oh my God, did that hurt. The weight of the world was on your shoulders.

Ben: Long after I was on my own two feet as an adult, I'd frequently get feedback from Dad about how well I was doing, and he'd tell me all the good things he'd heard about me from other people. Maybe I thought people were just being kind or polite, because these comments didn't have much of an impact. It wasn't until Dad described an account of a negative interaction of mine that I became suddenly far more tuned in to his commentary. He called and told me, "Ben, I was talking to a friend and I heard that you were dismissive, you were unkind..." It broke me, it just broke me. My first reaction was defence—who, when, what—but then I realized that wasn't the point. I was used to hearing these kinds of things from him as a teenager, but as an adult—those times are few and far between, and they have a big impact. Do they make me a better person? Of course. I am glad I can trust my dad for an honest appraisal.

Mark: As siblings, we also keep each other in check. If Ben's doing something that I think is a bad idea, I'll call him on it. He'll do the same for me. It's a great thing that we can do this, and it's the result of having the sturdiest parental relationship at the top, the closest of relationships as a model. Our parents didn't contradict each other, they stood behind each other. If you can't back your mum into a corner, you're certainly not going to back your dad into one. We have had our parents' example of how to deal with conflict—respectfully and without put-downs. We knew which direction *they* were rowing in, which meant we knew which way to row.

People assume we had a tough time as children. They say, "It must have been awful because your father was always away." The fact is I have no memory of him *not* being there. What I do remember clearly is a present father. When the opportunities were there, he was a full-on involved father. I don't recall him being inaccessible. If there was a problem and I called him, regardless of where he was he'd say, "It's my son on the phone, I have to take this." That was way before any other dads were making space for children in their careers. My dad was a trailblazer on that front. He'd have ministers in his office, but he'd allow me to interrupt, to give him a hug, to tell a story, and he never made me feel that I was secondary. "Okay," he'd say. "Dad's going to finish this meeting now. I'll see you for dinner. Have fun." He somehow made me feel special, valued. It was just normal for us, but now I know that he was—and is—exceptional.

Ben: I have a friend who works at *The Globe and Mail* and he asked me to write a piece for the paper when Justin Trudeau became prime minister. "I want you to write this as a letter to him," he told me, "because you have an appreciation for what it's like to be the child of a prime minister." I said pretty much what Mark remembers—we didn't have an absentee father and there was no reason Justin couldn't be the same for his kids. While our father wasn't always present, he was always a *presence*. You can be there twenty-four seven without connecting at all. We never felt with my dad that he put anything ahead of us. The responsibilities of running a government are enormous, but we grew up feeling that we were the main priority.

As a boy, I fell off a swing in the middle of winter when my parents were on a flight somewhere between Ottawa and Toronto. The information they got through the "broken telephone" was that I was paralyzed. They turned the plane around. It turned out that I had broken vertebrae in my neck and back, but I was okay. When I heard they were about to arrive I was imagining I'd be in big trouble—but

FROM LEFT: John, Ben, Brian and Ivy (IN FRONT)

that wasn't their style. I think all of it amounts to that secret sauce that everyone looks to replicate. Great families, great careers, great boundaries. Lively conversation at the dinner table, no phone calls, no papers or documents, not a screen in sight.

Mark: Any time I was handling something big in my life, I was Dad's biggest concern. He took me seriously. He wouldn't lose it.

Ben: He had a great way of giving us perspective. Many times we'd frame something as a big problem and he'd find a way to help us get around it, to make it smaller or to will it out of existence. Now I'm doing the same with my kids. I notice there are some people, parents, who take all their children's issues as worthy of consideration. Every thought and feeling that's verbalized is treated as valid and urgent, and as needing to be addressed. I'm a bit more old-school on that front.

Mark: When it was me causing the problem, what I feared most from Dad was the quiet. When his voice lowered, that's when you knew the hammer was going to drop. It was calm. There was no yelling. There were times I would've preferred some yelling over the quiet treatment. I wouldn't say he used discipline as much as he taught us self-discipline. Now, it's us that are dropping the hammer. We are super disciplined. We're also delicate. And accurate.

Ben: A lot of dads don't read the parenting books. The models many men have for parenting are women, mothers. But sometimes our roles complement those of women rather than replicate them. I am glad my father showed me how to be honest and straightforward with my kids. On *Your Morning*, it's me and a number of women co-hosts. We chat during the TV commercials. Once, I was explaining how my sons disappointed me and I dropped the shame hammer on them. These women said, "You can't do that to your children, that's not how you're supposed to do it." Who says? I had got just the result I wanted with my sons. I don't believe there is one model for parenting that you can always apply. There's no right way for every parent, or every child, every time.

Mark: I've always felt I had the best dad, and I've always felt I'll never be as good as him. But I also hope that my children feel that *they* have the best dad. As long as I am growing, getting better every day, we're good.

Ben: I am at work at four a.m. and I hit the ground running, but my day really gets going when school gets out. They're at that age now. Mark, his kids are in three different groups for soccer: he's got to be at the park nine a.m., ten a.m. and noon.

Mark: People look at you and say, "It's insane." Well, yes—it's *my* insane, this is *my* crazy. It's controlled chaos and I am embracing it with everything I've got! Being from a large family, we do things as a pack. If my siblings and I get invited to the same party, you won't find us at opposite ends of the room. It's as if there's a magnetic force that pulls us together. And with parental authority, we spread it around. If I step in and tell one of Ben's children to stop doing something, he'll back me up and tell them, "Uncle Marko has told you to stop." As my wife and I now have a large family, we get a lot of questions from new parents about how we make it work. I believe it all starts with a sturdy couple and teamwork. Everything flows more easily when we are on the same page. My wife and I have talked through our various roles (we call them "departments") and how to handle things.

Ben: My advice is to be 100 per cent wherever you are. I rarely touch email at home. Anything that comes in probably doesn't get a reply until the following day, and I don't feel bad about it. And then when I am at work, I am 100 per cent there. To be the best dad I can be, I sometimes have to be a little selfish. I sometimes need an hour to myself at home. I can tell the kids, "Daddy needs a break to decompress. There are many things around this house that you can do."

Mark: I've got to learn that one. It's easier to say than to do.

Ben: Because I have twins, there is no one else they'd rather be with than each other. I guess it's an easy sell for me. Ivy thinks she's an only child living with roommates! She has no problem playing alone with her toys.

Mark: I can't do that yet with a two-year-old. But those little footsteps coming down to our room—it's the nicest sound ever. Anytime I think about complaining, I always have the thought in the back of my head of how fleeting it is, this time of life. I just met a friend who's looking at universities with his daughter. He's saying, "I remember my baby; it was just like yesterday." Our first baby is about to turn eight. This is a slice of life that I know I need to focus on, not the future—but *now*—and I'm making sure I enjoy it as much as possible.

It's not as if there is any training for this job. All of a sudden it happens. You are launched into fatherhood and you realize what everyone has been talking about. There's no way you can be ready; you have to learn as you go along. By the time number four arrived, my wife and I felt like professionals! But seriously, are we ever truly ready?

Ben: I'll never forget that drive home from the hospital with the twins.

Mark: Yes, it's like this fragile package, you're asking yourself, *Can we really do this on our own?* By the time we had number four it was like, "Well, we have to head to soccer practice, get groceries on the way home..."

Ben: I think it's important not to take ourselves too seriously. I saw a vignette once of a mother dropping a soother on the ground, freaking out, picking it up, cleaning it off, boiling it, putting it in a plastic bag and freezing it before putting it back in the baby's mouth. By the time baby number two comes along, the soother drops and she wipes it on her jeans and puts it back in the child's mouth.

Mark: We were all put to work in the kitchen when we were kids, so I learned to cook. There's nothing about being a father and doing the everyday tasks of looking after kids and running the house that I balk at. It feels good to share roles. My wife Vanessa handles all the heavy lifting and I am more of a weekend warrior.

Ben: I'm prepared for all that fatherhood will involve—I know there will be a lot of letting go. It'll break my heart, but I am confident we'll have the kind of relationship that will bring them back to us. I took the boys to summer camp for the first time this year, two and a half weeks. I thought I'd be taking them to their cabin, getting them unpacked and sorted, but no, that's not how it's done anymore. They just took them away from me, I hadn't said my goodbyes—and I lost it. I just lost it. It was not pretty.

My children see me expressing emotion. I'm not holding anything back. They've seen me sad, frustrated, angry, fighting with my wife, making up again.

Mark: Same for me. And I don't try and erase or rescue them from their own difficult feelings. One thing that stands out for me is that in our family we're demonstrative, we do all the hugging and the kissing. That's one thing we'll never shy away from. My dad hugs and kisses us, always has. He'll say goodbye to me and give me a kiss. I give my kids lots of affection and I love how it feels.

Ben: Very important to express caring and love. Don't bottle it up. I know in some families the brakes get applied, especially for males.

Mark: We have some interesting issues to deal with that our parents didn't have when we were growing up. We stopped using screens three years ago—we only use them for travel. I appreciate what they can do for us, but they also keep us away from so much.

Ben: Screens are everywhere, it's hard to keep kids off them, it's hard to find the balance. We've made mistakes along the way. I think it's a universal byproduct for kids who are on screens too much;

Mark with father Brian and children (FROM LEFT) Maximillian, Dylan, Ronan and Mila, 2018

they become dependent, they lose interest in all other aspects of being a kid.

They are obviously a big benefit to parents, because you know a screen will keep a kid occupied for a few minutes. It's very alluring, so I have found it's a constant back-and-forth, almost like a war with myself. As a dad I'm thinking how much time can I devote to being hands-on, how much trust do I place in my kids, how do I reduce the addictive quality?

I've found this to be the diciest part of modern parenting, finding a way to incorporate what we know is an essential tool in their lives, knowing how fraught with pitfalls that relationship can be. It's not only that they want the screen so badly, it's the losing of passion for other things that worries me. When they are not using screens, they are watching the clock tick down for that moment when they can get the endorphin rush again.

I don't think a lot of parents saw this coming. They are a handy tool, gosh darn it—I got two hours of peace and quiet at home yesterday; that's something I've been craving for weeks. It's like, *How is that not a good thing?* But it's not a good thing because my kid hasn't picked up a book in two weeks.

Mark: There's also a lot of pressure on parents to do everything right these days: have the right stuff, the perfect home, all the coolest baby equipment. I can see why parents can feel overwhelmed. There are so many people giving advice and there's so much comparison on social media.

Ben: Don't be afraid to make mistakes—and admit them: "Oh, that went sideways on me today"; "I blew it"; "Didn't see that one coming!"

Mark: You have to be able to let things go and laugh at yourself. You're in the grey area a lot when you're a dad. You have to have confidence and trust your own judgement.

Roy Henry Vickers
Hazelton, British Columbia
Artist, 73

||||||||||||||||||||||||||||||||||||||||||||||||||||||||||||||||||||||||||||||||||||||||||||||

Roy Henry Vickers was born in 1946 in northern British Columbia. He has lived at various times in Victoria, Tofino, Kitkatla and Hazelton. He is an artist, author, recognized leader in the Indigenous community and advocate for those with issues of addiction and abuse. Roy lives on the banks of the Skeena River in northern BC with his wife, Andrea, and two of his seven children. In 1998 Roy received the Order of British Columbia and in 2006 he was made a member of the Order of Canada.

||||||||||||||||||||||||||||||||||||||||||||||||||||||||||||||||||||||||||||||||||||||||||||||

My dad was a residential school survivor. When I was a child he was always away and when he was home, he wasn't there. My mom tried to perform both roles but it was impossible. I could have used his help during my puberty years, when I craved that connection a lot. The old ways—ceremonies, initiation into adulthood—were long gone. My art was my salvation during those years. I took my sketchbook with me everywhere and got lost in my creativity.

My relationships with women were cursed from the beginning. I didn't have a mentor to show me how to be with women, or who to be. My idea of love was about a physical relationship with a woman. It got me into a whole lot of trouble. By the time I was forty-five I had been married and divorced four times. All failures. I didn't know what was missing. I hit bottom, utterly despondent and broken. I was suicidal.

My way out of that pit of despair came from reflecting on the teachings of different sides of my family, finally concluding that I couldn't end my life. The prevailing message was that the creator gave us life and we don't have the right to take it away. Instead, I drove myself into my artwork to keep my sanity and got myself into a treatment program. I got a lot of help, and began to look at my dad in a different way, to find qualities that I valued—his strength of character, determination...

One message he gave me was that you don't quit; if you start something, you finish it. Dad's been gone a long time—and here I am working at being the father I wish I'd had. My dad had many good qualities that I couldn't see for a long time because I was so angry with him. Once I got through the anger, I could see the beautiful man there underneath and have empathy for him because I was that man, too. I started a journey called life, and you don't quit!

It was a huge deal, my father being present at the sessions in my treatment program in Arizona. He was a proud man, very competitive, a strong sports figure. He had to humble himself to be there, and he apologized to me for being an absent father. I was the only one in a group of eight who had both parents show up; what a gift that was to send me on to the next stage of my life journey.

We had one session where the counsellor asked for all the names of people in my family and wrote them on a whiteboard. "Okay" she said, "I want you to tell me about addictive behaviours any of them have." We went through all my family members. Everyone had addictive behaviours. The counsellor challenged me: "Now Roy, do you think you had a chance to be anything other than the way you were?" That's when it became clear to me that I had a chance to change. My life was in my own hands.

After the recovery process, things changed for me. When you discover the strength, truth and beauty of who you are, it brings humility, and with that humility you can show empathy and include people in your life who may not be kind, who may not return your kindness. In the end, I got to be a mentor to my dad, to show him in my present marriage what a wonderful, authentic relationship I am in with my wife, Andrea! So now, after four marriages and

FROM LEFT: Jordan, Andrea, Grace, Wakas and Roy, 2015

seven children, I am working at being the father I always wanted. My advice for new fathers? Oh my, oh my—it's love. Love makes the world a better place, but it's not something you fall into, it's something you choose every conscious moment. It's not an emotion, it's an act of volition.

I knew the loneliness of not having a good relationship with my father, and didn't want my children to experience that. I've always tried to be there for them, even though it didn't always happen. I've never been a deadbeat dad. Recovering, uncovering the truth and beauty of who I am changed my relationships, but most especially it healed the relationship I have with my children. Andrea and I are partners in a relationship called a family. I don't separate myself as I did in the past; I gain so much being an equal. I see the magic now of raising children with two parents who are connected.

There are simple times that we share where we are overwhelmed with emotion. We may be sitting at the dining room table with our children, and the energy can be so beautiful that I have tears—Andrea as well. We both have the knowledge and the awareness of what we

Roy in the Roy Henry Vickers Gallery in Tofino

have, and what we are doing together, and can celebrate it in the moment—it is a great joy! Now I have no intention of being anyone else other than who I am. I work at it; now I have a whole new spiritual life without any church. I fast as my ancestors did, I spend time in the sweat lodge. I experience the breath of God, *inspiritus*.

Bernard Richard

Cap-Pelé, New Brunswick

Social worker, lawyer, 67

||||||||||||||||||||||||||||||||||||||||||||||||||||||||||||||||||||||||||||||||||||||||||

Bernard Richard grew up in Cap-Pelé, New Brunswick.
He became involved in municipal politics and in 1977 was
elected as a Liberal to the legislative assembly of New
Brunswick, where he served in various positions from 1991
to 2003 including Speaker of the House and minister of
education. In 2004 Bernard accepted the post of provincial
ombudsman, and in 2006 became New Brunswick's
first child and youth advocate. For two years he held
the position of representative for children and youth in
British Columbia, then returned to New Brunswick to be
closer to his father and to act as an advisor to Mi'kmaq
NB Child and Family Services. Bernard is married to
Annie, and they have four sons and eight grandchildren.

||||||||||||||||||||||||||||||||||||||||||||||||||||||||||||||||||||||||||||||||||||||||||

Trepidation is what I feel when I think about talking about my dad.
Did I really know him when I was a child? Do I really know him
now? We are an Acadian family, and when and where I grew up, all
the responsibility for child-rearing fell to women. My mother "did
the job" and my father was quite absent from our lives. He was a
mechanic, ran a service station and worked seven days a week. I
have happy memories of the times he managed to take off on Sunday
afternoon when my uncle would spell him so that we could visit my
grandparents in Cocagne Cape. They were wonderful times.

Skip to my generation: I had more time for fatherhood, but not that much. And for different reasons.

As a young man I played a lot of hockey, a ton of it, and baseball. We didn't have a gym or an arena, and I can't remember a time when my father attended a game, whereas my grandchildren have a family fan club that follow them around! They go to all the games!

There was never any doubt about my father's love. I never felt that he didn't want to be with us, but we weren't really in his day-to-day picture. He never spoke about the love, but we could feel it, clearly: he was encouraging, supportive, critical as well. Never forceful, but not very present.

When I became a father, I thought about how I wanted it to be different. I threw myself into it. I spent many, many hours as a hockey coach, baseball coach, president of minor hockey, minor baseball, busting myself as a lawyer all the time. I was very involved, but involved doesn't mean close. We'd go to church and there would be three, four people waiting to talk to me after the service. My wife would often end up going home with the boys without me. I was deputy mayor, and publishing a small weekly newspaper in my community; I don't know how I survived. Then when I was elected as a member of the legislature, I was consumed by the duties I took on.

I'd be the first to admit I missed out on a lot; in a way my style of parenting mimicked my dad's. I wish I'd spent more time with my boys. You can't get that back. I see now how it could have been different. Three of my four boys were born when I commuted every week to law school at the University of New Brunswick in Fredericton. It was a bit nuts and we were dirt poor. I remember we'd joke that I had the "Kraft Foods Scholarship" because during the week at law school I survived mostly on peanut butter sandwiches. I thought a thousand times about not finishing.

Once my dad retired there was a big shift in our relationship. After Mass my parents hosted Sunday lunch, and they were ever ready to babysit which, for us, was worth its weight in gold!

My mum died in 2005. We always thought dad would go first as he was the stress ball, but he's still going strong at ninety-four! He's quite a character, independent, disciplined, doesn't stop. He walks

Bernard Richard (SECOND ROW, THIRD FROM LEFT), his wife Annie (TO BERNARD'S LEFT) and his father Joseph (TO ANNIE'S LEFT), together with Bernard and Annie's four sons and their partners, and eight grandchildren

daily, gathers oysters and mussels, picks wild blueberries in the summer. He writes incisive letters to the editor. He only has a grade eight education, but ended his career as an environment inspector. He's never been a "by the book" kind of guy and I still meet people who come up to me and say, "Please say hi to your dad, he helped me when I was in a tough bind."

It wasn't until I was sixteen, seventeen and working at my father's garage that we spent any amount of time together one-on-one, but even then we didn't talk much. I think we were both quite uncomfortable with each other. There were other men around, hanging out. I'd wash cars, pump gas, listen to them. I paid attention, trying to learn what I could, but they didn't include me. They weren't going to allow me even though I tried. My father was so keen for me to be ambitious I think he worried that I'd stay working at the garage.

When I hear others tell stories about my father, I realize I missed something. I can't help wondering what I could have learned from him directly, if only we could have gone there. He's a relentless crusader for the little guy, and we have the same determination and thirst for social justice. But back then I was a rebel. I was reading Trudeau's book *Towards a Just Society*, knowing my father was a staunch Conservative and chairperson of the Conservative Association. "If Dad reacts," I thought, "that's all the better." I was desperate to be treated as a grown-up, even for the wrong reasons. When I ran for the Acadian Party at the age of twenty-three, he still didn't take me seriously.

I had to wait a long time to earn his respect. The relationship with him warmed after I was elected as an MLA, and then got better still after my mum died. He's superbly proud of me now and takes a big interest in my work and family. If he'd gone early in his sixties or seventies, we'd never have got the lovely relationship we now enjoy.

It was hard work to get out from under the Conservative umbrella of my father, my grandparents and great-grandparents. Dad believed that politics was like religion: if you are born Catholic you are always Catholic, and if your family is Conservative you are too. According to him, there's no changing your political stripes. It was pretty common to think that way at the time.

He didn't attend the events that punctuated my political career, because he was a Conservative. I joke publicly that I don't even know if he ever voted for me. I'm not sure...maybe in the privacy of the voting booth he chose me, but I wouldn't want to ask. Either he'd say no and that wouldn't be good, or he might lie and that would be bad, too.

There were never any hugs or kisses, no mention of love from Dad or other men when I was growing up. The community embraced such staunch beliefs. These were made clear each week in church by the purveyor of standards and values for the entire community, the priest. He ran the show in town for many years, acting as mayor before the village incorporated, even running the Boy Scout group. Years later we found out he'd been abusing dozens of boys, children he could manipulate. I worked with some of his victims, preparing their compensation claims to the diocese.

It was easier for me to get close to my children than it was for my father, but the apple doesn't fall so far from the tree. I have to work

Bernard Richard and his dad, Joseph

at it, and I know we could be closer emotionally. I watch my children spending time with their kids and I am in awe at the emotional connection they have developed. My eldest son has been a stay-at-home dad for several years. I could never have imagined doing that, and I admire him very much. My greatest pride is my children.

Still no hugs or kisses from my dad, no talk about love, but a few years ago we shared a beautiful moment when we were in church together: he put his hand on mine and our eyes met. I had just delivered my mother's eulogy. He didn't really say anything, but his look meant the world to me. I guess it's never too late for a father to let a son know he's loved, but it's best not to wait too long.

Lawrence Hill
Hamilton, Ontario
Author, 62

||||||||||||||||||||||||||||||||||||||||||||||||||||||||||||||||||||||||||||||||||||||||

Lawrence Hill was born in 1957 in Newmarket, Ontario, the son of American immigrants: a white mother and black father who came to Canada in 1953. Both of his parents were human rights activists, and his brother, Dan, is a renowned Canadian singer-songwriter. His sister, Karen, was also a writer (she died in 2014). Lawrence is a prize-winning novelist, essayist and memoirist, best known for his 2007 novel *The Book of Negroes*. He is married to writer Miranda Hill, and together they have five children: four girls and a boy.

||||||||||||||||||||||||||||||||||||||||||||||||||||||||||||||||||||||||||||||||||||||||||

My parents came to Canada from the States in 1953. Dad came to do his PhD. He was an activist, a public figure revered by many Ontarians who cared about human rights, civil liberties and black history, so I've often been stopped on the street by people who wanted to say how much they admired my father and to tell me about his charisma, humour and commitment to equality in Canada. Of course, they know the public side. But in addition to being a public servant, sociologist and writer about black history, Daniel G. Hill III was also my father—in a very private way.

Dad was an African-American who became a committed and engaged Canadian. Although he was an intellectual, he could act down home and folksy, deliberately underplaying his education—especially when he wanted to outmanoeuvre an antagonist. Just as he slid between academic language and street talk, he also switched between public and private behaviour.

Part of his approach to parenting had to do with the time when he grew up. He was born in 1923 in Independence, Missouri, the son of a strong-minded theologian and minister of the African Methodist Episcopal Church who brooked no opposition from his children. By the time my father was raising my older brother, younger sister and me, we were living in Toronto in the 1950s and 1960s. Many middle-class men—my father included—expected that they would be the sole breadwinner in the family, the undisputed boss of the family, and that their wives would stay home. For men like my father, there were a lot of *shoulds*. A father, he felt, should lead the way. He should not show doubt. He should lead by dominating.

I think Dad's sense of control and power was threatened because my mom wanted to work. While Dad was still pursuing his PhD at the University of Toronto, Mom had exciting employment with the Toronto Labour Committee for Human Rights, trying to persuade the provincial government to enact anti-discrimination legislation at a time when our political leaders were claiming, "We don't have discrimination in Ontario."

When my brother Dan was born in 1954, Mom gave up her work and stayed home full-time. Later she started teaching, but Dad made her stop work and return to the home. Dad loved his wife and children, and was committed to supporting us, but he loved us most happily when he ruled the roost and we did what he said.

He was an entertaining man, dynamic, charismatic, and when in public, his charm was utterly seductive. If he was happy, it was fun at home. He'd tell us wild bedtime stories: he knew when to withhold details to increase the suspense, had perfect timing and could even imitate the sounds of animals and a range of American and Canadian accents. In the living room, he and my mother would dance to jazz and blues. His favourites were Count Basie, Duke Ellington, Ella Fitzgerald and Joe Williams.

It would all go well as long as no one crossed him and he remained the undisputed ruler of the roost. If you didn't follow the path he'd set out, things could turn violent—physically and emotionally. He could quickly turn into the guy who'd punish you harshly and smack you around. In the case of my brother and me, the smacking took place in the garage, out of sight and hearing range of my mother. Dan and I never told her what he did to us in the garage. Although we as children usually figured out how to keep the peace with Dad, it was a dangerous relationship. It was hard to manage, because we never quite knew when he would remain in good humour or when he would blow up.

As a child, I was scholarly and athletic—in some ways following the mould he was proposing. At every opportunity I tried to make him proud of me, while knowing all along that he thought I couldn't do it. As a black man, he believed that pursuing higher education and becoming a professional was the best way to transcend the challenges of racism and inequality. He believed his children had to succeed profoundly. He sang the praises of other people's kids who were achieving and put enormous pressure on us to excel, yet I don't think he ever believed in us. Underneath was the message that we probably weren't capable of success.

There was something oddly competitive about his relationship with his children. When I was fourteen, I decided to write the exams to apply to the University of Toronto Schools (UTS), considered to be one of the top high schools in Canada. I told him I was going to write the test, but I regretted it right away because he told me, "That school is for bright kids. If you want to get in you'll have to read every volume of every *Encyclopædia Britannica*, but you still won't get in." I didn't feel confident or cocky about my ability, but his words made me more determined to write the exam.

I was a competitive runner, so one weekend in the spring I took part in a road race in High Park and then took the subway to the school to write the exam in my track clothes. I was a kid with darker skin, frizzy hair and track shoes, and I looked out of place among the white boys in jackets and ties who showed up to test their mettle that day. Of the six hundred who applied in 1971, I was one of the thirty-five offered a place. I began to take either my bike or the bus and subway downtown each day, and embraced high school life on the campus of the University of Toronto.

My father was proud to see me attend UTS, but his early, hurtful prediction that I would never qualify for the school made me shut him out. I stopped telling him what was going on in my life. I didn't share my victories or my losses. I hardly told him anything, though when he occasionally drove me downtown to school, I enjoyed listening to CBC News with him and talking about the state of the world. I do recall that once when I was younger, I had asked him when I would become responsible for the problems in the world. "Larry," he said, "as soon as you become aware of situations in the world, you become responsible for helping to solve them."

At times, when Dad was dictatorial, I stood up to him. I'm not a loud person, I don't generally like confrontation. I don't seek it; in fact I avoid it. But somehow, as a child I knew I couldn't let him flatten me. My brother would be much more devious; he'd say, "Yes, yes, yes, Dad," and then do whatever he wanted. I challenged him, for example, in person and by letter when he was cruel to my cat. And, in a move that served only to infuriate him, I once told him to leave my mother alone and to let her have her way, when she bought a painting of a nude woman and he made her take it back.

Mostly, though, if I wasn't standing up to Dad, I just withdrew. I ignored him or found ways around him. By the time I was sixteen, I was making my own money and my own decisions. I stopped giving him information. I didn't discuss where I was going to study or what I was going to study. I chose a Canadian university that was about as far from Toronto as possible.

I studied hard. I was writing fiction actively. I didn't give him anything I wrote, but I did share it with my mother who read it and commented avidly. I didn't tell him what I was invested in, or about the people in my life. I didn't want to open the door to the possibility of humiliation. My leaving home seemed to represent a loosening of the chains. Perhaps he no longer felt he had to be "the Man." He evolved from his former rigid, autocratic and repressive self into a much more open, relaxed and loving man. Whatever it was, he began to ease up on the gas pedal incrementally once he saw that he could no longer bully or control me.

Lawrence with children (LEFT TO RIGHT) Beatrice, Evangeline, Andrew, Caroline and Geneviève, 2018

I think about who he was as a young black man in America, being conscripted into the American army during the Second World War and living a segregated military experience. It rankled him to think that he was good enough to die for his country, but not to live as a free man in the United States. Shortly after the war ended, he decided that he would no longer live in his home country. He moved to study in Oslo, Norway for a year, and then he came to Canada where he obtained his MA and PhD in sociology at the University of Toronto and embarked on a lifelong career of human rights activism and the study and celebration of black history in Canada.

I think Dad had to prove himself over and over again, not just in his career but in his own home where he felt the necessity to be the alpha male. As we grew out of his sphere of influence, he relaxed.

All that was repressive and ugly in his character moved to the back burner, and the good in him was able to flourish and to flower.

As a younger parent, he told us again and again that he expected us to become professionals: doctors, lawyers or engineers. Anything less, he let us know, would constitute failure. However, as we entered adulthood he matured and was able to celebrate and be proud of us and of our choices to live as artists. He fully supported the lives we chose, encouraged us, and was full of conversation and curiosity about our work and travels.

We had great times. I got to ask him things I'd never dared to ask as a child or young adult, like, "I've got these two possibilities up ahead, Dad. What do you think?" Finally I felt free, and I could take his advice or leave it. Dad became a good and thoughtful listener who learned to suspend his own ego. The relationship also began to reward me professionally; the books I was writing touched on areas that he'd spent his life working on, like black history and human rights. He knew these mountains more than I did, and while I was writing the novel *Any Known Blood*, I was able to ask him, "What was it like for a black soldier to walk through the train station in Baltimore during the Second World War? What would he be feeling? Would he be allowed to take a taxi?" Dad had walked through Penn Station as a soldier, and he explained to me that a black man would have to leave the station and walk a block or two if he wanted to hail a taxi during the Second World War in Baltimore. He answered countless other questions about things I was writing about and if he couldn't answer them himself, he could steer me to someone who could. He became a huge resource in my writing career, and a loving conversationalist.

In time, we were able to speak about the love we shared. Our relationship became beautiful. He asked about what I was involved in, and shared his thoughts and encouragement without attempting to dominate, judge or control. He became an entirely different father—loving and supportive. I had never in my life had the opportunity to see such a radical mid-life transition in another person. I heard many times from my brother Dan and late sister Karen that the same thing happened with them. As we all graduated from adolescence, he grew up with us and became a better father, the man we so wanted him to be. I feel so grateful for the miracle of it all.

When Dad was dying in 2003, I felt very much at peace. In those last years of his life I didn't feel any abiding desire to throw how awful he had been back in his face. I had already told him all that when I was a child. So there was nothing to make right, no unfinished business. I have failings as a parent, but at least I didn't repeat my father's mistakes. I've never had an explosive personality. My fuse is long and slow. I don't erupt in my personal life or have fits of anger or violence, so as a father I haven't had to fight it.

I feel that parenting has been the most successful part of my life, in which my humanity has been most able to flourish. I didn't think about the details of becoming a dad. It was natural and easy. Babies and I understand each other. I was lucky to be a stay-at-home parent and took my first-born, Geneviève Aminata Savoie Hill, everywhere in the Snugli on the front of me. She slept to the sound of me typing, thrashing away at the keyboard.

Parenting requires an incredible amount of patience and the suspension of ego. You have to make parenting decisions based on who the children are, their thoughts and needs, not on *who you are* and who you want them to be—to understand *them*, not have them follow you. This was easy with my first two children, but put to the test by my third child, Andrew. When he was a toddler, if I asked him to turn left, he'd turn right; if I asked him to do *A*, he'd do *B*. I had to dig deep to understand his wiring and respond in a different way. I had to ask, *How can I reach this kid?* Being an effective dad required me to change strategies for Andrew. I had to let go of my need to have him conform. I learned to be more playful, and to engage him in silly games such as ball-throwing and wrestling.

Children do things that drive you crazy, disappoint or embarrass you. I remember when my children made choices I struggled with, making my own decision not to chastise them. If I said what I thought, what would be the point of the conversation? To express disappointment? To seek a change of behaviour? To make my child feel bad? I had to ask myself, *What am I trying to achieve?* At these points, I have opted to let go of control and to keep the relationship strong.

I'm close to my children. We have a loving relationship, and I'm quite certain they would say the same thing. As each child reached the age of nine or ten, I took them on a special trip, just me and them. At that age, a child can walk for hours, read panels in museums and art galleries, absorb new languages and understand much about the world. Those trips shine for me as the most glorious moments, and once I had done it with all five children, I cycled through them all again. As they grew up and left home to study and work, I went to spend time with them in their new spaces.

There's something I learned from my father that I have been able to give my children. Many people in the world don't have work, volunteerism or other activities that they *just love*. My father was entirely in love with his work. He was deeply passionate about not just his work leading the Ontario Human Rights Commission, setting up Canada's first human rights consulting firm, and serving as Ontario ombudsman, but also writing books about black history, co-founding the Ontario Black History Society and engaging the public in his talks.

He conveyed to me from the earliest age what it was like to live with gusto and passion. I have been able to experience that in my work, and I feel that living and parenting with passion is a gift to your children. This was my father's gift to me, and it feels wonderful to have passed it on. My children are all out there in the world doing things they can be passionate about. Not everybody gets to do that. Some never have the opportunity and others have a choice but don't take it.

The advice I'd give to new fathers is to *learn to get out of the way*. Don't project what you want. Let your child show you the way. Don't get stuck on "results." Kids are on loan to you. Your job is to show them how to be alone, show them the door and how to open it. Model love, kindness, passion and a willingness to listen. I learned much from both the frustrations and the joys of being my father's son, and becoming a father myself has been one of my greatest pleasures in life.

Acknowledgements

So many people have supported me since I set out to put this book together, with their ideas, introductions and words of encouragement. I am indebted to a whole village—my family, friends, colleagues at St. Michaels University School, and the dear parents of the children with whom I work. You believed in me, inspired me, offered feedback and helped me maintain my optimism. Thank you!

Robert (Lucky), thank you so much for helping me connect with Douglas & McIntyre. Thank you to the awesome D&M team: Anna, Silas, Nicola, Brianna, Emma and Cheryl, for your wisdom, astute editing skills, creativity and personal reflections, and for not missing a trick!

Big thanks to the venerable Peter MacKay who went to great lengths to support me while juggling work and family commitments and the arrival of a new baby. Thank you very much to the discerning Larry Goldenberg who believed in my project and lit my path in such important ways. Thank you Lawrence Hill, for your mentorship. Many thanks to Charlene Bearhead, who helped steer me, and to my good friends Michelle Simms, Nick van Orden, Maria Coffey, Susan Harrison and Marne St. Claire, who provided wise counsel.

I extend my sincere and heartfelt gratitude to the brave men, once perfect strangers, who were willing to sit down with me and discuss this intimate aspect of their lives. You welcomed me into your homes, introduced me to your families and friends, and allowed me to photograph you. You trusted me to tell your stories and were generous with your offers of support. Thank you for believing in the value of my endeavour and for opening your hearts. For this I will be forever grateful.

My family has been behind me every step of the way. Thank you to my daughters, Alissa, Jessica, Vanessa and Caitlin, for your valuable perspectives and insights, and for being my steadfast cheerleaders!

Finally, thanks to my darling husband, Peter, who kept me supplied with chocolate, tea, coffee and red wine at exactly the right moments, who gave me feedback on the first draft of every story, who made me think more deeply and critically, and who championed my mission from start to finish.

Tessa Lloyd

Photo Credits

Photos by Tessa Lloyd except as noted below:

Interior:
Page 8: Doyle family
Page 39: Adam Scotti
Page 67: Jeff Vinnick
Page 70: Demers family
Page 81: Bateman family
Page 83: Robert Bateman
Page 87: Masuda family
Page 95: Goldenberg family
Page 114: Office of
   the Premier
Page 117: Moe family
Page 125: Shenher family
Page 128: Erica McMaster
Page 133: Erica McMaster
Page 149: Evans family
Page 152: University
   of Manitoba
Page 157: Niigaan Sinclair
Page 184: Paul Gautreau
Page 189: Paul Sun-
   Hyung Lee
Page 203: Gordon Chan
Page 213: Newman family

Page 219: Charlie family
Page 225: Vij family
Page 231: Kissel family
Page 233: Ashley Hempel
Page 243: Peter Power/
   Globe and Mail
Page 253: Britney Gill
Page 255: Britney Gill
Page 259: McLean family
Page 267: Reid family
Page 275: George Pimentel
Page 277: Vanessa Mulroney
Page 285: Vickers family
Page 293: Richard family
Page 299: Miranda Hill

Dust jacket:
Top row, centre: Jeff Vinnick
Second row, centre:
   Doyle family
Third row, left: Erica McMaster
Fourth row, left: University
   of Manitoba